LEAVING
ALEXANDRIA

Also by Richard Holloway

Let God Arise (1972)

New Vision of Glory (1974)

A New Heaven (1979)

Beyond Belief (1981)

Signs of Glory (1982)

The Killing (1984)

The Anglican Tradition (ed.) (1984)

Paradoxes of Christian Faith and Life (1984)

The Sidelong Glance (1985)

The Way of the Cross (1986)

Seven to Flee, Seven to Follow (1986)

Crossfire: Faith and Doubt in an Age of Certainty (1988)

The Divine Risk (ed.) (1990)

Another Country, Another King (1991)

Who Needs Feminism? (ed.) (1991)

Anger, Sex, Doubt and Death (1992)

The Stranger in the Wings (1994)

Churches and How to Survive Them (1994)

Behold Your King (1995)

Limping Towards the Sunrise (1996)

Dancing on the Edge (1997)

Godless Morality: Keeping Religion out of Ethics (1999)

Doubts and Loves: What is Left of Christianity (2001)

On Forgiveness: How Can We Forgive the Unforgiveable? (2002)

Looking in the Distance: The Human Search for Meaning (2004)

How to Read the Bible (2006)

Between the Monster and the Saint: Reflections on the Human Condition (2008)

LEAVING ALEXANDRIA

A Memoir of Faith and Doubt

RICHARD HOLLOWAY

CANONGATE
Edinburgh · London

Published in Great Britain in 2012 by Canongate Books Ltd,
14 High Street, Edinburgh EH1 1TE

www.canongate.tv

3

Grateful acknowledgements are made to Anvil Press for 'Missing God' by
Dennis O'Driscoll (*New and Selected Poems*, 2004); Bloodaxe Books for 'Heaven'
by A.S.J. Tessimond (*Collected Poems*, 2010); Carcanet Press for 'The Two Parents'
by Hugh MacDiarmid (*Complete Poems, Volume I*); David Higham Associates for
'Mutations' by Louis MacNeice (*Collected Poems*, Faber & Faber); Faber & Faber
for 'Murder in the Cathedral' by T.S. Eliot; and The Literary Trustees of
Walter de la Mare and The Society of Authors as their representative for
'The Listeners' by Walter de la Mare.

British Library Cataloguing-in-Publication Data
A catalogue record for this book is available on
request from the British Library

ISBN 978 0 85786 073 6

Typeset in Garamond MT by Palimpsest Book Production Ltd,
Falkirk, Stirlingshire

Printed and bound in Great Britain by
CPI Group (UK) Ltd, Croydon CR0 4YY

Lorna and Gillen
For another day

Demas hath forsaken me, having loved
this present world.

2 Timothy 4:10

Come, come, whoever you are,
Wanderer, worshipper, lover of leaving,
It doesn't matter.
Ours is not a caravan of despair.
Come, come even if you have broken your vows
  a thousand times.
Come – come yet again, come.

Rumi

As one long prepared, and full of courage,
as is right for you who were given this kind of city,
go firmly to the window
and listen with deep emotion . . .
to the exquisite music of that strange procession,
and say goodbye to her, to the Alexandria
  you are losing.

C.P. Cavafy

ACKNOWLEDGEMENTS

It has been observed recently that editing books is a dying art, but that is far from the case at Canongate. Though I sometimes wearily resented the extra work involved, the attention Nick Davies brought to his reading of my book and the careful suggestions he made about how I might improve it have resulted in a far better book than it would have been had I been left to my own devices. I am most grateful to him – as I am to Octavia Reeve, who, at the copy editing stage, made some helpful suggestions as well.

CONTENTS

Prologue: The Graveyard

I: 1940–56

1. Carman Hill   23
2. Place of Sacrifice   46
3. The Fall   63
4. The Side Door   79

II: 1958–67

5. Tenements   101
6. Angel of the Gorbals   115
7. Broadway   131
8. The Absence   149

III: 1968–84

9. Thirty-Three Steps   173
10. Coming Through   198
11. A Double-Minded Man   226
12. Boston Common   247

IV: 1986–2000

13. New Cloth   269
14. Drifting   292
15. Leaving Alexandria   311

Epilogue: Scald Law   341

PROLOGUE

PROLOGUE

THE GRAVEYARD

If you come this way, not knowing where to look for it, you
will probably walk past the graveyard. It is hidden behind a
high and impenetrable hedge of yew that looks as if it had
been designed to keep out casual visitors. No sign points the
way in, and when you succeed in finding it, it looks more like
an untidy gap in a thicket than an official entrance. When I was
here as a boy, a lifetime ago, the way into the graveyard was
wide and clear. It had to be, because this was where we brought
our dead in solemn procession to lie in this earth, and here
they lie still. The leaflet published by Newark and Sherwood
District Council calls the path that takes you there King Charles
Walk, because of the tradition that Charles I strolled here while
he was held at Kelham Hall in May 1647, after surrendering to
the Scots during the Civil War. When I lived here 300 years
later, we called it not the King's but the Apostles' Walk, after
the clipped yew trees, twelve on each side, which lined the way.
We knew the story of the house, but we weren't much interested
in what had happened here before our arrival, so intent were
we on our own purposes. Kelham Hall was by then the mother
house of the Society of the Sacred Mission, an Anglican religious order that trained uneducated boys for the priesthood in
a monastic setting that was its own world, self-sufficient, entire

unto itself. Hoping to be a priest one day, I had been sent here at fourteen from a Scottish back street, and I fell in love with the place and the high purpose it served. After a probationary term in civvies, we were dressed in black cassocks and blue scapulars that set us apart from life outside the great oak gates of the old hall. Our life was military in its discipline and dedication, but it was also full of kindness and laughter. It is the laughter I remember as I walk here again today, taking the path I took so often then, now given back to the memory of the broken king. Change hurts. Or is it deeper than that: is it Time itself we mourn? Time has certainly wrought painful changes here.

The Hall in which Charles was held was rebuilt in 1728 by Bridget, the heiress of the Sutton family, the original owners. When the house Bridget built was gutted by fire in 1857, her descendant, John Henry Manners-Sutton, commissioned George Gilbert Scott to build him a replacement. Presented with what Mark Girouard described as 'an empty site, a compliant patron, and what seemed a long purse',[1] Scott went to work, and the present Hall was built between 1859 and 1862. The building Scott erected was a smaller, less manic version of Saint Pancras Hotel in London, built a few years after Kelham, and its hard red brick and surprising silhouette still dominate the flat Nottinghamshire landscape for miles around. When Manners-Sutton died in 1898, the mortgage on the property was foreclosed and it came into Chancery.

In 1903 the Society of the Sacred Mission acquired it as their mother house, where they trained boys and young men for the priesthood. In the 1920s, to accommodate increasing numbers, the Society added a new quadrangle, including a massive chapel, the outline of whose huge dome added a softer note to Scott's jagged skyline.[2] Internal difficulties within the Society, and the external pressure of Church of England politics, led to the closure of the college in 1972, and the Society left Kelham. Purchased by them in 1973, it is now the headquarters of Newark and Sherwood District Council, who use the great chapel as an events venue, described in their publicity material as the Dome. When they sold Kelham, the Society retained possession of their graveyard in the grounds, and members of the gradually diminishing order can still elect to be buried there. In their leaflet, Newark and Sherwood District Council describe it as the Monks' Graveyard. Coming across it unexpectedly must be like coming upon a corner of a foreign garden that has been set aside for the burial of British residents, and feeling a pang of sorrow that they are so far from home. Though the graveyard does not feel entirely forsaken, it does feel hidden now, which is maybe why I always have difficulty finding it when I make one of my pilgrimages here.

I arrived at Kelham in 1948, aged fourteen, from a small town in the west of Scotland called Alexandria. Knowing little of its past and nothing of its future, the great house, given over to its sacred mission, seemed to be a place of timeless order whose life would go on for ever. Though I thought I wanted to stay here for ever, in the end I spent only six years at Kelham. In 1956 the Society sent me to West Africa to be secretary to the newly appointed Bishop of Accra, a member of the order and the last white man to hold that office. I was meant to stay for two years and then return to my studies, but I never did make it back to Kelham. While I was in Africa I withdrew from membership in the Society, so it was to Scotland I returned when my time was up in Accra. I had been wearing a cassock for years, and had no other form of outdoor clothing, so I got a streetside tailor in Accra to run me up a suit. Wearing this, I came back to Britain in March 1958 on a noisy old cargo ship, and headed, shivering in the cold, for Scotland. Yet Kelham continued to haunt me, and I dreamt about it for years. When the Society departed in 1972, and the place was taken over by the Council, I would turn up and wander disconsolately around the house and grounds, as though looking for something I had left there and could not find. During my visits in the 1980s and 1990s I was able to do this on my own, but security was tightened in the 2000s and on my last visit I had to be conducted round the house by a guide.

The advantage of having an official tour was that I was able to get into the Cottage, the servants' quarters of the old Hall, used by the Society to accommodate the boys who had been admitted for preliminary training for the ministry. The Cottage refectory was the way I remembered it, but the dormitory had been carved up into a warren of small offices and it conjured up little sense of what it had been like when thirty of us slept there, windows open in all weathers. Father Peter was Cottage Master throughout my time, and what had been his room was still intact, though now shared by four officers of the Council. The ground floor of the House, where adult students and members of the Society resided, was largely unchanged. Because of the disaster of 1857, the new house Scott built was designed to be fire-proof, so all the rooms on the ground floor were rib-vaulted in stone and brick, and the corridor and staircase floors were of marble, tiles or cement. The public rooms on the ground floor of the old Hall had not been altered by the Society during its seventy years' residence, though they had been adapted to different purposes. The carriage court, at first used by them as a chapel, became the Society's refectory, the dining room and drawing room became libraries, the billiard room a lecture hall, the morning room an office, and the grandest room in the house, the music room, became the common room. With a cathedral arcade and triforium gallery down one side, and an enormous hooded chimneypiece on the other, it managed to be both grand and cosy at the same time.[3] This was the domestic heart of the community. Newspapers were kept here, there were easy chairs, and a log fire burned in winter on high days and holy days, when the usual routine was eased slightly. None of this has altered much, probably because these are the rooms that are hired out for weddings and other functions by the Council.

I said little as my guide showed me round, though she must have been aware of the emotions that were charging through me. She said that few old students ever visited Kelham now, and I was the first in a long time. It was the visit to the Great Chapel that undid me. Dedicated in 1928, it is a huge space, sixty-two feet square in the clear, with four superb arches supporting a massive dome sixty-eight feet high, the second largest concrete dome in England, leading Father Hilary – one of the younger members of the Society – to claim, not entirely facetiously, that:

> We give our life
> We give our all
> Inside this great big tennis ball.

Designed to instill a spirit of sacrifice and devotion in those who were summoned by bells to worship there several times a day, the chapel does not feel comfortable with its new purpose as an events venue, mainly because the dome overwhelms everything below it that does not acknowledge its own reach for transcendence. But that was not what did me in. Aware that I was holding back tears, my host led me into the narthex, which now contains the bar used during dances and other events in the Dome, wondering if I could solve a puzzle for her. There was a little door on the west side, just off the stairs to the gallery, which issued out onto the drive to the main gate just opposite the Fox Inn. Did I know what it was for? I shook my head, unable to speak. But I did know. This was the door through which a member of the Society left for work abroad, after a short service called missionary benediction. He would kneel on the step of the sanctuary, under the great rood arch, to receive the Director's blessing, and then he would walk alone to the door and into whatever the future held. I went through that door in March 1956, into a taxi that took me on the first leg of my journey to Africa, the final verses of Psalm 121 still echoing in my head:

> The Lord shall preserve thee from all evil: yea, it is
>   even he that shall keep thy soul.
> The Lord shall preserve thy going out, and thy coming
>   in: from this time forth for evermore.

There was a going out, certainly, but there was no coming in again for me, except this insistent returning to what is now an empty shell. I thanked my guide and made for the walk King Charles took on his last night here, the same walk that used to be taken by a member of the Society of the Sacred Mission to his grave, carried on the shoulders of students, in the certain knowledge that the sacred purpose of this place would endure long after they were dust.

The path takes you south away from the Hall, with the River Trent on your left to the east, though you can't see it from here through the trees. At the end of the walk, down some steps, is the orchard, tangled and neglected now, though still bearing fruit, as trees do long after there's no one left to eat it. Though they fed us well at Kelham, I was always hungry and grateful for the windfalls that lay on the ground beneath these trees many autumns ago. A remembered scrap of verse from Helen Waddell increases my melancholy.

> When I am gone
> And the house desolate,
> Yet do not thou, O plum tree by the eaves,
> The Spring forget.[4]

Beyond the orchard, the walk intersects with another path. Turn right and you come out at the playing fields; turn left and you get to the Trent and Forty Acre, a great meadow along the side of the river. Father Peter used to come here every day to fill in a meteorological chart he kept. Sometimes, when he had to be away from Kelham to hear the confessions of the nuns at Belper, I did it for him. He left me a picture book of clouds, and I would go into Forty Acre to identify the formations and enter their names in the logbook. Apart from his interest in recording the weather, Father Peter used it as an opportunity to teach me a bit of Latin. In his chuffly pipe-smoker's voice, he'd point out that clouds were classified by using Latin words to describe their appearance as seen from the earth. I haven't thought about it for years, but I can recall the four basic types: *cumulus* from the Latin for heap, *stratus* for layer, *cirrus* for a curl of hair and *nimbus* for rain. Looking up into the almost cloudless July sky today, I see a few wisps of white: *cirrus*. Remarkable what sticks.

It is hard to get into Forty Acre now, unless you bushwhack over a ditch and an ugly snarl of fences. It was a park to us and the place we went to swim in the Trent. Swimming was only permitted if there was a qualified life-saver present. I passed the test by going into the water with another student, flipping him onto his back, placing his hands on my shoulders, and pushing him towards the bank while I did an awkward version of the breast stroke. No one drowned during my time, but I wouldn't have been much good to anyone in real trouble.

It was an early example of being theoretically qualified to do something I was actually incapable of performing, something that has been a bit of a theme in my life. From somewhere, I have been afflicted with the gift of confidence, of appearing to be knowledgeable about something I am actually making up as I go along. My improvisations were based less on knowledge than on self-confidence allied to an easy fluency with words. I can see now that I spent a large part of my life winging it, and that some of the things I made up, some of the roles I tried to fill, I did because I admired the idea of them. The toughest lesson life teaches is the difference between who you *wanted* to be and who you actually *are*. And it can take a whole life to teach it. Funny, where a meditation on my incompetence as a life-saver has taken me.

The hard thing about coming to this place is glimpsing the young man I was fifty years ago, brimming with ideals, taking this same walk, earnestly conversing with a companion – and completely unaware of the spring and drive of his own character and where it would lead him. He thought then he had chosen a high road and would walk it to the end, whereas I know now that roads choose us and what they unfold before us is not the person we want to be, but the person we already are, the person time slowly discloses to us. Yet in spite of trying to learn this lesson, I still regret roads not taken. Is that why I keep coming back here? Am I trying to discern the outline of an alternative past, the most futile of pursuits? What is certain is that I am so far into my own head at the moment that I am not paying enough attention to what's going on around me; so I have come too far and passed the graveyard. I turn back down the walk, identify the untidy gap in the tall yew hedge and enter.

The graveyard of the Society of the Sacred Mission at Kelham is a shaded rectangle containing thirty-five simple grave-stones, irregularly spaced. From the gap in the

hedge	XXXXXXX
that	XXX
serves	XXX
as an	XXX
entrance,	XXX
the	XXX
arrangement	XXX
of graves	XXX
faces you like this . . .	XXX
	XX
	X

Apart from two erected recently, the stones are all covered in lichen and are hard to read, but I am able to decipher most of them.

I pause before the ones I remember. Here is Father Peter Clarke, my old Cottage Master, an ardent pipe-smoker who grew his own tobacco at Kelham – inevitably called 'Nobby weed' – to amplify the community ration of an ounce and a half a week. He taught history to the boys in the Cottage, very boringly, it has to be said. In fact, I do not remember any stimulating teaching at the elementary level, which may be why so few of the boys who went through the Cottage actually made it to ordination. It is hard to blame the Society for this, however. I doubt if they had a single trained teacher in their midst. They probably assumed that any educated man could pass on what he knew if he tried hard enough. It seemed to work for me, probably because, while I am not a teachable person, I am quite good at learning for myself if my interest is ignited. The teaching in the Cottage bored me, but the ethos of Kelham stimulated my imagination, which was probably more important in the long run. And what I remember about Peter Clarke, whose gravestone I am now trying to read, was his kindness and droll sense of humour – and that funny chuffly voice. His stone tells me he died on 25 November 1987, aged ninety-one, 'in the 65th year of his profession'. That means he was seventy-six when the Society left Kelham, which must have been tough for him, because he loved the place. 'Profession' relates to the ceremony, a bit like a wedding, at which a novice, whom we might think of as engaged but not yet married to the community, professed his vows of poverty, celibacy and obedience, and committed himself to the Society till death.

Each gravestone here tells how long the dead man had been professed in the Society. Most of the ones I remember were fortunate to die before the exodus from Kelham. I am particularly glad to see that Brother Edward did not live to see the move. He died in September 1965, aged seventy-eight, in the sixty-sixth year of his profession. Lay brothers in the Society, like non-commissioned officers in the Army, were the men who kept the system functioning. Edward was head gardener at Kelham, and a critic of sloppy work from the students. Since the Society hired no outside help, everyone pitched in to keep the place going. There were two types of work that no student escaped. 'Departments' were daily household chores, done after breakfast before study started, such as washing dishes, clearing up the refectory and sweeping corridors. 'House lists' were longer afternoon chores lasting a couple of hours, which might involve working for Brother Edward in the grounds, mucking out the piggery near Forty Acre, or scrubbing and polishing floors in the House. Two afternoons a week were dedicated to compulsory sport for everyone, football in the winter, cricket and tennis in the summer. The whole thing operated with military precision, though it was bells not bugles that summoned us to our duties. Suddenly I have an image of Brother Edward sitting on the big Atco motor mower, his spectacles glinting in the sunshine, going round and round the cricket pitch, getting it ready for the season.

Here's Brother Hugh. He died at eighty-one in 1957, while I was in Accra, in the sixty-first year of his profession. Hugh Pearson spent his life at Kelham, and was its indispensable handyman. A small, bent, scuttling figure, he was an authority on the Victorian plumbing system of the old house. He was known as 'Shoosty', because of the sibilant way he talked through ill-fitting false teeth – not that he said much, though he chortled a lot. Father Peter, who considered him a saint, once claimed that when there was a full moon his temper was vile.

Here's Father John Scutt. I remember him. He was a small, compact man, nimble on his feet. He taught us boxing in the Cottage, and gave us exercises to develop our biceps, feeling them at intervals to see how they were growing. I remember his verdict on mine after one examination: 'Small,' he said, 'small, but hard.' He died in October 1969, aged seventy-nine, in the forty-sixth year of his profession. Here is Richard Roseveare, the man I spent two years working for in Accra when he was bishop there. I am not sure when he left Ghana, as the Gold Coast became after Independence. Standing before his gravestone reminds me of Independence Day in Accra in 1957 and seeing Kwame Nkrumah hailed as the Great Liberator. Richard Roseveare, a great fan of Nkrumah in those blissful early days, later became critical of him as his megalomania turned him from freedom fighter into tyrant. That's when Richard was forced to leave and return to Kelham. A commanding figure, it must have been hard for him coming back, especially since his return coincided with the crisis that led to the departure of the Society. Anyway, here he is. His gravestone tells me he died in April 1972, aged sixty-nine, in the forty-fourth year of his profession, and three months before they decided to abandon Kelham. He got out just in time.

Stephen Bedale, died on 1 March 1961, aged seventy-nine, in the fortieth year of his profession. I revered him. He was Father Director while I was here. Tall, stooped, lean. The face of an eagle. 'Far ben wi' God,' they would have said of him in Scotland in the old days. And he had family connections with Scotland, with Inverness, according to my fellow student Aeneas Mackintosh, who came from there himself. I would conjure up a difficulty when I was a young novice, just so that I could take it to him and watch him look piercingly at me as he spoke. I remember wanting to be like him: austere, holy – a saint.

Implicit in all the devotional books I devoured at the time was the idea that sanctity was something I could achieve with practice: I could build myself into sainthood by my choices and actions. What I was actually good at was looking the part, staying in chapel longer than others and self-consciously cultivating what I imagined to be the unself-conscious demeanour of a saint. I thought that it would look like Stephen Bedale, before whose grave I am now standing. I think he liked me, the zealous young Scot. What would he make of me now, I wonder? Disappointed. He'd be disappointed in me. I hadn't stayed the course. I'd drifted, and not just from Kelham, maybe even from the Faith itself. I stay with him longer than with anyone else here. I scrape some of the lichen off his gravestone. Dead fifty years, and I can see his face, hear still his dramatic asthmatic delivery as he lectured on Paul's Letter to the Romans. An uncompromising man. Yes, he'd be disappointed in me. I'm disappointed in myself, despite knowing that – being who I am – I could not have done otherwise. I scrape off more lichen and move along.

Here's one whose funeral I clearly remember. Brian Sim's gravestone describes him as an 'associate', the term used to describe students and former students who were not members of the Society. He died in November 1954, aged twenty-five. I had been back in the House for a year after National Service in the army, and I can remember how alarmed we became at changes in Brian's behaviour as the Michaelmas term wore on. Normally reserved, he became uninhibited and talkative, before lapsing into a coma induced by a brain tumour. His death was a shock to the community, and he was given a full Society funeral, a solemn requiem mass that concluded with his coffin being shouldered out of the chapel by his fellow students, while we all chanted the Russian Kontakion of the Departed:

Give rest, O Christ, to thy servant with thy saints:
where sorrow and pain are no more;
neither sighing, but life everlasting.
Thou only art immortal, the Creator and Maker of man:
and we are mortal, formed of the earth,
and unto earth shall we return:
for so thou didst ordain, when thou createdst me, saying,
Dust thou art, and unto dust shalt thou return.
All we go down to the dust;
and, weeping o'er the grave, we make our song:
alleluia, alleluia, alleluia.[5]

The whole community, about a hundred and sixty of us, including the boys from the Cottage, followed Brian's body out of the chapel into the November mist drifting off the river, across the quadrangle, round the west side of the House onto Apostles' Walk, to lay him in the earth. Fifty-five years ago and remembered now by me in the penumbral quiet of this grave-yard in the middle of England. Suddenly, I feel cold. But I am not yet ready to leave. There is another grave I must find, another death I remember.

I am pretty certain it was at Halloween 1950. I was well into my third year in the Cottage and was keeper of the Cottage Log or diary for that Michaelmas term. We had been informed that Father Kelly, the Founder of the Society, was dying. Even those of us who had never seen him in the flesh knew that he was still an important presence in the House, confined to his room on B corridor, looked after by student 'batmen', including Aeneas Mackintosh, the only other Scot at Kelham. A day or two before he died, a little printed card appeared in everyone's place in chapel, containing his last message to us: 'The angels will look after you.' Angels were God's messengers. The Society of the Sacred Mission kept its Patronal Festival on 29 September, the feast of Saint Michael and All Angels, because its work was training God's message boys.

Herbert Hamilton Kelly, also known as HK or the Old Man, who in old age looked a bit like George Bernard Shaw, was born in 1860, the third son of a Church of England vicar, described as a non-quarrelsome Evangelical.[6] After Manchester Grammar School, he trained as an army officer at Woolwich, but increasing deafness made a military career impossible. While at Woolwich he had an Evangelical conversion, which prompted him to go to Oxford as the first step to ordination. Like some other geniuses before him, he did not fit the Oxford system – or any system, for that matter – and came away with a fourth-class degree in history, thereby justifying the rumour that Oxford gives plodders a third, while keeping the fourth for flawed brilliance.

It took Kelly a while to find his purpose in life, but he knew always that it would involve organising the power inherent in community to achieve a great end:

> ever since I was a cadet at Woolwich studying the art of war, I had been haunted by the dream of organised power . . . every part, large or small, grappling with its ever changing and different problems by its own independent intelligence and yet concentrating its determination under disciplined direction upon the attainment of one simple and common aim.[7]

The convoluted intensity of that passage says much about this complex man, who was always haunted by a sense of personal failure yet founded an institution that changed the lives of hundreds of boys and young men. Originally invited by the Anglican Bishop of Korea to train men for missionary work in the Far East, he was soon diverted into establishing a community that would, to quote the words of a Cambridge don at the time, 'make clergy of the humbler classes'. Kelly was not romantically attracted to the monastic life for its own sake, as I was later to become, but he did think that a community of men, committed to the traditional vows of holding all things in common – poverty; celibacy, remaining unmarried so that they could concentrate all their efforts on their work; and obedience, the submission of their wills to a common purpose – was the best way to achieve the vision that had ignited his imagination. The Society of the Sacred Mission was inaugurated in 1893, as Kelly put it:

> to start a college which would train for the ministry young men with no money and no special education . . . I was expected to follow the customary system. I never dreamt of doing so . . . These men were going to be teachers of a faith, given in a Creed. This is said to be correct, and that incorrect, but I do not care about these words. I would rather ask, why is this doctrine vital, and that fatal, to a man's soul and capacity to live? Someone said it was, and he ought to know. Very well, we must go to him, and find out why he found it so; then each man must look into his own soul, find in his own life its questions and difficulties, its perplexities and diversities.[8]

The Society started its life in south London, and then moved from the distractions of the city to Mildenhall in Suffolk. When that was outgrown they found Kelham, dismissively described by Kelly in these words:

> it is Gilbert Scott insanity on the model – or rather a previous model – of S. Pancras Hotel – one endless waste of paint, gilding, granite columns, vaulted ceilings and the *vilest* gothic. Extravagant, tasteless, unfeeling. Every capital throughout the house carved elaborately and vilely – with the sole object of spending money.[9]

HK always exaggerated, and there is little doubt that he came to love Kelham, though probably more for what was achieved in it, than for the setting itself. He called the community he had gathered together, which included boys and men from 'the humbler classes' as well as the professed members of the Society, 'an idea in the working', and it always had about it a sense of dynamic improvisation. Kelly had three characteristics that inhered themselves in the ethos at Kelham. A reverent agnosticism about all human claims, including morals; a tendency to teach and meditate in paradoxes; and a flippant attitude towards religion allied to a total commitment to the reality of God.[10] It all came together here at Kelham, where it took root, flourished gloriously for several generations, began to fade, and then was pulled violently from this ground. All that remains now is this graveyard and his gravestone, which I have just come upon.

> Herbert Hamilton Kelly
> Called to his Rest
> 31.X.1950
> Aged 90
> In the 57th year of his Profession

I had remembered correctly: it was All Hallows' Eve. I stand for a minute or two longer before making my way out of the graveyard back onto Apostles' Walk. I am still not sure what it is that keeps pulling me back to Kelham, but I do know what it was that brought me here in the first place– a whole lifetime ago.

I

1940–56

I

CARMAN HILL

My father always got up well before six. Sometimes, if I was sleeping in the kitchen, I'd watch him from the bed recess when he didn't know I was looking. I would notice how quiet and economical he was in his movements. The kettle goes on first to make a cup of tea, which he drinks standing up. Milk, no sugar. He takes nothing to eat. Fills his pipe with the wad of Walnut Plug he's rubbed up in his hands. Gets it going with one match. Then he stands looking out of the window, his left arm along his waist supporting his right elbow, his other arm upright, holding the pipe in his mouth with his right hand. I wonder what he's thinking as he stands there motionless. It's getting light. What's he seeing? He turns, opens the door quietly. With a sudden pang I realise what a considerate man he is. The door snecks softly shut behind him. He walks swiftly down Random Street, left along John Street, right down Bank Street to the Leven, then north along the riverbank to the Craft.

This is where he is from, the Vale of Leven, twenty miles north of Glasgow; but he'd been away a long time, walking the streets of Glasgow looking for work in what my mother always referred to as the Hungry Thirties. He'd try anything then to put something on the table for the five of us, including carrying his own weight in cheap coal up tenement stairs. It was the war that rescued him and brought us back to the Vale and his job in the Craft, the United Turkey Red factory in Alexandria. War work, he called it. To begin with we sublet two rooms in Bridge Street, but my mother importuned the house factors Burgess and MacLean to rent us a dilapidated old room and kitchen in Random Street. And we were happy there. Glad to be employed again, my father worked all the hours there were in the early years of the war, and we didn't see a lot of him. I too was glad to be back in the Vale, back among hills. And walking them became a passion, a passion that never faded.

It was my mother who started it. During the long double-summertime days of the war, she took me, my wee sister Helen and my big sister Gertie exploring the hills that surrounded us, and Carman was her favourite. We'd walk in through the woods of Poachy Glen, on the edge of Renton, till the path steepened on Millburn Muir and led us to the top, 800 feet up. From up there we could see in every direction, but my eyes always went north first, to Ben Lomond and the great loch over which it presided. At over 3,000 feet, it was massive rather than craggy, and from Carman it looked like a purple ziggurat. It sat halfway up the east side of the loch at Rowardennan, along the road from Balmaha, both stops on the voyage of the *Maid of the Loch,* the paddle-steamer that plied the loch throughout the summer months.

By the end of the war the family walks had petered out. Years of energetic smoking began to tell on my mother; and Gertie, five years older than me, left school at fourteen to work in a chemist shop in Renton and moved out of my orbit. Helen, three years younger, sometimes came with me; but she had pals of her own to play with and didn't always want to join me. I had pals too, but walking was something I preferred to do on my own, so even as a boy I was a solitary walker. Sometimes I went up Staney Mollan, near the loch at Balloch, or Pappert Hill over on the east side of the river; but most of the time it was Carman Hill I returned to, back to an early love. And it was always to the north I turned first when I got to the top, always to the Ben and its island-patterned Loch. Yet the view to the south was just as dramatic. The Leven met the Clyde at Dumbarton, a few miles away, and from Carman Hill I saw it coursing into the bigger river at Dumbarton Rock, a plug of volcanic basalt 240 feet high, and since the fifth century a fortress of the British Kingdom of Strathclyde – *Dùn Breatainn*. At school it always struck us as funny that Great Britain got its name from as dismal a town as Dumbarton. Turning to the south-west, I saw the river spreading itself into the Firth of Clyde as it flowed on into the distant sea. The Clyde was a majestic river, but she was a worker as well as a queen, and wherever my eyes followed her, up river to Glasgow or down river to Greenock, on a clear day I could make out the cranes of the shipyards that lined both sides of her banks. And I knew that down below me in a few hours, workers from Denny's in Dumbarton and John Brown's in Clydebank would be getting off the train at Alexandria. Bank Street would be loud with hundreds of men in tackety boots clattering home for their tea after a long shift in the yards. But the Vale of Leven had its own industries, drawn there by the river that gave the valley its name.

From Carman I could see the Leven flooding out of the Loch at Balloch Pier and snaking its way to the Clyde. It is only five miles from Balloch to Dumbarton as the crow flies, but the Leven takes seven serpentine miles to get there. Just down there, due east of Carman, it twisted completely back on itself at Cordale Point and again at Dalquhurn Point. And it was swift. We were told that only the Spey was faster, so we should respect our river. The Leven was swift not only because of the colossal force of the water that poured into it from Loch Lomond, the largest lake in Britain, but also because it flowed down, descending twenty-six feet from its source at Balloch to its exit into the Clyde at Dumbarton. All five towns along the river were obvious to me from up here. On the east side, going south from the loch, Balloch – really only a village – was clear; then came the small towns of Jamestown and Bonhill. Coming back west over the river, I could make out the Victorian hump of Bonhill Bridge, the link to Alexandria, the newest and biggest of the five towns of the Vale, a creature of the bleaching and dyeing industries that had established themselves along the Leven early in the eighteenth century. On this side of the river, back up the way to the loch, was the factory where my father worked. It had a Gaelic name, *Croftengea*, after a mighty oak tree that was reputed to have been a gathering place for the local clan, but to everyone in the Vale it was known as the Craft, a rambling, dilapidated dye works owned by the United Turkey Red Company.

Up on my hill, I pictured my father in there, dyeing bales of cloth hour after hour; and I would wonder what colour he'd come home tonight. He'd strip to the waist and wash himself down at the kitchen sink, and I'd furtively examine his small, wiry body. Then he'd eat the meal my mother had cooked for him, and fall asleep in his chair by the fireside. Everyone called him Wee Arthur because he was only a couple of inches over five foot. He was admired by everyone. I admired him too; but I longed for a more heroic figure for a father, big and heavily muscled like our neighbour John McGlashan, a physical training instructor in the army and a champion welterweight boxer. Mammy had told me that Daddy had been a long-distance runner when he was young, and that he would walk twenty miles a day without noticing it when he was looking for work before the war. I liked to hear that, but I wanted him to be bigger. He was back in the factory in which he had served his time as a block-printer when he was a boy – but not now as a tradesman. They no longer printed cloth by hand the way he had been taught. Though his trade was obsolete, he'd held on to the short lead mallets that were the tools of his craft. They were kept under the bed in the kitchen recess, wrapped in a bit of cloth. Why did he hold onto them? I wondered. He was a labourer now, maybe what they called a skilled labourer, but he did not complain. Actually, he didn't say much at all, except when he had a drink in him; then he could be talkative and amusing. I liked him, knew he was a good father. He worked hard for us. It was only that I wanted a more heroic figure, larger in scale. But Wee Arthur he was, working all the hours there were, down there in the Craft or *Croftengea*.

Alexandria was not a Gaelic name like *Croftengea*, nor was Renton, down the road from it on the west side of the Leven, the fifth of the towns along the river. The dominant family in the area in the eighteenth century were the Smolletts, the most famous of them being Tobias, the novelist. We were told that our street was named after his most famous novel, *Roderick Random* – whether true or not, it was certainly true that our town got its name from Lieutenant Colonel Alexander Smollett, Member of Parliament for Dunbartonshire in the late eighteenth century, and the son of Alexander Smollett and Celia Renton, after whom Renton was named.

It was easy to make out Random Street from Carman Hill.

All I had to do was find Alexandria Station, which was at the foot of the street, and trace it back up to where it met Mitchell Street, the crescent that linked Main Street with Bank Street. Random Street was one of the oldest streets in Alexandria. Bits of it went back to the early 1800s, and we lived in one of those bits, a row of red sandstone cottages, each habitation a room and kitchen, a 'but-and-ben' in local parlance. They went back to the days when farming was the only industry in the Vale. There was no lighting in the room at the back where the three of us children usually slept, apart from the window onto the back, but we had a gas light in the kitchen, above the fireplace. You turned the gas on with a wee tap at the side, applied a match flame to the white mantle in the lamp, and a quiet light suffused the room. That room was the scene of many sing-songs after the war. Uncle Harry, my father's favourite brother, was back from North Africa and working beside him in the Craft. They spent Saturday evenings together in the pub at the bottom of the street and brought a carry-out back to the house when the pub closed. The family told me I had a good voice, and I was urged to go through the repertoire of songs I had memorised from the wireless.

> Yours till the stars lose their glory
> Yours till the birds cease to sing
> Yours till the end of life's story
> This pledge to you, dear, I bring.

Then there was, 'You Are My Sunshine', and 'Bless This House O Lord We Pray'. As an encore, and without embarrassment, I'd sing:

My mother's name was Mary
She was so good and true
Because her name was Mary
She called me Mary too.

My mother, whose name *was* Mary, would watch me fiercely, drawing deeply on her Woodbine, eyes brimming. But she was the real singer. Though untrained, she had a true and powerful soprano voice that years of heavy smoking never diminished. She came into her own on Hogmanay, when we gathered round the fire in the kitchen to bring in the New Year. When midnight came and our first-foot had sunk his dram, someone would say, 'Mary, gie us a song' and all eyes would turn to her. She'd stub out her cigarette and start, and it was always the same song she'd start with:

Bonny Scotland I adore thee
tho' I'm far across the sea
and when loneliness creeps o'er me
my thoughts fly back tae thee
and in fancy I can see ye yet
your lovely heather braes
reminds me o' departed joys
brings back sweet memories
Scotland, Scotland,
Scotland aye sae braw
my hairt is aye in Scotland
tho' I'm sae far awa
take me back amang the wildwood
and roon the rowan tree
oh take me tae my ain wee hoose

> that's aye sae dear tae me
> sae dear tae me, sae dear tae me
> that's aye sae dear tae me.

And there wouldn't be a dry eye in the room. It was a strange thing, missing Scotland when we were right there in the middle of it, being overwhelmed with homesickness when we were sitting in our own kitchen before a blazing fire. Wherever it came from, this sadness is rooted in the Scottish soul:

> how strange was the sadness of Scotland's singing . . . the crying of men and women of the land who had seen their lives and loves sink away in the years . . . it was Scotland of the mist and rain and the crying sea that made the songs.[11]

The wee house my mother seemed to be mourning even as we lived there was 31 Random Street, and it became legendary in our memories. I have an old photograph of it, and am surprised to see that the pavement outside the cottage is not made up. Kerbstones separate it from the roadway, certainly, but the sidewalk is made of packed earth and crushed stones. On the opposite side of the street from us there was a terrace of two-storied tenements, with outside stairs round the back to the flats on the upper floor. They were characteristic of the town as a whole, and reflected its industrial growth. There were some handsome public buildings in the Vale, but most of the houses were in two-storied terraces like the ones in Random Street. Better-off people had bigger houses up the hill above Main Street – on Middleton Street and Smollett Street – but even here there wasn't much that was really grand or pretentious. And everything was near everything else. On a winter morning

I went up Mitchell Street and across Main Street to Rennie's Bakery to buy rolls. The shop wouldn't be open, so I'd go to the bakehouse round the back, where I'd stand in the warmth and watch them pulling the trays of hot rolls out of the ovens with long wooden poles. There was a Co-op store in Mitchell Street, and a fishmonger's and butcher's on Main Street. We bought sweeties at Goodwin's corner shop at the top of the street, where you could pay into a club for presents at Christmas. There was a greengrocer's in Bank Street, and other shops at the Fountain, a memorial to Alexander Smollett, which sat in the middle of the road between Main Street and Bank Street. But I haven't yet mentioned the buildings that were of particular interest to my mother and me, the picture houses.

My mother was addicted to the pictures, a habit I inherited. She usually took me with her twice a week, and Helen sometimes came too. Gertie was now a working woman with a boyfriend serving his time as a joiner, and they were both keen dancers, so the movie habit never hit my big sister. I got it badly and it stuck. Mammy and I would check the *Lennox Herald*, the local weekly paper, for the listings, but I don't think we were very discriminating and would sit through just about anything. It was an escape into romance and fantasy for me; but what was it for my mother? I suspect now it was the same for her. There was always something eager and unsatisfied about her, as if she was trying to compensate for a great loss somewhere and was filling her pockets before the sweetie shop closed for ever. An attractive, volatile, charismatic woman, she was the emotional centre of my life and I can still recall her most frequent endearment. She told me repeatedly that I was her wee ton of bricks. I loved her and hated to be separated from her. I knew the outline of her history, of course, but it was only after her death that I was able to fill in the detail.

At ten she had been orphaned and sent to Quarriers Home in Bridge of Weir, south-west of Glasgow. I have a copy of the page from the ledger of admissions that recorded her entry to the orphanage on 4 September 1917.

Mary Johnston Luke born 7th April 1907 at 12 Vernon Street, Glasgow & Violet Vallance born 30th January 1910 at 124 High Craighead Road. Presently in care of Mrs Docherty, 220 Possil Road, Glasgow. They were in contact with Whooping Cough and are just discharged from the Observation House, South York Street. Mary is by a former marriage but known as Vallance.

Father of Mary is James Luke, Iron Moulder, deceased. Father of Violet, William Vallance, No 8254 Pte. 46th Infantry Brigade B.E.F. France; presently in Stobhill Hospital.

Mother Christina Vallance, formerly Luke, M.S. Johnston, 37 years, died at 202 Possil Road on 6th Aug 1917 of Heart Failure. She had been drinking and pawned the children's clothing.

George, 3 years, is in Ruchill Hospital with Whooping Cough. He is to be cared for by Mrs John Kyle, 214 Possil Road by the father's arrangement.

The ledger states that there were no relatives willing to care for the three children, though the entry names an aunt and an uncle. The records at Quarriers note that Mr and Mrs Vallance had taken out an insurance policy against being unable to care for their children. Mr John Gray of the Hand in Hand Insurance

Society, 150 Hope Street, Glasgow, made the arrangements for the children's admission and for the appropriate allowance to be paid to Quarriers, then known as The Orphan Homes of Scotland. They also record that before his return to France, Private Vallance arranged for George's admission to the orphanage. Violet is noted as having 'Hip Joint Disease', for which she was wearing a plaster cast and using crutches to walk.

A later entry in the ledger goes on to record that on 7 May 1919, Mary and George were discharged to Mr William Vallance, then living in a 'damp' basement room at 30 Kelvinside Avenue, Maryhill. His occupation was given as a Lead Works Labourer, but the recorder noted that he had been unemployed since coming back from the war and was receiving Unemployment Benefit. My mother can hardly have known her stepfather when she and George were released into his care a month after her twelfth birthday. He had been a regular soldier in the HLI or Highland Light Infantry, the famous Glasgow regiment of wee hard men, and he had fought in France throughout the war. She was never explicit about what life was like for her in the basement in Kelvinside Avenue, but we could tell it hadn't been easy. By the time Violet was released to Bill Vallance on 26 September 1926 my mother was long gone. At eighteen she had already met and married my father. Violet and Granda went on living in the room on Kelvinside Avenue till his death in 1959, and Violet long after that. We visited them frequently on trips to Glasgow from the Vale. I remember going to the back of the close, then down a few steps to the basement room, which looked out onto the back court. Violet, who used crutches all her life, kept it 'scruptiously clean', as my mother put it. My memory of those Maryhill visits was of the heroic quantities of Scotch broth Violet made to celebrate our coming.

They were an unlikely couple, my parents, and not only because she was several inches taller. Where she was volatile, exciting, dangerous, Daddy was stoic, calm, uncomplaining, the steady parent. He was the third of eight children, five boys and three girls, born to Richard Holloway and Mary Buchanan, who had married in 1901. But there was a twist in his story, too. Sometime during the 1920s his father emigrated to New York, taking with him his son Dick and daughters Jessie and Beatty, leaving the other five – Tommy, Arthur, Joe, Gertie and Harry – in Scotland with my granny. There was a rumour that he had found another woman in America. Whatever the truth of it, he never came back, and for the rest of her life my granny was supported by the children who stayed in Scotland. Already intrigued by America from my movie habit, our own history made what lay on the other side of the Atlantic even more compelling. In fact, I sometimes felt I knew America better than Scotland.

What I knew, of course, was the America I saw on the screen at the Strand, the picture house in Bank Street to which I went too frequently, either on my own or with my mother. You could see what was presented on Monday, Tuesday, Wednesday, then go again when they changed the show for Thursday, Friday, Saturday. There were two houses each night, between which they cleared the cinema, though I sometimes managed to hide in the lavatory during the interval and see the show all over again. Most of my continuous movie memories are from the Strand. It was there I saw the Bud Abbott and Lou Costello comedies during the war, as well as the road movies featuring Bing Crosby, Bob Hope and Dorothy Lamour, whose very name triggered mysterious longings in me. And it was to the Strand we went for the Saturday morning matinees, whose audiences of children maintained a decibel level that drowned out the soundtrack.

There was another picture house in Alexandria, one that holds a particular memory. The Hall was down at the bottom of Bridge Street, directly opposite Bonhill Bridge. It was in the Hall that I remember clearly seeing *The Jolson Story*, because the event is attached to an electrifying memory. We were a group of twelve-year-old boys, but one of us was more developed than the rest of us and had a girlfriend, whom he brought with him to the Jolson film, and in whose hole, so he claimed later, he had kept his fingers throughout the film. You don't forget a boast as unthinkable as that, one that served to confirm the erotic complexity of going to the pictures. In a society that afforded little privacy, the darkness of the cinema was a good place for sexual exploration. A rigid protocol covered the moves, all of them made by the male: the arm casually draped along the back of the girl's seat; the dropping of the hand onto the girl's shoulder; if this is not repulsed, the hand clasps the shoulder and gently pulls the girl closer (easier if you are in the two-seat divans in the back row unofficially designated for necking couples). If you got that far, kissing could start, though it was years before I knew what else might follow. But the darkness of the cinema also provided scouting opportunities for sexual predators.

We were well equipped with picture houses in the Vale. As well as the Strand and the Hall in Alexandria, there was the Roxy in Renton, a fleapit of last resort entered only if there was nothing worth seeing elsewhere. It was Dumbarton that had the really classy places. Opposite the bridge that brought you into town was the Picture House, high above a grand staircase. It was there I saw *Blood and Sand* in the early years of the war, featuring Tyrone Power and Rita Hayworth, though it was Linda Darnell with whom I was smitten. At the other end of the town, in a vennel opposite the Burgh Hall, there was the Regent, which specialised in Westerns. In the middle of the town, in College Street, there was the Rialto, which I associated with sword and sandal epics, though it was there I saw *The Outlaw*, a Western whose main interest lay in shots of Jane Russell's cantilevered breasts. Though I can't remember the film I went to see on the occasion in question, it was in the Rialto I encountered the darker side of going to the movies.

Dumbarton was a bus ride away, and one I often took on my own in my excursions to the movies. I was heading for a Saturday afternoon show on this occasion, and I was feeling excited about life. Our local weekly, the *Lennox Herald*, had advertised the formation of a children's pipe band. Interested candidates were to sign on the following Tuesday evening at Renton Primary School. I told my parents I'd like to join, and my father said he'd take me up to register next week. Excited, I ran to Main Street for the bus. I got to the Rialto when the house lights were going down, just in time for the film, found a seat on the central aisle, next to a man with a young girl at his other side, and lost myself in the movie. Soon the man had taken my hand in his and was whispering to me. It's cold now the winter's in. You should wear gloves. I'll buy you a pair. I need to measure your hand to find out your size. Then he rubbed my hand up and down his erect penis, which was sticking out of his fly. I pulled away and ran to the lavatory. When I got home I told no one and thought little of the incident, though it must have left its mark, because it is one of the few clear recollections I have of my pre-teen years. On the following Tuesday my father took me to Renton to register for the pipe band. When we walked into the room I saw, behind the desk, the man from the Rialto. I turned and walked out. Ah've changed ma mind, Daddy, ah canny be bothered. My father didn't challenge me, and we went home. I never did learn to play the pipes, but nor did I ever tell anyone why I bailed out.

But it would have taken much more than that to stop me going to the movies. When I got my pocket money on a Friday it was a toss-up between Kinniburgh's bookshop and the Strand, both in Bank Street, though the movies usually won. I don't want to make pretentious claims about the impact of movies on young plastic minds, but I am certain they had an effect on mine. Maybe all they did was amplify a tendency to romantic daydreaming and discontent with the reality of my life, but they certainly did do that. More significantly, they increased a tendency to watch myself playing a role, rather than unself-consciously getting on with my life. And they instilled a sense that authentic life was a drama packed with struggle against adversity, in which only heroic figures emerged triumphant. Hardly surprising in an imaginative child feeding on a diet of emotional carbohydrates, served up as 'musicals, underworlders, westerners' and described thus by Vladimir Nabokov:

In the first, real singers and dancers had unreal stage careers in an essentially grief-proof sphere of existence wherefrom death and truth were banned, and where, at the end, white-haired, dewy-eyed, technically deathless, the initially reluctant father of a show-crazy girl always finished by applauding her apotheosis on fabulous Broadway. The underworld was a world apart: there, heroic newspapermen were tortured, telephone bills ran to billions, and, in a robust atmosphere of incompetent marksmanship, villains were chased through

sewers and store-houses by pathologically fearless cops . . .
Finally there was the mahogany landscape, the florid-faced,
blue-eyed roughriders, the prim pretty schoolteacher arriving
in Roaring Gulch, the rearing horse, the spectacular stampede,
the pistol thrust through the shivered windowpane, the
stupendous fist fight, the crashing mountain of dusty old-
fashioned furniture, the table used as a weapon, the timely
somersault, the pinned hand still groping for the dropped
bowie knife, the grunt, the sweet crash of fist against chin,
the kick in the belly, the flying tackle; and immediately after
a plethora of pain that would have hospitalized a Hercules,
nothing to show but the rather becoming bruise on the
bronzed cheek of the warmed-up hero embracing his
gorgeous frontier bride.[12]

This was the imaginary world that dominated my inner life and
its inchoate longings. The comedies didn't stimulate these iden-
tifications and projections to the same extent, but the thrillers
and Westerns fortified a tendency, later amplified by religion,
not only to hazard roles I was not cut out for, but also to see
life in theatrical rather than prosaic terms. Of course, there was
a consolatory side to the movie habit that was relatively benign.
I think that's what drew my mother. It was the movies that
afforded the poor their best way of escaping for an hour or
two from grey normality into colourful fantasy. This experience
was at its most therapeutically useful during and in the years
immediately following World War II, when most of my early
movie-going happened. Then something else happened. Not
only was I going to a lot of films, I started pretending I had
been to movies I hadn't seen.

We used to take two Sunday papers, the *Sunday Mail* and the

Sunday Post, the latter for the Broons and Oor Wullie. What drew me to the *Sunday Mail* were the dramatic advertisements for films showing in Glasgow. Glasgow loved the movies, and the city was populated with dozens of cinemas. From time to time, we went up to the city to shop at the big Woolworths and Lewis's stores on Argyle Street and to see the Christmas pantomime at the Metropole near Glasgow Green. Occasionally we went to the pictures. I loved the cinemas on Sauchiehall Street and Renfield Street; much grander than anything in the Vale. So I usually devoured the advertisements in the *Sunday Mail* for 'future presentations' in the Glasgow picture houses. One Monday morning I found myself describing to a group of boys an exciting movie I had not actually been to, but had seen advertised in the *Sunday Mail*. Soon I was locked into a playground routine on Monday mornings, as a group of boys gathered round me to hear about the movie I had 'seen' that Saturday. I became fluent at spinning stories based on the information I'd picked up from the previous day's paper; and I began to feel guilty about it. One night, in an agony of remorse, I woke my mother and poured out my difficulty. It's a' right, Dick, she said. You've jist got a good imagination. Don't worry about it. Go back to bed. And I went back absolved.

So maybe it was a true instinct that led me to choose a vocation that would make me a teller of stories that could be understood as containing their own meaning within them. What mattered to my friends in the playground on those Monday mornings was that I took them out of themselves with my fictions, not that I hadn't actually seen the movies I described to them. Implicit in my fraudulence was a theory of religion, though it would take me years to figure it out. I was to become fascinated by Saint Paul's description of Christian preachers as

'deceivers, yet true'. We become *true* deceivers when we understand the purpose of our deceptions, when we admit that the
stories we tell carry their own meaning within them, even if
there is no objective reality beyond them, no movie actually
seen, no stone actually rolled away from the tomb. Trouble
comes when we understand what's going on and start feeling
guilty about it. That's when we become *false* deceivers. To be a
true deceiver you have to believe your deception – the movie
actually seen, the stone actually rolled from the tomb by an
angel. Tell your listeners that there was no movie, no resurrection, but that the story itself has its own power to release them
– try to stop deceiving them, in fact – and they will turn on
you. This is why many preachers become imposters to themselves out of tenderness towards their hearers.

Some of the films I saw wrestled with these paradoxes,
showing just how astute movies could be. One cinematic trope
subverted the play-acting response that movies could provoke,
by showing how a fraud could move to authenticity and end
by filling the part he had started out counterfeiting: there was
the adventurer in hiding, pretending to be a priest, who ends
by sacrificing himself to save the community he was deluding;
there was the man, fleeing from his reputation as a coward back
home, who acts himself into bravery on a foreign field; there
is the kidnapper holding a young woman to ransom, who falls
in love with her and dies to save her life. These paradoxes are
all known to religious leaders who feel they have trapped themselves in a role they find difficult to sustain. A time would come
when I would nearly die of that covenanted deception, but for
years I was to revel in the power of stories to challenge and
console.

I don't think my walking in the hills and my movie-going

were unrelated. Both were prompted by a need for something that did not have a name, a longing for something that constantly eluded the searcher. How can you make yourself one with a landscape? You can tramp over it, become so familiar with its contours that you never need a map, but you can never possess it. It is always eluding your desire, just out of reach, beyond your possessing. I did not know the word at the time, or the idea that lay behind it, but on the hills I was experiencing *latency*, the sense of something hidden behind what is seen. How can you find words for what is beyond sound, make visible what vanishes when seen? Poets sometimes come close:

> . . . did we see that day the unseeable
> One glory of the everlasting world
> Perpetually at work, though never seen?[13]

The hills prompted that yearning. I was looking for something beyond myself, something *out there* that would take me out of *in here* – the life that was going on in my head. I was looking for transcendence, the *beyond* that is sometimes encountered in the midst of things, usually when we are not looking for it. This is the stab of awareness that causes us to turn on our heels to catch the shadow that is behind us. It is the sense of a presence, beyond any knowing, that we reach out towards. And it can be experienced as loneliness. We are missing something, either because it is not there or because we have not yet found it. It was neither the movies nor the hills that gave me what I thought I was looking for. It was something else entirely. And it was a death that brought me to it.

There were a lot of health scares about children during the war, the one I remember being a polio outbreak that had everyone in a panic because they thought it might have been passed on in the swimming baths all the children in the Vale went to. A boy across the street from us died of it, the first death I can remember. Random Street fell silent. Mothers clustered anxiously on doorsteps, desperate to protect their children, not sure how to. Then my cousin Mary Ann died, of meningitis. Polio and meningitis killed children, so anxiety tightened, and the street fell silent again. Because my mother was close to Mary Ann's mother, whose husband Dick was away at sea, my mother took over. Come to Cousin Mary's during your lunchbreak, she told me the day after the death, that's where you'll find me. I was still there, taking my soup, when the Rector of Saint Mungo's Episcopal Church called to comfort Cousin Mary and make arrangements for the funeral. When he was about to leave he turned to my mother. Who is that young man? That's my boy Dick, he's at the Academy. Can he sing? Dick's got a good voice. He turned to me. Dick, would you like to join the choir at Saint Mungo's? We need a good voice like yours. Aye, I said. Come on Sunday for ten thirty. There's a rehearsal before the eleven o'clock mass. The Rector was an extreme Anglo-Catholic. Tall and thin, with an elaborate comb-over hair style and a face that bore the residual lumps and scars of youthful acne, he was an unlikely hero for a movie-struck boy. Unmarried – and contemptuous of priests who married – he had turned his little red sandstone church into a Catholic shrine, heavy with incense and alive with lighted candles.

We weren't a church-going family. I knew the Holloways belonged to Saint Mungo's, but I can't recall ever going to the little church that sat on the edge of Alexandria at Burn Brae. I can remember school services in Main Street Parish Kirk that ignited no interest in me, and visits to little mission halls that had midweek meetings for children and were quite good fun. One was called the Ebenezer, and if you kept your eyes shut during the long prayer that followed the lantern slide show of Jesus performing miracles in Galilee, you got a cup of tea and a Paris bun afterwards.

My father was quietly but firmly unreligious, but my mother suggested there was a story behind his present position. He had been very religious as a young adult, she told me, but 'something had happened' – something that sounded like the death of a good friend in a fire – and he would have no truck with religion thereafter. So I was pretty much a blank page the day I encountered the Rector in Cousin Mary's kitchen in Mitchell Street.

On the following Sunday I turned up, as I said I would and fell in love. It wasn't with the wee church on the edge of town I fell in love, but with what it pointed towards. It was a place that suggested elsewhere. I had not realised what a lovely word that was, elsewhere. It hinted at a distant gate, slightly ajar, or a slit of light high up in a battlement, drawing me into the possibility of *something else*. And the compelling mystery of it all came with proud claims as to its efficacy and meaning.

I cannot remember much about any doctrine the Rector tried to teach me, though one detail lodged permanently in my imagination. He said that the Holy Catholic Church, of which St Mungo's was an outpost, existed in three dimensions: militant here on Earth; expectant in Purgatory; and triumphant in Heaven. Thus was I initiated into a drama that chimed with the themes I had picked up in the movies, and with the longings I had felt in my long tramps on the hills above the Vale. Though a drink problem was to see him removed from the

priesthood long after he left Scotland for England – the reason
I have a strong affection for broken priests – he painted a
picture of the priesthood as a heroic calling, reserved for those
with a *vocation*. A vocation was discerned by an inner troubling
that became a summons to be set apart for a great work. It
was a call to leave father and mother and all earthly ties and
give oneself to a high and lonely task. The priestly vocation
seemed a lot like the thrill and glamour of the movies that had
captivated me, with their lonely heroes expending themselves
to save the lives of others and bring them a contentment they
themselves would never possess.

After that encounter in Mitchell Street, I spent most of my
spare time at Saint Mungo's or working in the Rectory garden.
I was less at home in the Rectory itself, which was often full
of men, young and not so young, who came to take part in
one of the Rector's festivals. He loved the sanctuary full of
servers, of whom I became one, kneeling behind him to lift
the corner of his chasuble at the moment of consecration in
the mass. My imagination was kindled by the drama he had
called me into. He was not surprised when I told him I had
heard the summons and wanted to be a priest. Unlikely as it
seemed for a boy due to leave school, he did not hesitate for
a moment. There was a place in England that took boys like
me, but he'd have to speak to my parents before trying to get
me in. My mother was thrilled and took a job at O'Hare's fruit
shop to pay for the new clothes I'd need for where I was going
and the train fare to get me there. My father was compliant:
'We'll no' stand in his way.'

A few months later, not long after my fourteenth birthday,
the Rector announced my departure in the parish magazine in
his usual high sacerdotal style:

I have the greatest possible pleasure in telling you all that one of our Altar boys, Richard Holloway, has been accepted by the Kelham Fathers to train for the Sacred Priesthood of our Church. I think I am right in saying that since the Vale of Leven Mission was founded and raised to the status of an incumbency at the present St Mungo's, we have never produced a vocation to Holy Orders here. It should be with profound thankfulness to Almighty God that some of our prayers have been answered, at all events in part, and that we are now to have one of our own lads in residence in the famous seminary at Kelham. It remains with the boy himself now, with the help of God's grace, to vindicate the faith and trust that has been placed in him, and to make the best possible use of his eight years at the College of the Sacred Mission, accepting the rough with the smooth and the firm discipline with joy and spiritual longing. Dick leaves us in September and I feel sure he will receive your grateful prayers in his journey south, with the prayers of the faithful, that one day he shall return to Scotland and serve our Church in this dear land with perseverance, holiness, obedience and sacrifice.

2

PLACE OF SACRIFICE

On a crisp September day, with a suitcase full of new clothes, including garments I had never worn previously called underpants, and a brown dressing gown purchased from Burton's in Dumbarton, my mother took me up to Glasgow to put me on the train for Newark. We caught the SMT bus, sitting on the upper deck so that my mother could smoke. I knew the road well, but I'd never been on the bus so early or seen it so packed with men going to the shipyards on the Clyde. Most of them slept through the journey, but some of them knew my mother and chaffed her about travelling in such dodgy company. When we got off the nearly empty bus at the terminus on Waterloo Street in Glasgow, I felt the first chill of leaver's remorse, but kept it to myself. We cut up Hope Street and along West George Street to Queen Street Station. We didn't say much as we approached the station, but my mother held my hand tightly as we crossed the street to the entrance. I was a homesick boy who hated being separated from his mother, but I managed the parting without tears, though there was a lump in my throat as I leant out of the carriage window to wave goodbye.

Hours later I changed trains at Grantham in Lincolnshire, and a pile of returning Kelham students got into the same compartment, along with a priest in black cassock and red girdle whom they addressed as Father Victor. I sat quietly, cheered by their banter, wondering what the book being read by Father Victor could possibly be about – *The Plantaganets*. I followed them off the train at Newark Castle Station onto the Mansfield bus for Kelham – only a couple of miles away, they told me. The countryside was flat and boring, but soon I saw an astonishing silhouette pushing itself above the trees. A high clock tower without a clock but with a confident assertive steeple. A scatter of chimneys, tall triple chimneys, arranging themselves over acres of steep slated roof. Quick sight of a solid flat-topped tower. Then the road rose to the elegant span of a bridge over the Trent at the edge of the village and I caught a glimpse of expanses of red brick, quickly hidden by trees as we slowed to a stop opposite the Fox Inn at a cosy-looking gatehouse, a tiny echo of the great house itself. We streamed off the bus with our suitcases, I behind the rest. The men barged cheerfully under the high entrance arch through the great oak gates which lay open to the drive into the estate. I made to follow them up the main drive, but Father Victor told me to follow the path to the left that went behind the looming bulk of the chapel. He told me it would take me to what they called the Cottage, the boys' bit of the college, which was in a square at the back of the main house.

I followed his directions into a quadrangle of two-storey buildings at the north-east corner of the old Manners Sutton Hall, and knew I had arrived at the Cottage. These buildings had been the servants' quarters and ancillary storerooms of the old estate. Compared to the grandeur of the main house, everything here was on a smaller scale, but it looked elegant and imposing to me. I found my way to the Cottage Master's room where Father Peter was at his desk. I was the last of the boys to arrive, he told me, but there was time to get me settled in before Evensong. The Cottage Senior was summoned to help me. First he took me to the dormitory to stow my luggage and make my bed, showing me how to fold in the corners army style. Then he gave me a quick tour of the premises: the Common Room, the Refectory, the study I would share with two other boys, the showers and lavatories. When a distant bell sounded, he told me it was time for Evensong and we followed a stream of boys to join a flood of men, all heading for the chapel. No one spoke, but the noise of hundreds of hurrying shoes on stone floors was deafening. Coming into the Great Chapel stunned me; and for the first time I felt lonely and homesick; but I was borne on into the great space, which was soon filled with its black-cassocked and blue-scapulared congregation. We settled quietly in our places as a gong sounded. Then there was a knock on wood and we all stood. 'O Lord open thou our lips,' chanted a member of the Society from the stalls where the professed members of the Order sat. I knew the response to that and began to feel at ease: 'And our mouths shall shew forth thy praise.'

There were thirty boys in the Cottage, almost all of them from working-class parishes in the Midlands and north of England, with one or two from London and the south coast. And they were a cheery and talented bunch. There were some star footballers among them; there was a brilliant pianist who couldn't read a note of music but could play almost anything by ear on the old Cottage piano in the Common Room; and there were some great table-tennis players, a game we all played with ferocious seriousness. I could tell immediately that it was a kindly, considerate place, so it didn't take me long to adjust to the hive-like activity of my new home. I liked the way everything worked efficiently and a lot got done. Chapel, manual work and study consumed the day. We were summoned by bells to meals three times, and to chapel four times a day. To get everyone into chapel in time from the various corners of the sprawling complex of buildings was an exercise in military precision. There was the first electric bell, which rang in every corridor of the building to advise students that they had seven minutes to finish what they were doing and get moving. A second electric bell told them they had two minutes left to get into chapel. Then the duty bell-ringer moved purposefully to a large brass gong, like the one in the opening credits of films by J. Arthur Rank, which stood at the bottom of the stair in the main hall. When he struck it, its reverberations rolled throughout the house and stragglers caught behind the ringer were in trouble. Last of all, there was a small gong just inside the chapel door. Those who were not beyond this when the ringer hit it with officious finality were late and were not permitted to take their place in chapel. Instead, they had to sit the service out in the late pew against the wall, in the face of the whole community.

Central to the ethos of Kelham, what Father Kelly had called his *idea in the working*, was the conviction that the total life of the place was an integrated and significant whole in which no part was more important than any other. The necessary chores we all had to share were not thought of as unwelcome distractions from the holy purpose of the place. They were as important to its integrity as the services in the chapel or the lectures we attended. And sport was held to be as important to the spirituality of the place as meditation or learning to sing plainsong. It was said that we did not play *football* at Kelham; we played *theological* football. Nothing was thought to be holier than anything else. We employed no servants and used no outside help. We were entire unto ourselves. This meant that to get everything done that had to be done every second counted and they all had a purpose.

We were up at six thirty for a cold shower followed by mass and breakfast. After washing up and other household chores, we moved into study mode till the next visit to chapel in the middle of the day. After lunch, afternoons were given over to heavy labour, either scrubbing and shining floors in the house or labouring for Brother Edward in the grounds. Two afternoons a week went on sport, football in winter, tennis and cricket in summer. There was a relaxed cup of tea with bread and jam, sometimes with bread and dripping – an English taste I never developed a liking for – at half past three. In summer this was served outdoors on the long terrace to the east of the hall. Then it was back to study again at four, till bells summoned us to Evensong at six thirty. Then dinner, more washing up and more study. The day ended at nine thirty with Compline, followed by lights out. I liked the peace evoked by the last service of the day, *Completorium* in Latin, because it finished the round of prayer that framed the structure of life in a monastic community. The plainsong chants for Compline were haunting. They haunt me still. Plainsong is an ancient, monophonic way of singing an unac- companied line of melody in free rather than measured rhythm. It evolved over centuries, but it seemed as if it had been specifically designed to send waves of transcendent yearning round the great spaces of monastic churches and cathedrals. I loved not only its sound, but also its elegant black squared notes called *neums*. They conjured up images of cowled monks bent over parchment folios, inscribing ancient melodies handed down through the ages. We sang plainsong beautifully at Kelham, because Brother Edwin the choirmaster was a renowned authority on the subject, and he rehearsed us well. Each evening we left chapel in silence, under the spell of the fading plainsong that marked the ending of the day.

Silence was as important to the purpose of Kelham as every other aspect of our lives, and it had two modes. In Greater Silence, which ruled from Compline till the start of morning lectures, talking was forbidden everywhere. During Lesser Silence, which prevailed from the beginning of morning study till lunch, we were allowed to talk in our rooms, but not in the corridors or public spaces. Speaking was never permitted at breakfast except on special Feast Days, when the community got better food as well as time to relax.

Also central to the ethos of Kelham was a sacred under-standing of time, and not just in the way we tried to fill every minute of it with significance. The rhythm of our days was set by the Christian calendar, the ancient pattern devised by the Church to mark those events through which God had revealed himself to his people. It was this side of life at Kelham I cher-ished most. I loved the alternations of gladness and sorrow, light and shade that marked the passing of our days, as we followed the ancient cycle of feast and fast. The Church's Year started not at the beginning of January, but at the beginning of December, the season of Advent, when the readings and hymns trumpeted the imminent arrival of the One Who Was to Come to redeem the world. Advent reached its climax at Christmas, when the Church celebrated the fact that the One longed for, the Desire of All Nations, had slipped anonymously into history at an obscure outpost in Israel. Preachers have hammered the paradox to death, but there is still something heart-stopping about the claim that:

> . . . the wise eternal Word
> Like a weak infant cries!
> In the form of servant is the Lord,
> And God in cradle lies.[14]

The fact that this declaration can be taken literally by unbelievers as well as believers only adds to its power. For those who think religion is a human creation, our own attempt to offer an answer to the riddle of existence, then God has indeed become our child, conceived by our longing and cradled in our imagination. That is why it is still possible at Christmas for the godless to sing with sincerity the carols that celebrate the coming of God in human form. For them, God has indeed come down to earth from heaven – which means heaven itself is now empty. Knowing that can pierce even the confidently godless with occasional regret, the way we sometimes come across a postcard from a dead friend and remember all over again that she is gone for ever. The godless may no longer believe in God, but they can go on missing him when he leaves.

> Miss Him when a choked voice at
> the crematorium recites the poem
> about fearing no more the heat of the sun . . .

> Miss Him when we stumble on the breast lump
> for the first time and an involuntary prayer
> escapes our lips; when a shadow crosses
> our bodies on an X-ray screen . . .

> Miss Him when the linen-covered
> dining-table holds warm bread rolls,
> shiny glasses of red wine.[15]

In those waking days I was unaware of this kind of theological entropy. I loved the poetry of the liturgy and the way it led me through the story of Jesus week by week.

Advent and Christmas were succeeded by Lent, when we meditated on that period in the gospels when Jesus went into the wilderness for forty days to be tempted by Satan. The Lent term was meant to be a heavy time – and it was. This was the season for an outbreak of spiritual influenza known to religious communities the world over, anatomised by the fourth century monk Cassian.

Our sixth contending is with that which the Greeks call *akedia* and which we may describe as tedium or perturbation of heart. It is akin to dejection and especially felt by wandering monks and solitaries, a persistent and obnoxious enemy to such as dwell in the desert, disturbing the monk especially about midday, like a fever mounting at a regular time, and bringing the highest tide of inflammation at definite accustomed hours to the sick soul . . .

When this besieges the unhappy mind, it begets aversion from the place, boredom with one's cell, and scorn and contempt for one's brethren . . . towards any work that may be done within the enclosure of our own lair, we become listless and inert. It will not suffer us to stay in our cell, or attend to our reading: we lament that in all this while, living in the same spot, we have made no progress, we sigh and complain that bereft of sympathetic fellowship we have no spiritual fruit; and bewail ourselves as empty of spiritual profit, abiding vacant and useless in this place; and we that could guide others and be of value to multitudes have edified no man, enriched no man with our precept and example . . . one's mind is an irrational confusion, like the earth befogged in a mist, one is slothful and vacant in every spiritual activity, and no remedy, it seems, can be found for this state of siege than a visit from some brother, or the solace of sleep.[16]

At Kelham this affliction of the soul was called not *akedia*, but 'the Doom', and it rolled through the house in the early months of the year like the mists that came off the Trent in the same season. The rigours of Lent climaxed in Holy Week, when the life of the community focused exclusively on the ancient liturgies that had grown round the observance of the most solemn days in the Church's calendar. The pace slowed down to real time, as we followed Jesus from his entrance to Jerusalem on Palm Sunday, through the events of Holy Week, to his death in the afternoon of Good Friday, his lying in the tomb on Holy Saturday and his resurrection on Easter Sunday. We fasted on Good Friday and spent most of the day in chapel, the main event being the Three Hours preaching of the cross starting at noon, usually led by a visiting preacher. After the Three Hours we broke our fast at four, with a dish known as Kelham beans. The beans, bought in bulk from a supplier in Newark, were soaked overnight, covered in tomato paste and other secret ingredients known only to generations of Kelham cooks, and baked in the oven.

After the heavy trudge of Lent, April was the kindest month at Kelham, because it brought the release of Easter and the promise of vacation. Then there was the Summer Term, the most delightful time of all, when the cricket pitch was restored to use and the tennis courts brought back into play. Depending on the date of Easter, this could be a long term, though it usually sped past. Those were the green days: green for the tree-circled cricket pitch lovingly tended by Brother Edward and his team; and green for the colour of the vestments worn by the celebrants in chapel at mass, green being the colour of the season after Trinity that ran from Whitsun till the end of November, when we waited for the trumpets of Advent again.

> We have done with dogma and divinity
> Easter and Whitsun past,
> The long, long Sundays after Trinity
> Are with us at last;
> The passionless Sundays after Trinity,
> Neither feast-day nor fast.
>
> Christmas comes with plenty,
> Lent spreads out its pall,
> But these are five and twenty,
> The longest Sundays of all;
> The placid Sundays after Trinity,
> Wheat-harvest, fruit-harvest, Fall.[17]

Unrelenting though it was, there were periods of relaxation in all this activity. I liked the moments before things started, the interludes between duties, the way there was time after dinner in the summer before study for a stroll down Apostles' Walk to the orchard or a turn about the cricket pitch where swallows darted round the pavilion, their nests visible under the eaves. Those were sweet moments, because they were fleeting. I learnt that pleasure was caught on the slant. Contentment, if it happened, came when I wasn't looking for it and was intent on something else. Concentrate on the something else, the matter I was engaged on, and a sense of wellbeing might strike like a flash of sunlight from a frozen river. It never worked the other way round. Sometimes it was in the tumult of a football match on a winter afternoon, the crows settling noisily in the elms behind the Cottage, when my blood thrilled because I'd cleared the ball from our penalty area with a kick that took it to the other goal mouth. Sometimes it came in the clash of argument and the heady joy of the struggle with ideas. Sometimes it crept up on me in the hush of the day's ending.

Kelham was self-sufficient, autonomous, intent upon its own purpose, which was the doing of God's will – *whatever that might be*, as Father Kelly would have observed wickedly. It was a complete culture that appeared to be unconcerned with what went on outside its gates, which is maybe why it integrated working-class boys into its life without difficulty. Benign though the atmosphere was, it was impossible to ignore the emphatic use of the language of sacrifice in describing the purpose of the place. It was reported that when Father Kelly was showing a distinguished guest round the great chapel, he had responded to the visitor's dismay at the size of the altar by chuckling, 'We sacrifice young men on that altar!' And he wasn't joking. We were there to sacrifice our own wills and submit them to the will of God, so that He might forge us into instruments of his mission to win back a world that had forgotten his love. At the end of one Good Friday at Kelham, when the theme of sacrifice had been wound up to an almost unbearable degree by the monk who preached the Crucifixion to us during the Three Hours, I was so fired with spiritual zeal that I determined to write to my father and call him back to God. In the interlude between breaking our fast and returning to chapel for Evensong, at the very moment he would have been girding himself for the remaining three hours of his shift in the Craft, I wrote to him, pleading with him to come home to God. I had been teaching myself calligraphy that term, so it was with italicised self-consciousness that I crafted my summons. He had the tact never to refer to it. When my mother died years later, I found the letter among her papers and felt sick with shame when I read it.

It is hard not to see the motive behind an overture of this sort as a kind of spiritual conceit. It is probably okay to interfere in the lives of people we are close to if we feel they are endangering themselves in some way. On several occasions I have done what was called 'an intervention' in the lives of people I knew who were suffering from a drink problem that was becoming a danger to them and their families. It was always a painful thing to do, and was not always successful, but I justified it on the grounds that if I saw someone about to back off a cliff, I'd warn them of the danger and advise them to stop. What is the difference between that kind of warning, and exhortations to come to Jesus or submit to Allah? Believers will reply that backing off an eschatological cliff is precisely what the unrepentant sinner is about to do, hence the need to warn them of the danger they are in. The difference, of course, is between an actual cliff and a hypothetical one, which is why evangelists have to spend a lot of time persuading listeners that their imaginary cliff is real. Having persuaded them of the existence of an illusory world, they then offer them a deal on how to avoid the horrors that are part of its imaginary landscape. No wonder V.S. Naipaul said of the impact of Christian evangelism upon the native peoples of South America, 'The missionary must first teach self-contempt. It is the basis of the faith of the heathen convert.'[18]

57

To be fair to the religion I absorbed at Kelham, it rarely mentioned Hell as the final destination of all those who refuse to turn to God. I never found it hard to reject the vulgarity of the idea of Hell and see it only as human darkness made visible. We have made enough Hell on earth to know how creative human cruelty can be, not excluding its grimmer theological metaphors. It was never fear of Hell that was to haunt me. It was the lacerating sadness of disappointing God that hurt. The idea of the heartbroken God reaching out to his children for their love and being rejected by them is emotionally powerful. What I picked up at Kelham, and was never to lose, was a powerful theology of disappointment – the flipside of the sacrifice theme – and it was imparted more by what was left unsaid than by what was said. The Society had a history of people forsaking the life of sacrifice for the life of the world. The Kelham slang for this kind of failure was 'boshed'. Some students in every generation boshed over women. There was a strong celibate ethos in the place. Students were not allowed to establish relationships with women during the long years of their training, and they were expected to remain unmarried for at least five years after ordination. There were casualties. A student would fall in love while he was on vacation. He would be told by the authorities not to come back for the following term. We would come back and learn that he had boshed. A member of the Society would have difficulties and leave: and there would be disappointment that he had lifted his hands from the plough and looked back. There was a plangent phrase from Saint Paul's Second Letter to Timothy that used to make me shiver with anticipatory regret when it was read in chapel: 'Demas hath forsaken me, having loved this present world.'[19] The life we had chosen was a high and arduous one: would we stay the course or would we, too, bosh our appointment with God and fall into regret? He would not punish us if we did, but he would be *disappointed* in us. He'd still love us, but we'd know that his real friends were those who stayed with him till the end, like the beloved disciple in John's Gospel who was the only man brave enough to stand at the foot of the cross on which Jesus hung. One of Father Kelly's favourite sayings, written in capitals for emphasis, was NOTHING COUNTS BUT LIFETIMES.[20] The ones who counted were those who sacrificed themselves for life: celibate priests who stayed a lifetime in slum parishes or members of religious orders who made vows for life and kept them. For those of us who were to find ourselves incapable of that kind of steady heroism, there was to be the constant tug of disappointment. We were those who had made the great refusal and gone sadly away.

> For some people the day comes
> when they have to declare the great Yes
> or the great No. It's clear at once who has the Yes
> ready within him; and saying it,
>
> he goes from honour to honour, strong in his
>   conviction.
> He who refuses does not repent. Asked again,
> he'd still say no. Yet that no – the right no –
> drags him down all his life.[21]

This was some way in the future for me, but even then there were tremors of unease in my soul. Why did I feel the compulsion to write so strongly to my father that Good Friday afternoon? And why did I fall in love with the most extreme version of monasticism and even try to practise it at Kelham?

In my second year I was bewitched by *The Listeners,* a poem by Walter de la Mare. A traveller arrives at a house in the forest and gets no answer to his repeated knocking. We are never told if the house is empty – though the title suggests there may be listeners within – but no answer is given to the traveller's question:

> 'Is there anybody there?' said the Traveller,
> Knocking on the moonlit door;
> And his horse in the silence champed the grasses
> Of the forest's ferny floor;
> And a bird flew up out of the turret,
> Above the Traveller's head:
> And he smote upon the door again a second time;
> 'Is there anybody there?' he said.

He knocks for a third time, with no result.

> 'Tell them I came, and no one answered,
> That I kept my word', he said.

He gets back on his horse and rides away, and:

> . . . the silence surged solidly backward,
> When the plunging hoofs were gone.[22]

The forest is a frequent image in literature for the life of humanity, this wood we find ourselves traversing without map or compass, like amnesiac travellers who do not know where they came from or where they are going. Thrown into existence, gifted with the ambiguous power of consciousness, it is no surprise that we have been asking if there is anybody there since our synapses fired the first question at the universe, only for it to meet silence and invisibility. Yet there is also the mystery of latency I encountered in the hills above the Vale, the sense of something just out of reach, something unseen *that listens!* From that invisible listener a colossal demand has exerted itself upon some men and women, who then give themselves utterly away to it. Jesus called it Father and offered himself to it without condition. Since his death on its behalf countless others have followed his example. Always a minority, they provoke discomfort, even among believers, because most believers acquire only a mild version of faith and are made anxious by those who catch it badly. T.S. Eliot put their anxiety into the mouths of the women of Canterbury in *Murder in the Cathedral.*

> Forgive us, O Lord, we acknowledge ourselves as type
>   of the common man,
> Of the men and women who shut the door and sit by
>   the fire;
> Who fear the blessing of God, the loneliness of the
>   night of God, the surrender required, the deprivation
>   inflicted.[23]

I feared yet longed for the loneliness of the night of God, the surrender required, the deprivation inflicted. I wanted to be heroic, make the ultimate sacrifice, give my life away to the silent listener who haunted me but never spoke. I fell in love with the romance of extreme monasticism. I devoured books about it, especially if they contained photographs of monasteries tucked into the lee of mountains in remote places. I searched for glimpses of monks gliding into cold chapels to pray to the unseen listener while the world slept. I was particularly drawn to the Cistercian order, founded in 1098 to establish a form of the monastic life stricter and more arduous than any that then existed. Their life was one of secluded intercession and adoration in remote places, their churches plain and without ornament. My interest had been stimulated by the autobiography of a colourful American called Thomas Merton, which was published about the time I arrived at Kelham. Radically and rather patronisingly edited by Evelyn Waugh for the English edition of the book, *Elected Silence* told the story of Merton's conversion to Catholicism and his decision to become a Cistercian monk at Gethsemani Abbey in Kentucky.

Merton's spiritual journey was to take him far from the certainties he espoused at the time of his conversion, but his early story fired my imagination. I bought a Latin version of the Cistercian Breviary and for a whole term I crept out of bed at two in the morning and slipped into the Lady Chapel on the ground floor of the House to recite the Night Office. Having only rudimentary Latin, I was like a Madrasa student who knew no Arabic but recited the Quran by rote. The recitation of the words had a meaning for me apart from my understanding of them. I knew that at that moment, in monasteries hidden up forgotten lanes all over Europe, monks would be assembling in their cold churches to pray the Night Office because it was the hour of sorrow and despair for the wretched of the earth, the hour on the bridge above the river, the hour with the whisky bottle, the hour by the deathbed. That was what I thought I was honouring, as the Kelham community slept and I knelt in the Lady Chapel.

3

THE FALL

I didn't have to pay fees at Kelham, but it was expensive for my parents to keep me there for the four years before I was called up for National Service in the army at eighteen. There was the cost of three return trips to Newark every year, not to mention the extra clothes I needed when I started to stretch. By the time I was seventeen, in 1951, I was a foot taller than my father – free school milk, my mother said. My mother took on extra work to help, and Rosie Kirkpatrick, our local communist councillor, heard about our struggle and got me a grant to cover my expenses. Then a suggestion was made by the Rector. Admiral Mackenzie, one of his parishioners, had a small estate at Caldarvan, a few miles east of Loch Lomond near Gartocharn, and he arranged for him to give me work on the estate farm during the spring and summer vacations.

During my second year at Kelham, after my sixteenth birthday, the family moved into a new council house across the Leven on the edge of Jamestown, the beginning of a redevelopment process in the Vale that was to see the centre of Alexandria gutted and a string of housing schemes planted on the hills above the east side of the river. We were moved to one of the earlier schemes, still within walking distance of the amenities of the town centre. It was goodbye to Random Street and its camaraderie, compensated for by an inside lavatory and the bath that went with it, not to mention separate bedrooms for everyone. It was from this house in Elmbank Drive I cycled the five miles to Admiral Mackenzie's farm to do general labouring jobs in the spring vacation and help with the harvest in August. I would cut through the scheme to Jamestown, go round the edge of Balloch to the Stirling Road on the east side of the Loch, and after a couple of miles turn up a steep hill that led me to the farm at Caldarvan.

There was always a lot to do on the farm in the spring and summer vacations, but it was the August harvest a few months before my seventeenth birthday that I remember most vividly. When the crop was ready and the weather looked stable, Tam the ploughman scythed a corridor round the edge of the field. I followed Tam, gathering the corn into rough sheaves and binding them together with a rope of half a dozen strands of the fallen crop. Backbreaking work that opened the way for the Admiral's new Ferguson tractor to pull the Binder onto the field. When it was lined up against the standing corn, Tam dropped the lever and the Binder chomped its way round the field spewing out sheaves more elegantly bound than my ham-fisted efforts. Those of us who followed the binder picked the sheaves up two at a time and leant them against each other at an angle, their heads of grain mingling, eight sheaves to a stook – thirsty work in the heat and rough on the inside of the wrists, especially when we were harvesting barley. When the day's work was over I loved looking back at the rows of stooks on the harsh carpet of stubble, the evening sun sending their patterned shadows across the field. As the binder chomped its way round the field, the island of corn in the middle got smaller and the farm dogs got more excited. The whole population of the farm would gather round the tiny island that remained for the last cut. When the binder started the final swathe, out would hurtle a platoon of terrified rabbits and hares who had retreated to the last redoubt of corn against the advancing machine. The dogs, in an ecstasy of barking, caught as many rabbits as they could, though the hares usually managed to elude capture. That year Lassie got a hare nearly as big as herself, grabbing it by the back of the neck. One shake and its neck was broken. I rode proudly home with it on my bike that night, and my mother soon had it skinned and in the stew pot.

In contrast to the rhythm of life at Kelham, which was a blend of physical labour, intellectual effort and spiritual struggle, being back at home during the vacation was one-dimensional and I felt distanced from that other self. The beginning of a duality in my being? It is hard to say whether it was created then or whether the divided circumstance of my life began to make visible what had always lurked under the surface – two disconnected lives. At Kelham I was caught up in the transcendental romance of the religious life, heightened by the language of sacrifice and self-offering. I wore a black cassock with a blue scapular or apron over it to keep off the wear and tear: an ideal costume for the practice of visual piety. Jesus warned us not to practise our piety 'to be seen of men', but where was the fun in that? Uniforms are *meant* to draw attention, mark us out as different. I was genuinely drawn to the romance of the given-away life, but I was also fascinated by the theatre of it. I loved playing the part, and not always 'to be seen of men' – or why had I been getting up at two in the morning that term to act the Cistercian in the Lady Chapel? And at the end of each long term I would hang up the cassock and come back to the Vale, where I appeared to slot back in without effort. The Rector might have understood what was going on in me, but I had begun to feel a bit embarrassed by him. He had visited me at Kelham that summer term and insisted on playing tennis. Actually he wasn't bad at the game, with a quick, biting service, but his long comb-over fell out of place in the tumult of the rallies and floated in distracting tendrils round his head. It was hard not to feel ashamed for him. There would always be a bond of affection, but there was now a reticence on my part as well. Soon he left the Vale for England and we lost touch, though news about him filtered through from time to time, some of it sad. With my family it was easier to reconnect, but only because I resumed my place as the only son and reverted to the old pattern. I would entertain them with stories of the eccentrics at Kelham, do the voices and gestures of the *dramatis personae* of the place; but I could not talk about the other life that haunted me, a life that seemed unreal in this placc on these streets below these hills. They saw changes in me: my accent shifting, my body lengthening, my habits changing. My mother noticed that I had started using a nail file instead of scissors and hoped I wasn't getting above myself. Behind the barb I knew she was afraid of losing me. It was Gertie who saved the day by pointing out that filing stopped nails splitting, so it was better than cutting, and she used a file too. But there had been a shift away from the old unself-conscious closeness. I was different; they were the same. The same was true when I tried to reconnect with my pals from school, all working men in apprenticeships to local tradesmen now. We went to the movies together, but nothing of that different self I carried ever intruded here. When the pictures came out we would stand at the bus stop eating fish and chips before saying good-night, and I would look up at Carman Hill, over there on the other side of my life.

And that summer was the time of Brenda the Land Girl.
Land girls were a wartime invention, aimed at helping farmers
whose labourers had been called up, and they stayed around
for a bit in peacetime. Brenda came from Bridgeton in the east
end of Glasgow, and she was a fixture at Caldarvan that summer.
She was a large, cheery young woman, about three years older
than me, probably pushing twenty. And she enjoyed teasing me,
the college boy. Shy at first, I soon got into the pushing and
shoving game young men play when they want to touch a
woman but lack the confidence to do it openly. My favourite
ruse was to come up behind her, wrap my arms round her waist
and lift her off her feet. She played her part in the charade
enthusiastically, shoving her backside against me in mock resistance as I performed the clumsy manoeuvre. On the day I
remember, the two of us were in a field on our own in the
early morning when it was still too damp to start harvesting.
Sometimes we were sent to repair stooks that had fallen over
in the night, the kind of make-work farmers did while they
waited for the right weather for the main event. There the two
of us were, out in the field, no one around. She bent over to
pick up a couple of fallen sheaves, and I felt a shift in me as
though a valve had opened somewhere. As I wrapped my arms
round her waist to lift her off her feet, she giggling against me
in the accustomed way, I was swept by a wave of pleasure so
acute it took my breath away. I held on, pressing against her,
while it rolled through me to its climax. I had no idea what
had happened, but it happened again that night when I was
face down on my bed, remembering Brenda in the field that
morning. This time the pleasure was more intense and the
consequence more obvious. When it was over I lay there stunned
and depleted, already guilty at having 'burst into fulfilment's

desolate attic'.[24] That was the secret shame I brought back to Kelham that September when the vacation ended.

I didn't come right out and ask Father Peter about it, but he must have recognised the change in me, because he called me to his study to tell me the facts of life. He was as embarrassed as I was, but he ploughed on, giving me a rudimentary sketch of the biology of reproduction, and leaving me with the distinct impression that God himself regarded the whole business as regrettable and wished he had invented a less troublesome way of guaranteeing the continuance of the species. There was no guidance on how I might deal with the impact of the reproductive imperative on my own body; nor did I ask him about the moral status of the secret pleasure that was dominating my attention, probably because I had already concluded that it must be a sin. What settled it for me was the little going away present the Rector had given me two years before. The Centenary Prayer Book, blue cloth, octavo size, had been published originally in 1933, the hundredth anniversary of the beginning of the Oxford Movement, from which the Catholic revival had started in the Anglican Church. In one handy volume it contained all the prayers and devotions the self-conscious Anglo Catholic needed, including a guide for making one's confession. This was a practice the Rector had encouraged me to start, informing me that it was an essential element in the spiritual life of an *ordinand*, the mystical estate into which I had entered when I left Alexandria. It was a practice Kelham also encouraged, so it was soon part of my routine to make my confession once a month. Until that day at Caldarvan going to confession had hardly been a pleasure, but it had been straightforward and easily accomplished, a bit like getting in the cold shower that started the day at Kelham. I would go to the little side chapel in the gallery of the Great Chapel where I would kneel beside Father Peter, facing the form printed on the prayer desk, he sitting in a chair facing the other way, with a purple stole round his neck. I would begin: 'Bless me, Father, for I have sinned.'

Father Peter would reply: 'The Lord be in thy heart and on thy lips that thou mayest truthfully confess all thy sins, in the name of the Father and of the Son and of the Holy Spirit.'

Following this admonition, I would recite the formula on the card in front of me, admitting that I had sinned in thought, word and deed, since my last confession, in the following ways. Then I would read out the laundry list of particular sins, ending the recitation: 'For these and all my other sins which I cannot now remember, I am heartily sorry, firmly purpose amendment of life, and humbly ask of you, Father, penance, advice and absolution.'

Father Peter would offer a few words of advice, a penance to recite – usually a psalm – then, by the authority given to him to forgive sins, he would absolve me in the name of the Father and of the Son and of the Holy Ghost, and end: 'Go in peace, the Lord hath put away all thy sins, and pray for me a sinner.'

Auricular confession, confession to the ear or *auriculam* of a priest, as opposed to *general confession*, which is the kind of group act that takes place in public worship, is a controversial subject around which many legends have grown. Some have seen it as a device by which the priesthood has maintained control over a quiescent laity, and while there may be something in that, it strikes me as too conspiratorial a view, and one that does not fit my own experience from either side of the confessional. Private or auricular confession has never been compulsory in the Anglican Church, where the working principle has always been: all may; none must; some should. The some who should are those who are burdened with guilt for serious offences, for whom absolution can be a liberating and life-changing experience that enables them to put the past behind them and move on into the future.

One of the most tragic things about us is that we commit irreversible acts with no power to undo them and no way to rewind to the moment before the event that may have stolen another's joy and destroyed our own peace of mind. The remedy for the irreversibility of our actions is the ability to forgive them or be forgiven for them. The most terrible effect of bad conduct is its ability to steal the future by trapping us in a futile loop that endlessly rehearses what was done to us or what we have done to another. Confession can stop the constant replay of the past and allow the future to open before us again. That is the truth that lies at the heart of a practice that is capable of both abuse and trivialisation. The ecclesiastical monopoly of the process has been over for a long time, and the practice of it has been largely secularised by the psycho-therapeutic professions, which have taken over as the main ports at which the cargos of human despair are now unloaded. After that morning in the field at Caldarvan my practice of confession became unhealthy, because it locked me into the classic Christian trap of freighting sexual sins with a weight of shame that did not attach itself to other, arguably more serious ones. And that is an old song that is still being sung.

All of which brings me back to that little blue prayer book. Not only did it contain a handy form for the rite of confession, it included lists of sins aimed at helping forgetful souls remember what they'd been up to. There are lots of stories about the childish misuse of these lists, including one about a ten-year-old girl who confessed to having neglected her diocese, having reached a section of a prayer book clearly aimed at peccant bishops. The Centenary Prayer Book contained a whole section on *impurity*, the word that began to flash accusingly at me after my encounter with Brenda. There it was in black and white: 'Have you been impure in thought, word or . . .' – the big one – '. . . deed?' Yes to *thought*. Definitely. *Thinking* about what had happened in that field was how it all started. Another verb used was *harboured,* as though impure thoughts were pirate ships or smugglers' vessels seeking somewhere to dock and land their illicit goods. That was another idea that convicted me. I knew I had harboured impure thoughts in my head. More than that: I had signalled to them and invited them to sail in and drop anchor in my mind, where they rolled in the swell of my imagination. No one ever told me how to prevent them from sailing in like that; no one told me where to find the coastguard vessels that would head them off before they could slip by my defences and drop anchor in my mind. And once they sailed in, I *harboured* them. There was more to come, much more. There was another word that accused me in the prayer book: had I *entertained* these thoughts? Movie fan that I was, that was a word I knew and rated highly. I loved to be entertained in the picture house, letting the show take me out of myself. I loved the trailers that promised *future entertainments*. I was definitely doing that here. I encouraged the little regatta to sail in and put on a show for me. I both harboured impure thoughts and *entertained* them, though it would have been more accurate to say they entertained me, by flooding my mind with an erotic cabaret. There was no doubt I had been flagrantly impure in *thought*. They caught me on that, repeatedly; and it was an unpleasant one to have to confess, because it made me feel furtive and secretive.

But they never caught me on the next one. I was never impure in *word*, never. The one thing I didn't do, couldn't do, was *talk* about this stuff. To anyone. As far as I knew, I was the only person at Kelham, where I was surrounded by holy people whose minds were on higher things, who was bothered by any of this. So there was no way I was going to talk about sex to anyone, apart from my furtive whispers in Father Peter's ear, which didn't count as talk and which couldn't ever be alluded to elsewhere because of the seal of the confessional. Sex was the secret that never became Word. Well, never the spoken Word. I did start trying to read about it. There was a good library in the Cottage and I spent a lot of time in there on my own, combing through novels for mentions of that which could not be said but might be read. What I found confirmed me in thinking that sex was as deadly as it was fascinating. Graham Greene made it sound inescapable – and desolating. It was a curse that drove people out of happiness, the way it had driven Adam and Eve from Eden. Even the doing of it, when it finally did get done in the books I read, was heavy with loss and pain. In his Afterword to Nabokov's *Lolita*, Craig Raine describes the unavoidable duality of sex as 'the imperative and the accusative, the sexually romantic and the sated regret'.[25] My reading intensified my fascination with this ancient struggle in the human psyche, but I never spoke about it and was always uncomfortable when others alluded to it, however cryptically, such as the day a boy pointed out to me that the dictionary said *friction* was the rubbing of one body against another. I shivered with embarrassment, because that was the very thing I spent a lot of time thinking about. But my disgraceful secret was secure. I was never impure in *word*.

I had been guilty in thought, but not in word. Next there

was *deed*, which was what all that harbouring and entertaining led to, a deed that stained my conscience as it stained my body. Shame had come into my world.

A shame that started at sixteen
And spread to everything.[26]

It removed much of the joy I had known at Kelham during my first two years there. Outwardly things were the same. I went about my work and tried to say my prayers, but I was now carrying a secret burden. I knew I was a fraud. I was like the whited sepulchre excoriated by Jesus, which appeared beautiful outwardly, but within was full of dead men's bones. There were a few days a month when I was at peace. Technically, I was then in *a state of grace*, because I had confessed my sins and scrubbed them off like mud stains from my football kit. I would approach confession with dread, while looking forward to the feeling of release, once it was all over, that would accompany me out of the little chapel up there in the gallery.

I always began with the easy stuff: the gossip about others, the lack of charity, the unkind words spoken, the occasional moment of anger. Then, my voice getting hoarser and lower, I would record my secret shame, though not every incident. I usually grossed the incidents up, only to worry about the effect of my evasive circumlocutions. Would each act of impurity actually be forgiven if I lumped them together? Or was each act noted individually and kept on my record unshriven by God like unpaid taxes, because I had been too embarrassed to offer a precise accounting? I never did sort that one out, but since Father Peter never asked *how many times?* I assumed I was okay and would leave the confessional unburdened by shame

– sometimes for a whole week. That was my record: in a state of grace for seven days, hoping the habit was finally kicked. Till the despicable little fleet sailed into the harbour of my mind again and the shameful ritual recommenced. In the brief advice he offered me in his coughy smoker's voice at the end of my recitation of shame, Father Peter never alluded to this aspect of my confession, so I assumed his silence consented to the seriousness of my self-accusation. Peter Clarke was a kind man, but he was unable to find words to reduce or explain away my misery. As far as human anguish goes, it was at the lower end of the spectrum, but it was pain enough, and it left a shadow. I have often wished I had met someone then, maybe someone like the priest I became later, who could have told me to relax, that it was natural, just don't turn it into a full-time occupation.

Sadly, Christianity has been more intent on repressing and misrepresenting sex than on helping people manage it wisely. It wouldn't have been so bad if the Church had said to the children of the earth: 'We know you are going to be enthralled by the mystery of sexuality, which is hardly surprising since it is the energy of life itself. We know it will have the power to take you over for its own purposes, and we know you won't always be able to resist it. Try at least to think about its possible conse-quences. Recognise that sex has the potential to hurt and devas-tate, as well as the capacity to thrill. Understand that it will get all tied up with your need for consolation and acceptance. And never forget the sheer fucking insanity of it all.' Sadly that's not how they put it, and their response has bedevilled Christianity's relationship with humanity ever since. The tragic thing is that what they actually said was based on a wilful misreading of an ancient myth and a profound mistake about human origins. Bad enough in themselves – and causing centuries of anguish for many human souls – these mistakes also provide us with a classic example of religion's difficulty in admitting that it has ever been profoundly mistaken about anything.

There were two elements to the mistake the early fathers made about sex, one more excusable than the other. The less excusable mistake was their failure to understand the nature of myth, which is the narrative form of all religions. The power of myth lies in its ability to *represent* ourselves to ourselves. A myth is a story that expresses but does not explain a universal human experience. You only have to look at a cartoon of a naked couple gazing at the enticing fruit on a tree, while a serpent wraps itself seductively round their legs, to understand the message. The best myths have immediacy. We get them, see ourselves through them. They are mirrors. The early Church read the myth of the expulsion of Adam and Eve from the Garden of Eden as a historic event, and projected onto it a theological interpretation it was never meant to have. Not only did this primordial act of disobedience happen, everyone born since it occurred has inherited the guilt of the primal act. *In Adam all have sinned.* And here's the kicker: *sex is its mode of transmission!* Henceforth, sex is not just a natural drive that can be misused; it is intrinsically disordered, wrong in itself. The main architect of this reading of the myth of the Fall was Augustine, Bishop of Hippo in North Africa in the fifth century, one of the geniuses of early Christianity. Augustine believed that had Adam and Eve never eaten of the tree, they would have propagated children without what he called concupiscence, the desire that is the engine of sexuality.

Against this drive, which is in tension with the *law of the mind,* all chastity must fight . . . This urge, had it existed in

Paradise . . . would . . . have never run beyond the bidding of the will . . . It would never have forced itself upon the mind with thoughts of inappropriate and impermissible delights. It would not have had to be held upon the leash by married moderation, or fought to a draw by ascetic labour. Rather, when once called for, it would have followed the will of the person with all the ease of a single-hearted act of obedience.[27]

If the first element in this misreading of sexuality is hard to excuse, the second is forgivable, because it was based on igno-rance of human origins and the unimaginably long processes of natural evolution. *We* know that sex could never have been the consequence of the fall of man from an original state of pre-sexual innocence, because sex existed long before humanity appeared on the scene, and it came along not because it was prompted by the serpent, but because it was the answer to a problem. In his book, *The Language of the Genes,* Steve Jones asks why sex appeared on the evolutionary scene. Some crea-tures manage with just females, so that every individual produces copies of herself. Why bother with males and introduce the inevitable struggle and strife they will bring to the equation of life? According to Jones, sex is:

a way of producing individuals who contain genes from more than one line of descent, so that inherited information from different ancestors is brought together each generation. In an asexual creature everyone has one mother, one grand-mother, one great-grandmother, and so on in an unbroken chain of direct descent from the ur-mother who began the lineage.[28]

The reason why life is not female and therefore sexless has to do with the hazards of mutation. If a sexless organism had a harmful change to her DNA it would be handed on to all her descendants, none of whom would ever get rid of it, and the decay of the genetic message would set in as one generation succeeded another. However, in a sexual creature the new mutation can be purged as it passes to some descendants but not to others. Sex has a positive effect on evolution, because the new combinations of genes are better able to cope with the challenges of a changing environment. Creatures that give up males may save themselves some conflict in the short term, but only at the price of killing themselves off in the long run.

Far from being the corruptor the early fathers said it was, sex is the mechanism that evolved in nature to pass life on as vigorously and effectively as it could. It is the sexless life that turns out to be a dead end. Sex is the imperative that drives life. At its primal level it is pre-moral and uninterested in its impact on those it uses to keep itself going. Nevertheless, though they were wrong in their understanding of the origins of sex, the early fathers were right in recognising the havoc it can play with humans who cannot restrain their own desires. The heart-breaking thing is that, because of its gross misunderstanding of the real nature of sex, Christianity has become a dangerous and untrustworthy guide on the subject. This is why sex continues to be a source of shame and abuse in Christian societies; and it is why it is forced to operate in the dark, with frequently tragic consequences.

And it is why I brought back to Kelham for the Michaelmas term after that Caldarvan summer a new heaviness and a more pronounced duality. Good at compartmentalising, I do not think it showed. I went about my work as I had before. I prayed in chapel and continued to read books about the monastic life. I enjoyed playing right back in the Second Eleven football team, with occasional outings for the First Eleven. I was a cheerful presence about the place during the day. Then the night came, and it was different. The little flotilla would float into my mind and drop anchor. The show would begin. The term before, I'd started getting up at two in the morning to read the Cistercian Night Office in the Lady Chapel. This term I started getting up at two in the morning to go to a different place and do a different thing. I would creep down to the shower room, take off my pyjamas and lie on the cold concrete floor. And I would pray. Not the Night Office. This was a prayer of desperation, a prayer to God to expel the little fleet of impure images that insisted on sailing into my mind. Sometimes it worked.

4

THE SIDE DOOR

I tried to make a run for it just before my eighteenth birthday. The signs of restlessness were there for the reading during my last year in the Cottage, little premonitions of departure that I tried to ignore. I had a significant break in front of me, anyway. Before moving from the Cottage to the House to start the four-year theology course that led to ordination, we all had to do two years of National Service, starting as soon as practicable after our eighteenth birthdays. Mine was in late November, so I was expected to complete a final Michaelmas term in the Cottage and head into the army after the Christmas vacation. My final year I'd been coasting. I'd already passed the School Certificate, so I was in a one-boy Sixth Form with no exams to face, but with lots of interesting reading to do.

Things were in transition at home in the Vale as well. Admiral Mackenzie had died at the turn of the year and his estate was wound up. During the Easter vacation I had gone to Caldarvan not to work on the farm, but to help them get the contents of the house and estate ready for sale. On the day, the house was full of dealers as well as ordinary citizens chasing bargains, and I was surprised at how upset I was by their presence – not that I had spent much time in the house during the years I had worked for the Admiral. It was not a particularly grand house, but I had always liked its comfortable elegance. History has largely abolished the minor gentry from the land and the delectable properties they cherished for centuries in our countryside; but only the coldest heart could be immune to the sadness of their passing. Though he had been kind to me, the Admiral's people were not my people, and I had always felt intimidated by their accents and effortless assurance. Nevertheless, I recognised that a way of life that had carried important values was passing, and I was susceptible to the sorrow of endings.

When I returned to Kelham after that Easter vacation, I wrote an essay on the sale of the estate for a new English tutor who had joined the Society, a priest who tried the life for a couple of years before joining the ranks of the leavers. We were both surprised by the essay. It turned out to be an act of mourning and a cry of protest at the passing of things. Though the Old Man had told us that nothing counted but lifetimes, I was starting to suspect that I would turn out to be one of life's leavers, and I began to anticipate the sadness of partings. I had discovered the poetry of Gerard Manley Hopkins. It was an unfortunate discovery on one level, because it prompted me to write reams of imitative poetry, heavy with alliteration and sodden with spirituality. That phase went. What endured was a debt to Hopkins for the way he prepared us for the passing of everything.

> Margaret, are you grieving
> Over Goldengrove unleaving?
>
> It is the blight man was born for,
> It is Margaret you mourn for.[29]

The blight man was born for is not just time and the way it conducts us to the big exit at the end of the road, but the way it makes us rehearse that departure over and over again through other partings, other losses. It is possible to be an accomplished leaver, yet for something in us to cry out at the violence of separation. A few years ago a friend told me of the night he left his wife. As he opened the front door to go away, his children were leaning over the upstairs banister screaming, don't leave daddy don't leave don't leave don't leave daddy daddy don't leave. But leave he did, their grief pounding in his ears, stricken and guilty, a monster in his own eyes, yet incapable of staying. Sometimes parting is more about moving on than moving out, but even here regret can undo us. Cardinal Newman, recalling his departure from the Church of England, remembered the snapdragon that grew on the walls opposite his rooms at Trinity an emblem, he thought, of a life in Oxford from which only death could remove him. It was not death, but his conscience that took him away. After he became a Roman Catholic he never saw Oxford again, 'excepting its spires, as they are seen from the railway'. Our heart may want to root us in friendly soil for ever, but our mind or our will or forces we neither welcome nor understand may call us away.

After losing Caldarvan that spring, I had an elegiac summer term at Kelham, transfigured by a melancholy infatuation. Living in the Cottage afforded us frequent glimpses of the coming and going of local business people delivering food to the kitchen that backed onto the courtyard. One of the regulars was the daughter of the baker from Newark who supplied us with bread. Good brown bread it was, and there was something brown and nutlike about her as well. Dark hair, hazel eyes. Small, compact body. I was Cottage Senior, unconstrained by others, following my own course of study, so it wasn't difficult to be in the courtyard when her van turned up. Helping with the trays of bread, I would follow her up the stairs to the pantry. She became an object of longing, as much for what she represented as for her beauty. She was the world that married and was given in marriage. The world of the back row in the picture house. The world of the walk along the riverside to the secluded place in the wood. The world of breasts and thighs and the consolation and desolation they promised. The honest world unhaunted by the divine demand. We hardly spoke. A smile, a 'taraa' as she got behind the wheel of the van, that was all. I discovered that the pain of longing was not without its consolations, as I carried my sadness through the green days of summer. The term ended. I went back to the Vale for my last Cottage vacation, National Service not far away on the horizon.

The manager at Caldarvan had recommended me to Muirhead's farm, just outside Balloch. It was there I spent the last summer of my boyhood in 1951. There were three others employed to help with the harvest that year of intense and unusual heat, all women from a notorious street in the Vale, known for its pubs and punch-ups after closing time. They were a cheerful trio, and there was a lot of banter, much of it at my expense. The youngest of the three fired my senses. Unlike the quiet demeanour of the baker's daughter, who absorbed my admiration but gave off no discernible response, Lily fired back. She was a couple of years older than me, about twenty, and I found it difficult to keep my eyes off her, particularly when the day heated up and she peeled off her jersey, then her shirt, under which she wore a cotton swimming costume. We were always dripping with sweat from the stooking by the time of the afternoon break, when the farmer's wife left milk cans full of cold water for us under the trees at the edge of the field. After we'd drunk as much water as we wanted, Lily would soak a cloth in what was left and mop her face and chest. I tried not to look, but it was a losing battle. I had never seen a woman's breasts before. The oldest woman would be on to me, telling Lily to gie me a wee shufti at her chest since I couldn't keep my eyes off her. Lily announced that students were a' the same, laughing as she said it, her breasts obvious against the wet cotton. I sat there, stunned. And I saw what my life would be like. An endless struggle with the flesh.

> Let not sin therefore reign in your mortal body, that ye should obey it in the lusts thereof. Neither yield ye your members as instruments of unrighteousness unto sin.[30]

Was I in for this my whole life long? Psychologically unsophisticated, I had enough insight to grasp that it was the very intensity of my battle with the flesh that gave it such power over me, made it such a preoccupying torment. Obsessively denying yourself something you desperately want can be as addictive as being enslaved to its performance.

> For the good that I would I do not: but the evil which I would not, that I do. Now if I do that I would not, it is no more I that do it, but sin that dwelleth in me. I find then a law, that, when I would do good, evil is present with me. For I delight in the law of God after the inward man: but I see another law in my members, warring against the law of my mind, and bringing me into captivity to the law of sin which is in my members.[31]

Paul might have been writing about me. The difference between us was that he claimed that Christ had made him free from the law of sin. Well, he hadn't made me free of it, and I was tired of the fight. How had I landed myself in such a predicament? Something in me still longed for surrender to God and the great abnegation – *nothing counts but lifetimes* – but that desire was at war with my nature and its lusts. I couldn't square the circle. No one had warned me that this was what I was letting myself in for when I was sent to Kelham:

With this tormented mind tormenting yet.[32]

But it wasn't only religion that saw my longing for ordinary belonging in the world as unheroic. The celibates who had tried to draw me into their fellowship were like the heroes of my favourite Westerns: like Jesus, they were men who had no place to lay their heads. Living on the edge of settled society, called in from time to time to overcome threats to communities they could never belong to, they were destined always to ride away from the woman standing by the white picket fence. The hot Western of the time was *Shane,* the loner who saves the peace of a little prairie community then rides off into the sunset because he himself is never allowed to settle down. In spite of little Joey's cries – 'Shane, Shane, come back, Shane, come back' – he rides away. I realised at the edge of the woods on Muirhead's farm that I was tired of trying to be Father Shane. I wanted to find out about the world I had renounced before I knew anything about its lures and attractions. I wanted to be able to look at Lily without feeling guilty. Actually, I wanted more than that.

A few days later I wrote to the Cottage Master.

Dear Father Peter,

I have decided not to stay at Kelham, so I won't be coming back for the new term. I have already told the authorities and I am expecting my call-up papers any day now. Thank you for all the help and kindness you have given me over the last three years.

Yours affectionately,

Dick

The day I posted it I realised I had made a mistake. I knew that the consolation of Lily's breasts could not last a lifetime – and nothing counted but lifetimes – so I immediately wrote again, telling him I had changed my mind and asking to come back. He replied, kindly, advising me to do my National Service and come back when I was demobbed. So into the army I went, to a boring and uneventful couple of years. The army discovered that, though I was not officer material, I was good at square-bashing, so they slapped stripes on me and made me a drill instructor. The one useful thing I retained from the repetitive routine of my service was the ability to project my voice over great distances. I still have the old drill sergeant's impatience with public speakers who cannot make themselves heard.

Demobbed in time for the Michaelmas term in 1953, I couldn't wait to get back to Kelham. This time I was determined to stay – for ever. During my years in the Cottage I had shuttled between two opposing demands, represented by Kelham and the Vale. The Vale, and Lily's breasts, had nearly won. But now that I was going into the House after National Service, I could remove the Vale from the equation, get rid of the tug of war, by joining the Society and making Kelham my home. The first step would be to apply to join the Novitiate – the apprenticeship for professed life in a religious order that is like a formal engagement to be married to the community. During a short service in the Great Chapel I would commit myself to the vows of poverty, chastity and obedience, and after three years training and formation I would be professed and take my final vows – a bit like getting married after a long engagement. And as soon as I reached Kelham after the army got rid of me that is what I applied to do. But there was a snag. Being only nineteen and therefore underage, the Novice Master sent me home to discuss it with my parents and get their permission. I caught the night train to Scotland. For the last time, I thought, as I boarded it at Newark Castle.

One of the sorrows of the cultural emigration on which I had embarked when I left Alexandria was the way it took me to places I could not share with my parents. What was left between us was the past – love and the past. I told them what I wanted to do. My father said he thought it was unnatural to choose that kind of life, but they wouldn't stand in my way. I knew that's what they'd say. That's what they'd always said. Not that they knew me now, this son they loved but no longer fully understood. What puzzles me now is that no one in the Society probed me about my decision, either. I have always suffered from the confident man's ability to make people think I know what I am talking about. Sometimes I do, more often I don't. In this case I didn't. Back then there was no such thing as a psychometric test to measure a person's suitability for a job. SSM didn't probe my motives. Maybe they didn't realise how divided I was. More likely they knew it too well to want to interfere with it. Father Kelly had advised us never to examine our motives, anyway. Just assume they are wrong. God can work through our muddles and delusions, as long as we don't take ourselves too seriously. I had applied to join the order. They thought I was worth a try. And so when I returned to Kelham from Scotland with the paperwork completed and signed by my father, they put me in a black cassock, wrapped a red girdle round it, suspended a crucifix from it, and admitted me to the Novitiate.

There were over a hundred students in the House at the time, of whom the fifteen novices were a sub-set who were necessarily thrown together more than the others. The biggest difference was that novices did not get vacations like the other students. Kelham was our home, so we stayed there during vacations with the fully professed members of the Society – apart from a couple of weeks a year when we were allowed to visit our families. Life at Kelham had a different feel during vacations. The community was smaller and more intimate. There was a greater family atmosphere, and the routine, though still severe, was more relaxed than during term time. And novices provided a useful maintenance and repair crew during the holidays. One of the novices was a qualified painter and decorator who supervised the rest of us repainting rooms and corridors while the students were away. There was time for long walks with other novices and members of the Society in the local countryside, sometimes towards the bumps on the horizon that the map called Kelham Hills, reached along the road opposite the main gate that went north towards the village of Muskham.

Towards the end of vacation there was always a sense of waiting for the main event to start, and for students to pile off the bus and fill the place with noise and enthusiasm. The great stage of the House really only came into its own during term time, when it buzzed and throbbed with life like a theatre in the middle of a brilliant season – though life in a residential drama school might be a better analogy. All that being on show, that acting before an audience of one's peers, that close attention to the style and mannerisms of others. There were a number of stages on which we acted: sports fields, lecture rooms, the common room and library, not to mention the opportunity for observing and being observed provided by the long drives and walkways, the benches placed before romantic vistas for gazing into the distance. There was plenty of time for watching others and being watched by them just about everywhere. But the supreme stage was the Chapel, itself absolute in its theatricality. Designed to maximise the impact of great processional liturgies, the chapel was the main arena in which we watched and assessed, admired and appraised each other. At the time I assumed I was the only person doing this. Everyone else, I supposed, was unself-consciously getting on with being holy, attentive only to the captivating presence of the God for whom I longed but whose presence continued to elude me. I felt the demand of God, but little of his promised consolation. But wasn't that the part I had been chosen to play? I had seen too many movies and they had made me too conscious of the temptation to act a part, play a role. Monastic religion offered an enormous stage on which to perform. The props of the religious life were themselves dramatic. Cassocks and cowls, red girdles and crucifixes, the theatre of the liturgy with its *corps de ballet* of acolytes and sacred ministers, its brocaded vestments wreathed round with clouds of incense and waves of plainchant. The rhetoric of demand and surrender was the discourse of the life, and the constant call to deny the self and give it away to God. Only the truly holy and unself-conscious could be immune to the temptation to strut their stuff on this tumultuous stage, and I was neither.

The theatrical subtext was even present in Kelham slang for serving at the Sunday High Mass. Before they erected their great basilica in the 1920s, the Society had used the carriage courtyard of the old Hall as a chapel, in which the sanctuary – the stage on which the liturgy is enacted – had a wooden floor. To serve at High Mass on Sundays was to be 'on boards', literally speaking. That usage flitted to the new chapel, so that to serve the Sunday liturgy was still to be 'on boards', even though the new sanctuary was made of stone. I was all too conscious of the opportunity the chapel provided for putting on a show of self-conscious unself-consciousness and practised spontaneity. I was sure that the others were unaware of themselves when they came back to their seats from receiving Holy Communion at the edge of the sanctuary, traversing the great space in blissful unawareness that their demeanour was the object of fascinated interest. Some returned with downcast eyes, their unself-consciousness slightly betrayed by the sudden theatricality of their genuflection to the altar, back erect, head tilted inconsequentially to one side, both hands posed briefly on the left knee, thigh parallel to the floor, before sweeping round to continue the long trek to their seat, where the intensity of inwardness was maintained for as long as possible, the body upright, till the bottom sagged gratefully onto the edge of the seat and the head fell into the hands in the usual posture of semi-somnolence. American colleges had big men on campus. Our alpha males were athletes of the spirit, their devotional form studied keenly. The equivalent of inter-collegiate matches were the big set pieces on Sundays and high holy days 'on boards', when the solemn liturgy required highly trained squads of acolytes to carry candles and crosses and incense thuribles stoked with burning charcoal. There was an occasion when I sabotaged the precision of it all. Unintentionally? That's what I thought at the time.

I was the thurifer, the man in charge of the incense pot. They usually chose someone on the tall side for this role in the drama. The thurifer was accompanied by a boat bearer, usually a boy from the Cottage, who carried the incense in a boat-shaped vessel. Incense, fragrant resins that leave behind them – after they have been consumed in fire – clouds of perfumed smoke, first used as a fumigant to counteract the odours that accompanied animal sacrifice in primitive worship, has become a metaphor for the soul's longing to ascend to God. Its use in these solemn liturgies was carefully schooled and choreographed. The big moment for the thurifer and boat boy was the censing of the principal celebrants of the liturgy, followed by a general censing of the community in their stalls in the chapel. This was the one movement in the routine that provided an opportunity for a mild display of individualism. There was no set way to swing the thurible at this moment in the choreography. Conventional performers swung it with metronomic vigour, two swings to each side, then bowed and returned to their chairs in the sanctuary. On the occasion I am remembering, I was experimenting with a more introverted mystical approach, which involved holding the pot slightly above my head before giving it a few limp jiggles. This manoeuvre was meant to suggest my detachment from the whole process. I was too engaged in the spirituality of the task to be aware that I was there at all, hence the rather abstracted nature of my double swings. I am still not sure whether I was copying or parodying one of the biggest souls on campus, a contemplative whose demeanour was at its most abstracted when he handled the thurible, which he held with a sort of helpless dismay, as though he were being forced to wave a week-old haddock at the congregation. It was a style that provoked as much admiration as derision. After the devotional pirouette of the censing, we returned to our chairs in the sanctuary. This was another precisely configured manoeuvre. We moved across the chapel floor by pushing our slippered feet along the polished black rubber, thereby maintaining a perfectly even posture. We bowed to the altar, turned left and walked to the side of the stone-flagged sanctuary where two heavy wooden stools were placed for our use. We stopped parallel to our respective stools, about nine inches away from them, turned right to face the centre, paused, stepped back the requisite nine inches and sat down, bodies erect, eyes to the front. Parade-ground stuff. Carefully drilled. Always immaculately performed. Never a hitch. Except that day.

We performed the manoeuvre, the boat bearer and I, in complete unison. He found his chair with accustomed precision. I missed mine and hit the floor, my legs in the air – arse over amice, as someone later described it. The chanting in the chapel ceased, except for a few short-sighted souls. In spite of the best attempts of the celebrant, that service never recovered. One or two people claimed they'd bribed me to do it. I knew it was an accident, and that was the received view of my superiors. But are there any genuine accidents? Was a part of me at work unconsciously disturbing the pattern, sabotaging the effect? If the incident in the sanctuary can be understood as a metaphor for the way life can interrupt our most cherished plans, then maybe it was also a reminder that circumstances are indifferent to our ideals and intentions. And sometimes the circumstance are inside us like buried mines waiting to explode. The main threats to the contented mind come from the mind itself. Enemies within, compulsions we did not know about, because our life did not come with a map of its inner topography enclosed, a guide to its psychic weave. The shuttle on the loom had been at work on us long before we thought we had taken charge of its design ourselves. It was about to dart a surprise at me.

I thought I was where I wanted to be, back:

> Where no storms come,
> Where the green swell is in the havens dumb,
> And out of the swing of the sea.[33]

It did not last. I became emotionally fixated on another novice. It crept over me like sadness, more like falling in regret than falling in love. He was a year ahead of me, so I became aware of his presence only gradually. Easy to overlook, he was short, slight and almost nun-like in his demeanour. It wasn't hard to believe that when he made the journey back to his seat from the sanctuary after communion he was genuinely oblivious to those around him. He moved quietly, economically, with short, quick steps, head tilted slightly forward, eyes downcast. The eyes were my undoing. They were large, a startlingly pale blue, fringed with long black lashes. His black hair, kept short, was wiry. But that was not the word I wanted to use. It suggested hardness, tautness, whereas he had the kind of beauty that evoked protectiveness, and a desire to shelter such delicacy from life's storms. His skin was smooth and almost beardless, with a suggestion of light emanating from it.

I was surprised the first time I heard him speak. I expected a high voice. Instead I heard this creamy baritone that was so unexpected I wanted to hear him laugh. I can't remember anything he ever said, but I can remember how he said it. He had none of the faux intellectuality of a lot of the other students. He didn't think of himself as clever or bright or with anything particularly interesting to say. He was sideways and quirky in his angle on things, and there was something absolutely right about his take on people. No phoniness. Nothing posed. Utterly himself. I was bewitched by the completeness of the man, the oneness of the inner with the outer, the physical beauty that perfectly expressed his sweet and unexpected strangeness. It would be wrong to say that he did not have a man's body, though it would be truer to say that he did not yet have a man's body. He had the beautifully unformed body of a boy, neither soft nor hard, neither male nor female. He was a year ahead of me, yet I felt a century older. I was intensely drawn to him, yet his beauty reduced me to incoherence. For what could I do with such a feeling? It reduced everything else to emptiness. I don't think I wanted to possess him physically, or not in any sense I understood or could express. All I wanted was to be with him or at least be near him. Actually, I wanted never to be anywhere else. Since this was impossible, my life became a kind of mourning. As the weeks passed I withdrew into dejection. If I could not be with him always then I must just be by myself. Increasingly, I was. Life at Kelham was busy, but it did allow time to hang out with friends, to walk with them, share a joke, gossip. I became a ghost to all of that, wandering round the edges. When I wasn't reading gloomy Russian novels, I took it on myself, uninvited by anyone in authority, to do extra gardening jobs in the grounds, cutting weeds, hacking at overgrown bushes, raking gravel paths, anything that used up energy, though nothing ever turned off the ache of wanting to be with him, only with him.

I didn't know how he felt about me. He must have known about the impact he had on people, must have known that they flirted with him, that he flirted back. He never flirted with me, though sometimes when I came out of the woods in which I was brooding and approached him he would smile with delight, though I was always too awkward to stay around him for long. These inconclusive encounters were almost as painful as my long silent absences. Then, though I can't remember how it came about, it was agreed that we would take our two weeks' summer leave together in Cornwall, ending with a visit to his widowed mother in Plymouth. We would hitch-hike south, taking our time, stopping at bed and break-fast places along the way. It was late August, and drivers were inclined to stop for two men in cassocks. I was quietly happy just being with him. We had the kind of ease in each other's company that allowed us to be silent when there was nothing to be said or when neither of us felt like speaking. The rosebay willowherb, flaming by the roadside, was beginning to send its seeds into the warm autumn wind. The drivers who picked us up chatted inconsequentially, asking us what religion we were. I hardly noticed. We got to Cornwall on a Saturday evening and found it hard to find a place to stay. One friendly B&B proprietor told us it would be busy everywhere in Polp-erro that weekend, but his cousin a few miles out of town on a farm sometimes took people in. Would we like him to phone? It was a three-mile walk through lush green country-side. The farmer's wife gave us high tea when we arrived, after showing us the room. It was the only one they had available and would we mind sharing the double bed? We accepted the arrangement and took a walk over the fields after the meal. We were supposed to wear our cassocks everywhere in public, but was this public? We left them in the room and walked in our shorts and shirts.

After the walk we decided to head for bed. It had been a tiring day, with a lot of hiking between lifts. To my surprise, he suggested that we should sleep on different sides of the top sheet. I was already under it, so he got into bed on top of it, under the blanket, thereby creating a frail yet absolute barrier between us. I was puzzled by his insistence, but didn't question it, didn't ask why it concerned him. I had not figured that in bed one plus one can sometimes equal one. We did not enact that arithmetic, but I sometimes wonder what would have followed had we done so All I know is that my need for his presence was not assuaged by our days together. Back at Kelham I plunged into the old sadness and started again to wander disconsolately round the edges of the community, so much so that the Warden called me in to see him.

The Warden was a man given to watching. When he sat in his place on the high table during silent meals his eyes always seemed to be surveying the refectory like a searchlight playing over a maximum security prison. They were deep-set eyes, appraising, discomfiting. I had been aware that they had been on me for some time. After the summons, I knocked on his door on B Corridor and he told me to enter. Ah, Dick, he said, Dick, I've been watching you. He wondered why I, cut out to be a leader, absented myself from the life and politics and rhythm of the place. He mentioned another student, a man who was well respected, a man who more than pulled his weight in the life of the community, a man others looked up to. I could be like that. Had it in me to be a personality about the place. Instead, I kept to myself, did not engage, wandered about like a wraith. They were grateful for the extra gardening and labouring I was doing round the place, but it was unimportant, would get done anyway. It hit me. I knew it was true. What he did not do was ask why, to probe the helpless love that had overwhelmed me. I wonder if he knew the reason and was scared to explore it. I admitted the symptoms but said nothing about the cause. I gave assurances. I would engage with others again, become part of the family. I tried. I was around more. I loosened up a bit and tried to engage with others. I knew I was being watched.

Then, not long after my session with the Warden of the College, I was summoned to a meeting with the Father Director of the Society. He told me that Father Richard Roseveare, Provincial of the Society in the South African Province, had been elected Bishop of Accra in the Gold Coast in West Africa. He wanted the Society to send him a priest to be his personal assistant. None was available, so they proposed to send me. It would be for two years, after which I would return to Kelham and continue my studies in the Novitiate. I would have to prepare myself for the post. I would be expected to deal with the bishop's considerable correspondence, so must teach myself to type. Brother Noel, the Kelham Secretary, would give me a Pitman's typing manual and access to a typewriter. I had six weeks to master it. They would also send me for driving lessons in Newark, because that would be useful, too. What did I think?

I was excited. Another part to play – the dedicated young missionary. 'Here am I. Send me.'[34] I don't know what was in their minds in proposing this move. Was it a make-or-break tactic? Get him away from that emotional entanglement – not that it had ever been mentioned. A lot wasn't mentioned, by them or by me, or maybe they would have had second thoughts about sending to Africa a young man struggling to crucify his own insistent libido. I left the Director's room, immediately got to work with Pitman's and mastered touch-typing. Typing this now on a computer, I remember the big sit-up-and-beg Underwood I hammered away on for weeks in the Kelham office, the old Business Room on the ground floor of the Manners Sutton establishment. Typing was a skill I developed quickly. Unlike driving. On my test in Newark I ran the driving school's car into the corner of a baker's van and was failed on the spot. Back at Kelham I enjoyed describing the white face and shaky hands of the examiner.

The day of my departure came around quickly. I was to take the train to Liverpool and spend the night in a B&B near the docks so that next morning I could get on board the Elder Dempster ship that served all the West African ports from Freetown to Lagos. On a March morning after breakfast I followed the community into the Chapel for my missionary benediction. Because I was leaving for foreign service, I was the only man in chapel without the blue scapular over his cassock. I was called forward by the Director, who was standing in front of the altar on which Father Kelly said they sacrificed young men. I knelt in front of him while the community sang Psalm 121 in poignant plainsong.

> I will lift up mine eyes unto the hills: from whence
>   cometh my help.
> My help cometh even from the Lord: who hath made
>   heaven and earth.
> He will not suffer thy foot to be moved: and he that
>   keepeth thee will not sleep.
> Behold, he that keepeth Israel: shall neither slumber nor
>   sleep.

The Lord himself is thy keeper: the Lord is thy defence
   upon thy right hand;
So that the sun shall not burn thee by day: neither the
   moon by night.
The Lord shall preserve thee from all evil: yea, it is
   even he that shall keep thy soul.
The Lord shall preserve thy going out, and thy coming
   in: from this time forth for evermore.

The Director blessed me. I stood, and pulled back my shoulders. The Director smiled at me. I turned and walked, alone, under the great dome, across the expanse of polished black rubber out of the Chapel into the narthex. I turned right and made my way through a little side door on the east side.

Outside, a car was waiting for me, already loaded with a trunk full of books for Bishop's House Accra and my few possessions, including two white cotton cassocks suitable for the tropics. We drove down the drive, through the great oak gates, and took a right over the bridge onto the road to Newark. I turned in my seat and looked back at the remembered silhouette pushing itself above the trees. A high clock tower without a clock but with a confident assertive steeple. A scatter of chimneys, tall triple chimneys, arranging themselves over acres of steep, slated roof. Quick sight of a solid flat-topped tower. Then it fell from view, as I was taken towards Africa and my future. But it was not to be the future I thought God had intended for me. This was certainly my going out from Kelham; but there was to be no coming in again. It was to Glasgow I would return when the time came.

II

1958–67

5

TENEMENTS

I had a strange awakening after my first night in Abbotsford Place. Everything around was quiet that Saturday morning. I could sense that no one else in the street was up, yet I was sure the sound of singing had wakened me. Then I heard it again, coming from the back court. A strong voice, singing one of Scotland's sad songs.

> Ca' the yowes to the knowes,
> Ca' them where the heather grows,
> Ca' them where the burnie rows,
> My bonnie dearie.

Collected by Robert Burns, it is a folk song sung to a tune that breaks the heart, and it was echoing off the back walls of Abbotsford Place that chilly morning. I pulled my curtains aside and looked down into the back. He was standing beside the midden, head up, eyes closed, singing his heart out in a rich baritone. And he was a striking figure. An old man. Tiny, under five feet I guessed from up here on the third floor, wearing a tweed suit and waistcoat, well worn and old-fashioned. 'Perjink' is the term in Scots that best described him, and the sound of the word carries its meaning. Why was he there and what did he think he was doing? It was too early for busking, and it was a daft place to do it, anyway. Was he mourning something in his past? Was he lamenting the slow dying of Gorbals, performing a Kontakion for a death foretold? Later I discovered that no one else on the stair heard him. I was up early. I heard him. I can hear him still. Every time I look at a photograph of a backcourt of one of Glasgow's vanished tenements I hear him again.

Maybe I heard him because I knew that back courts were mystical places. A week after I moved in there was a knock at the door. When I opened it, a wee boy handed me a cheque made out to me for £27, my stipend for the month, which had found its way into my waste paper basket by mistake and out into the bins at the back. I had myself played lucky middens as a boy, hunting for discarded treasures in other people's rubbish. I was glad Glasgow children were still doing it. The boy whooped down the stair with a half crown in his pocket, and my pay cheque was soon deposited in the Bank of Scotland.

Children played everywhere in Gorbals, but the back court was their real kingdom. The backs had been originally planned as drying greens, with brick sheds against the far wall for the ashes of the coal that burned in fireplaces all over the city, the smoke from a million lums blackening the buildings and filling the air with a soft deadly sweetness. There was nothing green in the back courts of Gorbals in the second half of the twentieth century, but the packed earth and rusty remains of the posts on which they had once slung the drying lines offered endless possibilities to the imaginations of children.

They appealed to my imagination too. I'd been born in one of Glasgow's tenements, so they were in my DNA. My mother also came from them, and she had been orphaned in one of them. Sometimes I thought I saw her as a child in these streets. And from somewhere came a memory of the two of us, my small hand in hers, hurrying anxiously along a road flanked by pubs and pawnshops. Whether it was us I don't know, but the image contained its own truth. On these streets there was a lot of weeping and leaving, as well as a lot of laughing and forgetting. It was children who brought the laughter and sometimes the forgetting, children playing on grey streets in their mothers' hats and shoes, singing out: 'Wait till she sees this, but . . .' I had been on my way back here a long time and hadn't known it. It could have been to another street. In fact, it could have been to anywhere in Glasgow, a city packed with tenements, four storeys high, black with soot and bright with life, but it was to this spot, to this room in a flat used as a day nursery for Gorbals children. Which is why it was quiet that Saturday morning as I stood at my window looking into the backcourt, listening to the wee man singing. Who was he? Why was he singing to a sleeping street?

I dressed and sped quietly down the stairs, scooped and worn by lives sunk away in the years, past the assertive ugliness of gang slogans scrawled on the walls – 'Cumbie Ya Baas, Tong Ya Baas' – through the close to the back. He wasn't there. I ran to the front of the close into the street. It was empty, except for my neighbour Lilias's green van Jemima and my motorbike parked at the kerb. It had rained in the night and the black surface of the roadway glistened, reflecting the long stretch of tenements on the other side, marching south in an unbroken line to Cumberland Street. The original sandstone of the terrace was discernible only through streaks in the soot, but the row was still handsome and solid-looking. The railings that once defined the tidy gardens in front of each address were gone,

103

and the gardens were patches of mud outlined by the jagged remains of low walls. Six elegant gas lamps survived in the street, three on this side, three on the other, lit by a lamplighter before darkness fell, testament to what had once been a distinguished address.

At the end of the eighteenth century a couple of builders had lured the middle classes of Glasgow to a new suburb on the south side of the Clyde, a quick walk from the city centre. The aristocratic names on the grid of streets they built testified to their ambitions for the area: Bedford, Norfolk, Cumberland, Oxford, Cavendish. The vision of the Laurie brothers was never fully realised, but the area remained a prosperous district till well into the nineteenth century. Abbotsford Place was built in 1830, a four-storied terrace of large apartments, with a mews for horse carriages round the back. It had gone well down in the world by the time I stood outside number 10 that Saturday morning, wondering how my mystic balladeer could have disappeared so completely. I needed rolls for breakfast, so I went over Bedford, the cross street between Abbotsford Place and South Portland, to the dairy at the corner. South Portland Street ran up to the river that defined the northern boundary of Gorbals:

> . . . the real Clyde, with a dishrag dawn
> it rinses the horrors of the night
> but cannot make them clean . . .[35]

It was raining steadily as I took the rolls back upstairs and put the kettle on for tea. Maybe it would be over by the time I left for the Vale in the middle of the day. I had a plan to discuss with my parents. Bernard would be moving into his last term at the Academy after the Easter holidays, with a place at Glasgow University secured for the autumn. Why not let him join me in Abbotsford Place in another room in Lilias's nursery? It would take the pressure off them and get Bernard used to Glasgow. A few months commuting to the Vale wouldn't be a problem in the better weather. That was the plan we agreed to, and Bernard joined me in Gorbals at the beginning of the summer holidays.

Now a distinguished novelist and poet in the African modernist tradition, Bernard Kojo Laing had been a skinny ten-year-old boy when he left Accra to live with my parents and go to school in Alexandria. It was a silly Scottish boast that caused the move. Bernard's parents had been complaining to me about how difficult it was to educate their large family. They were worried, in particular, about what to do for ten-year-old Bernard. Send him to Scotland, I said, it has the best education system in the world. I reminded George, Bernard's father, who was Provost of Holy Trinity Cathedral, Accra, that his great grandfather had come from Scotland as a surveyor in the late nineteenth century. Maybe it was time he connected with his ancestral roots. It never occurred to me that my parents would balk at the idea of taking on an African boy they'd never met. Nor did they. Nine months before my own return, a friend of the Laings, an English businessman working in Accra, took Bernard with him on one of his flights to Britain and brought him to Elmbank Drive. It wasn't easy for him at first, but by the time of my own return to Scotland he was well settled and the Vale had taken him to its heart.

Those years in Accra had been life-changing for me as well as for Bernard. They were also complicated and lonely. Bishop's House was an attractive white colonial building near the

Cathedral. It was on a cliff overlooking the South Atlantic. I soon discovered that gazing out to sea is a great prompter of melancholy. The house had been situated to catch the breezes that made life more comfortable for Europeans in what was still known as the white man's grave, because of the tropical climate and the diseases and infections that went with it. Every day we took a prophylactic called Paludrin, and slept under mosquito nets at night in the bright airy house, though the precautions did not stop me getting a bad bout of malaria. I ran the Bishop's office by myself, and held the fort when he was away on one of his frequent treks. I was quick at the work, so it left time for a bit of youth work in local churches and a lot of time for reading and exploring. It was reading that precipitated the crisis.

I had hoped to leave my troubles behind when I sailed for Africa. Instead, I brought them with me. I was still battling the flesh, trying to beat my body into submission to the spirit. And I soon realised that Africa was not the place to win the battle. On our way out from Liverpool we had tied up at Freetown in Sierra Leone for the best part of a day, and I had spent the time exploring the quaint Victorian city. I was electrified by the number of bare-breasted women I saw going unself-consciously about their business in the midst of people who seemed unaware of this stunning and arousing fact. My attention was quickened, my senses heightened. I had never seen anything so beautiful or so tormenting. It filled me with a longing that was as much sadness as lust. I did not then understand how unsatisfiable romantic yearning was, and how addicted to the search for hidden doors and whispered avowals. It was no better when I finally got to Accra, where I spent much of my time in a state of embarrassed arousal.

The reading I plundered in the well-stocked local library in an attempt to distract my mind did not help. The mistake was to discover James Joyce. Soon my official reports to the Novice Master at Kelham became stream-of-consciousness descriptions of my reactions to what I was seeing as I wandered the streets and prowled the beaches of Accra. At last I was talking about the subject that had secretly obsessed me for years, but my talk alarmed him. James Joyce was not recommended reading for a young Novice struggling to control a galloping libido, so he ordered my immediate return to Kelham. I refused. I would not leave the Bishop in the lurch. I would stick to the plan and go back after two years. Then I must withdraw from the Novitiate, he replied. I refused this order as well. All of this was transacted on blue airmail letters, and we were clearly at an impasse. It was my duty to collect the mail from the Central Post Office in Accra where we had a box. One day I collected a letter for the Bishop from the Father Director at Kelham. Unusually, it was marked 'strictly personal and confidential'; and I was pretty sure it was about me. The Bishop sat on it for a day before inviting me into his office. He'd been informed about the correspondence that was flying between me and the Novice Master, and he knew about the standoff between us. The Society did not want to throw me out, so the Director had asked him to resolve the issue one way or the other, either by sending me back to Kelham immediately or, if I insisted on staying, persuading me to withdraw from the community. Maybe the fact that he needed me to complete the two years he'd been promised influenced his judgement, but he went on to say he did not think I was capable of the kind of implicit obedience life in a religious order required – there was no mention of celibacy – so wouldn't it be better if I faced facts and withdrew from the Society? It was my decision, but I had to make it today, one way or the other.

I went out into our clifftop garden and gazed at the breaking sea for ten minutes. Then I went to my room and put together a little package containing my red girdle, the crucifix that used to hang from it, Father Kelly's Constitution of the Society, and a letter announcing my voluntary withdrawal from the Novitiate. I sent the parcel off to the Novice Master, House of the Sacred Mission, Kelham, Newark, Nottinghamshire, England. I knew it would take a month to arrive via the Elder Dempster Line, which had regular sailings between Takoradi and Liverpool. As I left it at the big post office in the teeming centre of Accra, I pictured it landing on Brother Noel's desk in the office at Kelham where I had taught myself to type on his old Underwood. I saw him place it, with all the other mail, on the large wooden table at the bottom of the great stair, where it would be picked up by the Novice Master after breakfast one morning weeks away. I am sure that's what happened; but I never did hear if it got there.

So it was in Accra that I finally lost the direction I thought my life was supposed to take. It was there I said 'No' to the great demand, there I realised what a disappointment I must be to God. And it was there I began to recognise how incommensurate my character was to my own ideals and aspirations. It's hard when you discover that the person you are is not someone you admire; not the person you want to be; not cut out to be a saint. But there were compensations. The biggest discovery was that there was a world outside religion. I had been so intent on following God that I had paid little attention to the world he was supposed to love. That changed radically in Accra. I was present at the liberation of the first African colony and saw Kwame Nkrumah, Africa's first Big Man, carried by his supporters into history as the Gold Coast became Ghana. 'Seek ye first the political kingdom,' he paraphrased, 'and all these things will be added unto you.' It was in Africa's first independent nation that I discovered the ferment of European politics. I devoured the *Overseas Weekly Guardian* and *New Statesman* when they arrived at Bishop's House, and kept in touch with news of the Suez fiasco and the birth of CND on a shortwave radio. There was an exciting world outside the monastery, a conflicted and unequal world. Maybe it would offer me opportunities for other types of heroism, other ways to play the given-away life, other stages on which to strut. Though the tug of disappointment never left me, now the world was all before me. Where would the road lead me as I took my solitary way?

It never occurred to me that it would lead to the priesthood. I had forgotten the aspiration that originally brought me to Kelham. It had long since been subsumed in the higher purpose of the monastic life, and with that at an end I thought the enchantment of the religious dream was over for me. I decided that when I got back to Scotland I would head for university. I secured a place to read philosophy at Aberdeen, though they told me I'd have to brush up my Latin. I can't remember why I felt it necessary to tell him what had been going on in my life, but I wrote to the Bishop of Glasgow to bring him up to date. By airmail return he cancelled my plans. Forget about Aberdeen. When you return you will do a year's study at the College of the Scottish Church in Edinburgh, then I'll ordain you. When you are back, get in touch and we'll fix it. Yours, Francis Moncreiff. I had not, after all, completely lost the habit of obedience. I went along with his plan.

So it was that a year after I left Accra I was, to my surprise, ordained by the Bishop of Glasgow and posted to a curacy under the saintly Rector of St Ninian's Albert Drive, down the road from Gorbals. After a year kicking around in digs in Pollokshields, I moved into Gorbals where I had already been helping out at Lilias's youth club in Bedford Street Lane, a minute's walk from her flat in Abbotsford Place. It provided me with a new theatre in which to try on a different role, one closer to my own roots, one I felt I was returning to rather than coming to for the first time. And the religious dimension had shifted too. I had found another Jesus. Not Jesus the celibate abandoning himself to the loneliness of the night of God. This Jesus was the rebel taking up arms against the night of the world, a night in which the poor mourned and cursed the darkness. I was still afflicted with the old duality, one me watching the other me strutting on a new set of boards. But I also discovered something more authentic amidst the posturing, something I had not encountered before: anger at how the world ordered itself. What had previously been used as devotional tropes, instruments for spiritual self-laceration, I understood now as challenges to the powerful of the world, a world whose values Jesus had tried to turn upside down: 'Blessed be ye poor . . . Blessed are ye that hunger now . . . Blessed are ye that weep.'[36] Gorbals was like the world Jesus blessed and cursed. It was a good place for a fight, and something in me wanted a fight.

Not that I ever felt personally in danger. Young men fought among themselves with 'chibs' (blades) and hammers for the thrill of it certainly, but they rarely turned on civilians. The only regular violence I had to cope with was when Raveena, the young daughter of the Singh family on the floor below me, came up for me at the weekend to deal with her parents. Mr Singh got drunk on Friday nights, as did many Gorbals men, who came home when the pubs closed at ten and made life hell for their families. I tried to do something about it by starting a Friday night movie club, for men whose wives wanted me to keep them out of the pub before the pay packet was wasted and they staggered home in a guilty rage. I took them round the corner to the New Bedford in Eglinton Street, a jazzy cinema from 1932 that showed a lot of Westerns. But Jack Lemmon in *Cowboy* and Alan Ladd in *Shane* couldn't compete with the tradition of getting 'stōshus' at the weekend, so the club folded after a few weeks. And Mr Singh had never joined us anyway. When Raveena came for me that first Friday night I feared the worst for her mother because Mr Singh was an enormous man. I needn't have worried. I found him lying on the kitchen floor, turban off, hair unwound, with his wife banging his head on the linoleum as she cursed him in passionate Punjabi. Cheered by this cultural reversal, I helped them carry Mr Singh's groaning bulk to bed – and not for the last time. But it wasn't violence within the community – sad as it was – that really angered me. It was violence done to the community by forces outside its control that angered me more. A violence that, in the end, would destroy the physical fabric of the community itself. And it had been brewing a long time.

The arrival of the suburban railway system in nineteenth-century Glasgow started the flight of the middle classes from Gorbals, but the population of the district was constantly increased by new arrivals, immigrant groups fleeing starvation in Ireland or persecution in Europe or poverty in Asia. By World War II the population was over 50,000 in an area the size of a dozen football pitches.[37] It was what came after the

111

war that began the destruction. Glasgow's housing stock was in an apocalyptic state. An official survey established that 98,000 houses were unfit for human habitation. Most of the old tenements had no hot water, internal lavatories or baths, and they were all tired and dilapidated. It was the era of the slum landlord, most of whom were incompetent as well as grasping, and some of whom were actively criminal and warehoused the poor into derelict buildings of last resort when there was nowhere else for them to go. And South Portland Street was the epicentre of the problem.

It was my route into the city centre. It was where I did my laundry at the local Bagwash once a week. I would dry my load in one of the machines and then take a pillow case full of clean clothes back to my room and shove it in a corner from which I fished out clothes as I needed them. South Portland Street also housed the local library, a handsome red sandstone building, bustling and well lit. But it was also the main operating zone of a housing racket run by a well-known Glasgow boxing dynasty. I organised a survey of stairs owned by them. In each room of every five-room flat I found a family with children, all sharing a single WC, and with little in the way of cooking facilities. What city officials described as *multiple occupation* was intense in the street. In one flat I found sixty-seven people sharing a single WC. When I was raising money for a housing association we started in order to reclaim the old tenements from the depredations of the planners and racketeers, I featured a photograph of this lavatory in an advertisement in *The Lady* magazine. Under the heading *Ideal Homes,* the ad told readers, 'Last winter 67 people were using this W.C. in a tenement not far from the centre of Glasgow.' The ad brought in a satisfying amount of money, as did another of our advertisements: 'Room to let. 12 feet by 10 – do family of 10; coal fire provided for cooking; share cold water tap and W.C. with three other families; only 19 other families on stair (99 people); convenient for Glasgow city centre. RENT – £2 a week.' As well as raising money for the cause, that advertisement also elicited applications to us from families who thought we were the landlords and wanted to rent the flat. The real landlords had a family in it a few days after it had fallen vacant.

The best way of getting at slum landlords was to take them to the Rent Tribunal. By the terms of the contract with their tenants they were supposed to keep their properties 'wind and water tight'. That clause offered the opportunity of a challenge, which, while it could never remedy the overall situation, achieved some redress for the tenants in the form of reduced rents. I organised a series of rent strikes in South Portland Street, which I defended at the Rent Tribunal on the grounds that the landlords made no attempt to do even minor repairs. During the strikes I made sure the tenants paid their rents to me, so that the landlord could not counter sue them for withholding. We always won these actions, but they were only successful skirmishes in a war that was already lost.

No one doubted that something had to be done to respond to Glasgow's housing crisis. I thought that the best response was to modernise and rehabilitate the existing stock. With others, including sociologists and town-planners from the university, our campaign reminded people that Glasgow's tenements had been a good solution to population density at the time they were built. The streets of grey and red sandstone seemed organic to the landscape and climate of our northern nation. Even the cheaper ones were built to last, and they looked as though they belonged where they stood – and knew it. Why not keep them, improve them, modernise them? Had they been consulted, that is what the natives themselves would have gone for, but social engineers are famous for their indifference to the views of the subjects of their experiments. No one bothered to ask the people who actually lived in Gorbals. Glasgow wanted to do something dramatic to counter its reputation as the slum capital of Europe, so they opted for what they called comprehensive redevelopment, the complete flattening of the district and the erection of an entirely new housing pattern. They blitzed the traditional horizontal grid of streets and sent them into the sky in the famous twenty-storey high-rises. It was an astonishingly violent solution, and once a district was sentenced to it a deadly blight descended on it. It was like putting a whole neighbourhood on death row for decades before muscling it onto the electric chair. Was that what my wee singer in the backcourt had been lamenting? That here could be no abiding city? That here was another place where not one stone would be left upon another?

6

ANGEL OF THE GORBALS

When Lilias first got in touch I was living in digs in Kenmure Street near Maxwell Drive where the 59 tram woke me at midnight screeching round the corner on its long clank to Mosspark. She needed a man to help with her youth club in Abbotsford Lane. Would I be interested? I'd heard of her, of course. Everyone in Glasgow had. The *Daily Record* called her 'the Angel of the Gorbals', but to the clergy of the Diocese of Glasgow she was Miss Graham the Welfare Worker. Gorbals wasn't far away, but I wrapped myself in the big fawn duffle coat I'd bought in an Army & Navy Store when I got back from Africa and went there on my motorbike.

There were thick fogs in Glasgow that winter and it was easier to weave through them behind the headlight of a motor-bike than to stumble around on the sidewalk. I inched my way down Maxwell Drive to Eglinton Toll. Turned right off Eglinton Street at Cumberland Street. Next left down Abbotsford Place. The gas lamps shed a halo as I ghosted along the street to Bedford. I turned right and parked. The lane ran between Bedford and Cumberland streets parallel to Abbotsford Place. Its cobbled surface and low buildings identified it as one of the mews of Victorian Gorbals. Most of the old stables were wrecks, but some survived as workshops and garages. Lilias's club was upstairs in one of the less dilapidated buildings right on Bedford Street. Its low ceiling and rectangular shape made it a cosy place in which to hang out. The equipment was basic, like thousands of youth clubs at the time. A record player and billiard table was about it. But there was 'Ginger', the generic West of Scotland name for soft drinks, mainly Irn-Bru and American Cream Soda, a drink no one from the USA would have recognised. And crisps, potato crisps. Boxes of them. The contrast with the youth fellowship I ran at Saint Ninian's, less than a mile away, was startling. The Pollokshields teenagers were a confident group, getting ready for university or college, all of them with secure futures ahead of them. The boys in Lilias's club were already alumni of young offenders' institutions, and most of them would soon graduate to prison. The brighter and more energetic they were, the more trouble they seemed to attract and the more hopeless their future seemed to be. I was to spend a lot of time at the Sheriff Court on the other side of the Clyde near Glasgow Green, speaking up for these boys, usually to no avail. Off they went defiantly to gaol, their careers as Glasgow hard men marked out as predictably as the future dentists and engineers and schoolteachers of Pollokshields. Everyone had been dealt a hand in life, but it was obvious that the dealer had rigged the deck against those born in this postcode.

After the club, before heading back to Kenmure Street, I went back to Lilias's for hot chocolate. Up a grotty stair into the flat she shared with a teacher friend, the hallway full of boxes of baby clothes and children's toys, the living room warm and cheerful, a fire burning in the grate. It wasn't long before I decided to move in next door. Across the landing was the nursery Lilias had started to give single mothers a break.

Not that 'single mothers' was the phrase in use. Social workers talked then about families where the father was *not present*. Some of them were not present because they'd done a runner, others were in prison. A lot of washing and delousing of children went on in that flat, but it was a happy place. With the help of private gifts and support from Save the Children and a squad of volunteers, they cared for sixty children. The flats on the stair all had the same layout. Going clockwise in Lilias's flat, anticlockwise in the nursery, the kitchen was immediately next to the front door, facing the back court, followed by the bathroom and another room at the back. To the front there was a large living room and two other rooms, one quite small. In Glasgow housing lingo, these flats were four rooms and a kitchen. I moved into the back bedroom of the nursery. It was noisy during the day, but I had it to myself in the evenings and at weekends. The only furniture I owned was an old-fashioned desk. A friend donated a single bed that had been made for his brother, about my height he said. I rigged up a bookcase, acquired a two-bar electric fire, an old easy chair, a wastepaper basket, and moved in on a Friday afternoon. I was happy to be Lilias's neighbour, and she was happy to have a man on the stair.

Lilias Graham came from a family that descended from King Robert III of Scotland. Among her ancestors was Graham of Claverhouse, mortally wounded at the Battle of Killiecrankie in 1689 while fighting on the Stuart side against the Hanoverians. Maybe that accounted for the hint of Jacobite panache in Lilias. Born in London in the last year of World War I, her family moved to an Elizabethan farmhouse in Suffolk in 1923, where she was educated at home. When she was four she visited her grandmother, the Duchess of Montrose, at Buchanan Castle on the banks of Loch Lomond, where she announced that she intended to live in Scotland when she grew up. It took her thirty years to get there. Before that was work in the Docklands in East London and as a cook sergeant in the ATS during the war. After the war she worked with the United Nations Refugee and Relief Agency in Egypt, Palestine and Greece. Then to Klagenfurt in the British Zone in Austria, still working for UNRRA in refugee camps. She got back to Britain in 1948, worn out and suffering from a brain tumour, which was successfully operated on. It was then she made good that promise to herself to come home to Scotland. She wrote to the Bishop of Glasgow, asking if she could live and work in Gorbals. The Bishop, thrilled by the offer, told her he would be happy to license her for *work* in the Gorbals, but she could not possibly live there because it would be too dangerous. After a year of commuting from Ibrox, Lilias courteously informed him that she was going in. She moved into Abbotsford Place in 1954 and stayed till the slum clearances of the early 1970s. During those years she became a legend among the Glasgow poor.

What impressed me most about her was the contrast she posed to the imperatives of my own nature. Schooled in the monastic routine of filling every minute with purposeful activity, I was impressed by Lilias's relaxed attitude to life. She did not give the impression of *working* at all. She never seemed to be on or off duty. She was just *there*, so things happened around her. Children played in her flat. There was the youth club in Abbotsford Lane. The Auld Hens, a women's group, met one night a week in her sitting room. There was the nursery next door. There was a holiday scheme for children – most of whom had never been out of Gorbals – who were billeted with families in the countryside for a couple of weeks during the summer holidays. Streams of trainee social workers from the London School of Economics came to learn what they could about working in deprived communities without patronising the poor. And there was a constant flow of callers to her famous red door. Throughout this she emanated no sense of strain.

She slept late most days, something I was mildly shocked by. She went to concerts, loved expensive chocolates, took holidays abroad, particularly in Austria and Greece, countries the war had taught her to love. She was a toff. She sounded like a toff – I tried unsuccessfully to copy her pronunciation of cross as 'crawss' – but there was not the slightest shred of class-consciousness in her. I witnessed this ease of being with compli-cated admiration. She was a whole person, integrated, unself-conscious. I was divided, self-aware, watching myself playing this new game. And still crawling off to confession to unload the latest cargo of guilt, still living:

> . . . this tormented mind
> With this tormented mind tormenting yet.[38]

Lilias never talked about why she was there, and never gave the slightest impression that she thought there was anything unusual in living in one of the most notorious slums in Europe. Afflicted with the theological habit, I wanted an explanation for her presence in a community that was galaxies away from her own background. I found it, to my own satisfaction, if not to hers, in the word *presence* itself, which was emerging at the time as a descriptive term for a radical approach to the Christian Faith that acted rather than spoke. There was concern that the Church was being pushed out of the inner city into the suburbs. A movement that had started among the dispossessed now seemed to flourish only among the middle classes. And a deeper anxiety was burgeoning. A sense was growing that the old ways of understanding and talking about God were being eroded by a secular self-confidence that had no need of God to explain the world. It was getting uncomfortably close to me. The paradox of my own relationship with God was an increasing sense of loss accompanied by an undiminished sense of demand. Half the time I wasn't sure God was there, yet a powerful sense of obligation *to something* remained. What remained was Jesus. Whether *he* was God, as the Church claimed – whether, indeed, there was a God for him to be – a demand came through Jesus that could be separated from questions about God, a demand isolated by Jesus himself when he said it was actions not words that God was interested in, mercy and justice not professions of belief. He left us with the paradox of what sounded like God's atheism: it wasn't creeds he wanted, but the battle against oppression.

It was obvious that, with or without belief in God, what Jesus demanded was needed as much in our time as in his. This was still a cruel unequal world, as cruel as when Jesus had startled its leaders by telling them God was not on their side, but on the side of those they trampled on. The beautiful thing about this line was that it parked the supernatural question in a lay-by – permanently. You no longer needed to play conceptual games with God. What you had to do was clothe the naked, feed the hungry and give cold water to the thirsty. God was no longer on his supernatural throne. The place to find him was among the dispossessed, among the wretched of the earth. And the idea of *presence* expressed both ends of this paradox. Henceforth, God would be found among the poor. If you were seeking him, only there would you find him. The other end of the paradox was even sharper: if you want to make God known to the poor, don't speak to them about *him*, become poor like *them*, be *present* beside them. The flow was from word to work, from theory to practice, from theology to action. This was the narrative that had driven Albert Schweitzer to Africa. He wrote of this period in his life:

> I wanted to be a doctor that I might be able to work without having to talk. For years I had been giving myself out in words . . . this new form of activity I could not represent to myself as being talking about the religion of love, but only as an actual putting it into practice.[39]

In 1913 he went with his wife to Lambaréné, in what was then the French colony of Gabon, as a doctor. He spent his life there, no longer talking about Jesus but following his way of practical love. *Presence!*

Lilias was like and unlike Schweitzer. Like him she did not talk about faith, she acted. But she was unlike him in that there seemed to be no heavy theological motive for her presence in Gorbals, no wrestling with an elusive God, no bargaining. She was intrigued by my need to theologise everything, to darken everything with thought. That was because there was an uncomplicated goodness about her, a transparency that cast no shadow. Her relationship with organised religion could have been described as affectionate toleration. She liked going to Church, but not too often and never for too long. She enjoyed the quiet rituals of the Christian year. She was the only person I knew who decorated her Christmas tree with real candles, a tradition she'd learned in Austria. She liked these practices because they added grace and beauty to life. The poetry of quiet religion appealed to her. The doctrinal obsessions of noisy religion bored her. She ignored the wars between the rival priesthoods in Christianity, and she herself was never interested in joining the uniformed branch of the Church – not that it would have been open to her had she wanted it. She lived in Gorbals not out of grim duty but out of Franciscan gaiety. She intrigued me because she completely lacked the theological angst I had in abundance. The paradox of the god who abandoned metaphysics for identification with the dispossessed would have been too 'highfalutin' for her. But there was another remarkable person in Gorbals who was no stranger to agonistic theology. And I found him both compelling and threatening. Lilias's uncomplicated goodness did not threaten me. Geoff Shaw, a more complex figure, did.

A few years after Lilias moved into Gorbals, a group of Church of Scotland ministers followed her into the area. They had been given permission by the Kirk to establish a ministry in Gorbals outside normal parish structures. There were three ordained ministers in the group: Walter Fyfe, John Jardine and Geoff Shaw. Walter and John were married. Geoff was single. The Fyfes took a house at the top of Abbotsford Lane. The Jardines moved into the flat in Abbotsford Place, which became Lilias's nursery later when they left the group. Geoff moved into a small flat in Cleland Street, close to the Crown Street Baths, which he used for his ablutions. Geoff and Walter had done a year's graduate study at Union Theological Seminary in New York, where they had been influenced by the work of the East Harlem Protestant Parish. Abandoning church-based ministry, the East Harlem ministers and their families lived in apartments in the violent neighbourhood and operated from store-front ministries. And that was the pattern Geoff and Walter wanted to replicate in Gorbals.

It soon became obvious to me that Geoff was the counterpart and counterpoise to Lilias. He wasn't a toff, but he came from a privileged family and had been educated at Edinburgh's most prestigious private school. While Lilias went her way with blitheness and grace, there was a turbulence in Geoff that suggested inner struggle. Charming and handsome, he was a glamorous figure who could be moody and silent towards his colleagues; but he was always there for the troubled. For them he had unlimited patience. They invaded his life and kipped on the floor of his Cleland Street flat, boys on the lam, families at their wits' end. Unlike Lilias who never seemed to be on duty, Geoff never seemed to be off duty, or never allowed himself to be. I found him intellectually more interesting than Lilias, and temperamentally closer. Lilias was as transparent as a well of clear water; but for a divided nature like mine her purity sometimes prompted the sadness of self-reproach. With Geoff it was different. I sensed that he also wrestled with demons. I remember discussing a story in a radical Christian magazine about a gay American priest with a drink problem who, in spite of his self-loathing, had become an instrument of grace and redemption to a street gang in one of New York's most violent slums. I confessed to Geoff that there was a verse in the gospels that troubled and consoled me in equal measure. It was what the religious leaders had spat at Jesus as he hung on the cross: *He saved others; himself he cannot save.* Geoff understood that tension. He understood the paradox of grace: that through their very flaws, troubled men could become instruments of grace for others but never for themselves. *They saved others; themselves they cannot save.* It was part of that other paradox, that God was found only among the poor. In existential terms, that meant finding him in our own poverty. It was not the devout and morally successful who had understood Jesus and gathered round him. It was the desperate and defeated, the people who had let themselves down – the disappointed.

One of the hot theologians at the time was an exile from Nazi Germany who had made his reputation in the United States, where he was a professor at Union Theological Seminary in New York, at which Geoff and Walter had studied. Paul Tillich understood inner duality and the anguish of longing for a state of being he was incapable of achieving. Going the rounds was a sermon he had preached on the subject:

> Do we know what it means to be struck by grace? It does *not* mean that we suddenly believe that God exists, or that Jesus is the Saviour, or that the Bible contains the truth. Grace strikes us when we are in great pain and restlessness. It strikes us when we walk through the dark valley of a meaningless and empty life. It strikes us when we feel that our separation is deeper than usual . . . It strikes us when our disgust for our own being, our indifference, our weakness, our hostility, and our lack of direction and composure have become intolerable to us. It strikes us when, year after year, the longed-for perfection of life does not appear, when the old compulsions reign within us as they have for decades, when despair destroys all joy and courage.[40]

This made sense to Geoff and me. It made sense to follow what might have been described as a theology of failure, because it not only captured our own confusion, it also seemed to be true to the downside-up message of Jesus. Theologically close we might have been, but the big difference between us was that

Geoff also had a heroic commitment to what he did. We could use the same theological language, but our actions were different. I was a dabbler. He went deep. I was a leaver. He was a stayer. I knew I was a bit of a fraud. Like Lilias, Geoff was the real thing.

What I did not understand at the time was that the essential difference between me and Lilias and Geoff was my low boredom threshold. Unlike them, I was no good at the steady grind of routine caring. I was drawn to the excitement of campaigning because it ignited my interest and suppressed the boredom that squatted deep inside me like a toad in a well. It would be the same when I had children of my own and was left in charge of them. I was hopeless. I either excited them to the point of hysteria with the games we played, or had them asleep before bedtime so that I could get on with what interested me. Poets notice these things. It was with a pang I discovered Hugh MacDiarmid's words on the subject and realised what opportunities I had lost by my inability to endure.

I love my little son, and yet when he was ill
I could not confine myself to his bedside.
I was impatient of his squalid little needs,
His laboured breathing and the fretful way he cried
And longed for my wide range of interests again,
Whereas his mother sank without another care
To that dread level of nothing but life itself
And stayed day and night, till he was better, there.

Women may pretend, yet they always dismiss
Everything but mere being just like this.[41]

Lilias and Geoff were always capable of the patience of 'mere being just like this'. I never was. I lacked constancy. Constancy is an endowment of the self that marks the good off from the rest of fitful, flitting humanity. I wanted to be good, but knew I wasn't. Yet here I was, working with two people of different but equally remarkable goodness. Unsurprisingly, I occasionally fell into dejection as I compared myself with them.

Since heroically good people are rare, it is hardly surprising that they provoke envy in the rest of us. Envy has been described as 'sorrow at another's good', which is why it is the saddest sin in the book. Because it is such a mean affair, we rarely admit to it. We may confess other, more positive sins with relish, but we are rarely prepared to admit that another's grace has made us sad. We find corrosive envy expressed in other spheres, such as the critic, perhaps an unsuccessful writer, who is caustic in his criticism of a better writer who has won acclaim. But the saddest manifestation of this human fault has to be envy of the *good* for being good. It is really a sorrow for *ourselves* that life has dealt us a less attractive hand to play. Moral goodness is not unlike those other accidents of the genetic and social lottery, good looks. Some people are physically beautiful, most people are not. Rather than rejoicing that the good and the beautiful exist at all, it is all too human to fall into sadness because we ourselves have not been so endowed – understandable, but unattractive. Indeed, envy at the endowments of others has ugly physical manifestations: a tightening of the features, as the face constricts into a sneer; behind the eyes a lurking sorrow and from the mouth an ugly contempt. I remember a friend responding to another's justified reputation for goodness, 'And I suppose he shits custard'.

In thinking about human goodness, I have found something

said by the philosopher William James helpful. He divided religious geniuses into once-born and twice-born types. The once-born were people of uncomplicated goodness who were uninterested in themselves and were therefore easily taken for granted. They may find themselves in situations of conflict and moral complexity, but their calm integrity is impervious to the pressures and temptations that can wreck the lives of more conflicted characters. Their spiritual lives flow like quiet rivers to the sea. The lives of the twice-born are more tumultuous, which is why they are usually more interesting. Their personalities are often a problem to them, and their lives are often marked by crisis and conflict. Unlike the untroubled constancy of the once-born, the twice-born have to rush over waterfalls and crash among rocks before making it to the sea.

James's typology is too stark to capture the variety of human types, even in religion, but his once-born description did fit Lilias. Unlike many people who dedicate themselves to the service of others, there was no sense of strain in her, no aura of grim attendance to duty. Radical behaviourists say there is no such thing as pure altruism; there is always a payback; an answer to some kind of need is always being met. This dismissal of disinterested altruism – which has been called 'the hermeneutics of condescension' – is usually a variant of envy, but sometimes it fits the bill. The clue to the payback-altruist is self-consciousness: 'I am labouring heroically to make the world a better place and you are enjoying yourself – shame on you.' This is the result of tension in the committed because there is no effortless flow of goodness in them. Their commitment comes from conscience not compassion, the head not the heart, which is why it can come over as cold and unattractive. True and unaffected goodness is more intestinal than cerebral in origin, which is something the Bible understands. In the Parable of the Good Samaritan, an explosive Greek verb lies at the heart of the story. We are told that after the Priest and the Levite pass by the man fallen among thieves, the Samaritan goes to his aid because *he is moved with compassion*. Behind the verb used here, *esplanknise,* there lies a noun meaning entrails or bowels. At the sight of the naked man bleeding at the road-side, the Samaritan's guts were wrenched with such empathy that it obliterated all self-protective caution and calculation. History has many examples of such passionate behaviour, much of it contrary to the survival instinct that is supposed to control all our actions.

We are close here to the difference between intuitive and intentional goodness. Unlike someone like Lilias, who was intuitively good, the intentionally good have to work hard at it. And it can show. They may perfect the acts of love but they never learn the dance because they never lose themselves. The intuitively good are unaware of themselves in these costly trans-actions, the intentionally good always are, which is why they are destined always to be Salieri and never Mozart. Though there is something admirable in the determination of the inten-tional person to act well, they can be difficult to be around, especially if you yourself are harbouring doubts about your own capacity for unself-conscious goodness. There was none of that sense of strain in Lilias, no guilt-inducing emanations, no detectable twists or corkscrews in her psyche, no heaviness of purpose or duty. She was unself-consciously, joyously herself. I knew I was a phoney, a priest actor trying out a different part. Phonies are envious of the genuine and either keep their distance or are powerfully attracted to them. Lilias fascinated me because it was obvious she was the genuine article. What was that phrase from the Letter to James that had always puzzled me? 'No shadow cast by turning.'[42] My turnings cast shadows, not least in my own mind. I could detect no shadow in Lilias.

Geoff's goodness was different, more agonistic, which is why I found him both more interesting and more threatening. I was certain he struggled with his commitment to be available to those who needed him, but he never seemed to be defeated by the struggle. And he was no stranger to theological crisis, either. In fact, he seemed to me to be close to Schweitzer both in his actions and in the theological conflict that precipitated them. He no longer wanted to talk about God or religion; he wanted to act. His life became active goodness. There was effort in that goodness, but it never seemed to fade or need time out, as mine did. A sadly precise little memory captures the difference between us.

We were all members of the Campaign for Nuclear Disarmament, and Geoff was the Glasgow Chairman. As well as local demonstrations, including some imaginative dramatisations of the effects of Hiroshima and Nagasaki crafted by Geoff for performance in Glasgow's George Square, we decided one year to join the annual Aldermaston March in London. I saw it as an opportunity to go to the movies after the march in one of the great London picture palaces, and headed south on my own. Geoff saw it as an opportunity to give some of his teen-agers a jaunt to England, so he drove a gang of them down in his old Bedford van. When we met, as planned, after the march he asked if I would come back north with them in the van that night to share the driving. He was knackered. Goodbye to my plans for a night in London. Sure, I said. He got us out of London. I took over while he dozed. I couldn't manage his vehicle, which was an eccentric monster to drive. After one hair-raising swerve out of danger that had the guys in the back cheering, Geoff woke up and took over. No complaint. He drove with determination for eight hours while I sat beside him fretting at losing a night at the movies while contributing nothing to the journey home. It said it all.

7

BROADWAY

When I was ten I tried to start a correspondence with a pen pal. I got his name from an American comic paper bought from Kinniburgh's in Bank Street. His address was in Arizona, and that was enough for me. *Arizona* was a very un-Scottish word – we didn't have zeds in the middle of names – but I felt I knew it as well as I knew the Loch and the Ben. It featured in the novels of Zane Gray – and wasn't *Zane* itself a great name? A zed in it too. The library in Alexandria had his novels, most of which I had devoured, and many of them had been turned into movies, movies I had seen, movies set in the mythic South-West, land of sagebrush and tumbleweed and lonely drifting heroes. Wyoming. Utah. Those names also conjured up the myth of the American West, but none more so than Arizona, a word that rolled more easily off the Scottish tongue – though Colorado was pretty good, too, with that great *rrrr* in the middle. But it wasn't just Zane Gray. The Vale library had an enormous collection of Westerns, most of which I read: Louis L'Amour, Max Brand . . . But for me Luke Short was the chief. He had even more movies to his credit than Zane Gray, and I found more of an edge to his writing than the stately Zane's. Luke Short's *Ramrod* was made into a good film, starring Joel McRea and Veronica Lake, but it was *Blood on the*

131

Moon with the lazy-eyed Robert Mitchum that grabbed me. I lived that classic theme in my imagination. Far away from Alexandria I drift along the American frontier on my faithful horse, the only friend I have. One day I ride into a community held in the grip of fear by a rancher whose cowboys shoot up the town and terrorise its citizens. His only opposition is a small farmer and his beautiful but determined daughter. I sort out the bad guys and win the heart of the farmer's daughter. But what followed varied. Sometimes I settled down with her and hung up my gun, but sometimes I had to bid her a reluctant farewell, for I was not as other men were and had to move on to other challenges. Before the credits came up at the end of my private movie, she stood behind the white picket fence and waved me onto another lonely adventure. I roamed the hills of the Vale in my body, but in my imagination I was in America far across the sea, in the words of my mother's Hogmanay lament. America seemed far away and very close, thousands of miles across the sea, yet just round the corner at the Strand in Bank Street or up the road at the library in Gilmour Street.

So I was excited by the prospect of having an American pen pal, especially one who lived in Arizona. I wrote to him during one of the long double summertime evenings of the war when it never got dark, sitting on the doorstep of 31 Random Street, composing onto a page of my school jotter. I wasn't sure how to end the letter till a mild deception occurred to me. There were a number of ways to calibrate social distinctions in the Vale, the most obvious of which was whether your lavatory was inside your house or outside like ours. Another distinction was having hot water. We didn't. But for children the real difference was having *stairs* in your house. The big establishments up the hill had upstairs and downstairs *inside,* while the houses below Main Street were all on one level, whether tenements, cottages, or two-storey terraces with outside stairs. To have stairs *inside* distinguished you from the lives of people who had to live their days on one level. I decided to impress the boy from Arizona with a piece of sophistry. There were two steps outside our door, and I was sitting on the wider bottom one to write. I decided to end my letter to Arizona with a pretentious flourish: 'Now I must finish this and go upstairs to bed. Goodnight.'

The fact that he never replied did nothing to quench my interest in America. I was intrigued by the knowledge that I had an unknown grandfather somewhere over there. Even at Kelham the interest in America had not waned. It was Thomas Merton, the American monk, who had stimulated my interest in the Cistercians. Apart from the romance of American monasticism, there were always the movies, as close now as they had been in my Random Street days, with the New Bedford and the Coliseum just round the corner in Eglinton Street to keep the habit going. So it is not surprising that at the beginning of my second year in Gorbals I was excited by an advertisement announcing four travelling scholarships to the USA under the auspices of the English Speaking Union. I saw the ad in the *Glasgow Herald,* calling for applications from young Scots likely to benefit from a month in the USA exploring areas of work similar to their own. Though he left me to my own devices, I was still technically a curate under Canon Bullough at Saint Ninian's in Pollokshields. As tolerant as ever, he encouraged me to have a go. I got my application in early, was called to interview and weeks later heard I'd been successful. *I was going to America!*

Four of us, two men from Glasgow and two women from Edinburgh, set off from Prestwick at the end of September 1961. The cheapest way to fly to America in those days was also the slowest: thirteen hours by Icelandic Air in prop planes, with several hours spent on the ground in the airport in Reykjavik. None of us minded. It was the first time I'd been off the ground, so the journey was as exciting as the destination. We were aiming for Philadelphia, where most of our time would be spent, with side visits to Baltimore and Washington. But it was the prospect of four days in New York City at the end of the trip that caught my interest. They billeted us with wealthy families in Philadelphia's Mainline, most of whom were conservative Republicans, but one host was a founder member of Americans for Democratic Action, a liberal pressure group in the Democratic Party. I liked the whole family, but it was the daughter who provoked me into a fit of Hopkinsian verse. 'Meredith wore her hair in a wind flung far flown flash of flame', and more of the same. She was unmoved by the effusion. I was secretly relieved. It was America I was falling for, not her. I was taken to my first drive-in movie by another young woman, a prominent lawyer's daughter. The sight of the closed steamed-up windows of the other cars at the drive-in was promising, but Brooke reminded me that our outing was a cultural exchange not a date. We parked beside one of the hearing posts, placed the speaker on the middle of the dashboard, put the tub of popcorn on the seat between us, and watched the movie, sucking on our root beers – with the windows open to the balmy night.

But it was Manhattan I'd really come to see, and when we got there at the end of October it did not disappoint. When we arrived at the mid-town office of the ESU I was told they'd billeted me with Dr Kennedy, 'a lovely man', at Union Theological Seminary, a place whose reputation I knew something about. Union was a well-known postgraduate destination for Scottish Divinity students, for whom a number of attractive scholarships were on offer. It was while they had been at Union that Geoff and Walter had been inspired to start the Gorbals Group. UTS was up on Broadway between West 120th and West 122nd Street, not far from the Columbia University Subway stop. Designed in the English Gothic style, it was a handsome brick and limestone campus that covered several blocks, with a large elegant quadrangular garden in the middle. The Kennedys lived in a large apartment in the complex, at 606 West 122nd Street, and they were solicitous hosts. Dr Kennedy was Secretary of the Seminary. After a distinguished ministry in various Presbyterian congregations, ending at Englewood in New Jersey, just across the Hudson from upper Manhattan, he had been invited by his old seminary to come back as its chief administrator. Proud of his ancestry, he took a particular interest in Scottish students who came to Union on fellowships from Scottish universities. I was the wrong denomination but the right nationality. He and his wife Ann welcomed me warmly to my final fling in America.

In Philadelphia we'd mixed sightseeing and pleasure with research into our chosen areas of interest, and we were expected to write a report after our return. In New York we were free to do what we liked. I'd been looking at this city for years in darkened cinemas. I could do the accent and the walk. What I wanted to do with my three days was explore as much of the city as I could on foot. I walked the length of Broadway the first day and Fifth Avenue the second. But it was on the third day it hit me. I was walking across town from Greenwich Village to the East Side. I crossed the Bowery, picking my way over drunks who might have been positioned by a set designer, and turned into a little street that ran between the Bowery and Tompkins Square. The sense of time and place shifted. A shop sign announced itself as the *Ukrainian Bazaar*. In the window there were carved hens sitting on painted eggs. There were rows of holy pictures and old photographs of girls in peasant costumes. It had the look of a small-town museum, a small town in Ukraine. At the end of the street, Tompkins Square was a shot of contemporary America, with its concrete benches and kids playing baseball. And sitting in the middle of the square were scores of old Ukrainians, women in black dresses with scarves round their heads, and old men in black suits leaning on sticks. No one spoke. They sat there, out of place and out of time, in silence, waiting. Maybe they had grandchildren in Queens who went to the ball games and thrashed along in the American mainstream, but they themselves did not belong here. Exiled was the word, a word that always hurts me.

Maybe the pain I found in the word had more to do with me than with the old Ukrainians. A fear of finding myself in the wrong place? Not quite. A fear of being cast out of the good place, the place of abiding? Closer. Or maybe it was a prospective sorrow at the thought of *dying* in the wrong place. Twenty years later, when I was a parish priest in Massachusetts, I was asked to take the funeral of a man who had died in a rooming house in Boston's Fenway. He had no relatives, no friends, no next of kin. I asked the undertakers what information they had about him, anything that would help me make the rite of consigning him to the flames more personal, a way of noticing that he'd been here, even if it was only as an inflection in my own mind. All they had on him was that he had been born in London sixty-seven years before and hadn't been in the US long. No one came to the funeral. As I read the service I couldn't stop thinking of him dying alone in the wrong country. Shakespeare was running through my mind. *I am dying in Egypt, dying.* I checked the quote afterwards and saw I'd got it wrong. Anthony actually said, 'I am dying, Egypt, dying.' I'd supplied the adverb. To me, the sorrow lay not in dying, but in dying in the wrong place; dying in Egypt not Rome, in Boston not London, in the Bowery not the Ukraine.

I was surprised that my walk had left me feeling so melancholy. But I knew it was a deeper thing than the mood provoked by those old Ukrainians waiting for death in Tompkins Square. For all its energy and confidence, there was something unsettled about America and it chimed with my own spiritual state. The frontier was an abiding theme of American culture, a theme I knew from my addiction to Western movies. It was also a theme I was beginning to recognise in my own nature. The romantic's curse, to be searching for an abiding good place that constantly disappears over the horizon. America's restlessness mirrored my own restlessness – with one significant difference. God was the exception to America's search for the green valley over the next hill. Americans carried God the way the Israelites carried the Ark of the Covenant, through the wilderness of their wanderings. One of the influential books of the time was a study of how immigrant groups accounted for America's religious conservatism as well as its ethnic dynamism. In *Protestant Catholic Jew,* Will Herberg proved that America believed in belief. It was belief that brought them here, belief that sustained them through disappointment in the promised land. It wasn't *what* you believed that mattered either, but *that* you believed. *ProtestantCatholicJew!* And some aspects of this belief in belief seemed worlds away from the downside-up theology of Jesus. There was a lot of agitation in American newspapers about nuclear fallout shelters at the time, and I was disconcerted to see that a not uncommon topic for sermons was whether prudent builders of shelters had the moral right to shoot their imprudent neighbours trying to enter their shelter when the bombs were falling. Britain was different. It wasn't so sure about anything. Even Kelham hadn't been so sure. Indeed, it was the sense of gambling one's whole life on what was far from a sure bet that had been part of the appeal of Kelham theology.

I wasn't sure either. I was beginning to wonder if God was not the ultimate object of desire of the romantic imagination? It was God's elusiveness that seemed to be part of his appeal. The idea that there existed an immutable Good that drew the heart and made it unsatisfied till it rested in it was one of the themes of Christian theology, and the romantic Augustine of Hippo was its poet. He began his Confessions with an address to the God who haunted the human imagination and made our hearts restless till they rested in him. *Inquietum.* Restless. Inconstant. I knew I had an unquiet heart. Thomas Merton had had an unquiet heart till he found rest at Gethsemani. While I was a boy at Kelham I'd read the book he'd written about his journey and had longed for that kind of abiding for myself. I did not know as I walked the streets of Manhattan how unquiet Merton's own heart had become away down there in his abbey in Kentucky. All I knew was that my own heart was unquiet and always searching for what R.S. Thomas called 'the glimpsed good place permanent'[43] – and never finding it. And America, eager, questing, unsatisfied America made me more conscious of it than ever.

When I got back to the Kennedys that evening I let myself

into their apartment in Knox Hall on 122nd Street and walked the length of their ninety-foot hallway to the guest room to dump my stuff. If I shoved my head out of the guest room window and craned to the right I could see where the Subway emerged from underground and became the Elevated, running from Harlem, a few streets north, all the way up to the Bronx. My last night in America. I lingered at the window. I noticed how cold it was becoming. Dr Kennedy knocked on the door. Tea? A sandwich? Something more substantial? I followed him down the hall to the kitchen, a large cheerful room, well equipped in the American way, with a fridge the size of a small truck. Seated at the table were Mrs Kennedy and the younger of their two daughters, Jean. She told me, much later, that when she heard me enter the apartment she got up to leave, not wanting to be seen in the curlers she was wearing. Her mother told her not to bother. He's the dedicated type. He won't notice. She was wrong. I had noticed.

After the brilliance of New York in the Fall, Glasgow was dreich and colourless on my return. Rain was sheeting down. The close at number 10 was grimmer than I remembered. Back in my room I fingered my souvenirs, hung a print of Brooklyn Bridge on the wall, and wrote some thank-you letters, including one to Jean Kennedy, who had volunteered to parcel up the books I had collected and couldn't fit into my suitcase. At last I had an American pen pal. By Christmas we had decided that she would come to Gorbals the summer of 1962, when she had finished her Master's degree at Columbia, to do voluntary work with us for a couple of months.

When that summer arrived, I decided to spend my vacation motorcycling to Greece. Back in Britain three weeks later on a busted machine with only one brake working and with Jean shortly to arrive, I took the Great North Road to Scotland. Near Newark I caught sight of that remembered silhouette, and soon found myself crossing the old bridge over the Trent and turning through the gate into Kelham. It was the first week of the summer vacation, so there were no students around and not many professed, so the House was quiet. Their welcome was not effusive – I had boshed six years ago – but they offered me a bed for the night. I was just in time for Evensong, said not sung because there weren't enough in residence to carry the music. Though softened by the summer light that drifted in through the open door, the Great Chapel was as over-whelming as ever. I remembered how we had looked at stran-gers when they visited us and wondered about their lives, poor lives not led here where life was at its richest and most mean-ingful. Scruffy in my flannels and anorak, mine was a poor life now, no longer lived here in the intensity of the sacred mission. I looked up at the dome and felt small. Not the humble small-ness we were encouraged to practise here as a spiritual exercise. This was the smallness of my failure. I was a disappointment. *Demas hath forsaken me, having loved this present world.* I was now the stranger, the one looked at and wondered about. Yet the place still tugged at my unquiet heart. After supper I had half an hour with a contemporary who was now the Cottage Master. We sat in his big bright room under the east end of the Cottage dorm smoking our pipes while he told me of the changes they were making. Better teaching. A-levels now. The same ethos, of course. That could not change. The spirit of the Society. 'We sacrifice young men on that altar!' And how was I? Glasgow was it? Now, could I please excuse him? Things to finish before Compline. Lovely to have caught up.

I wandered down Apostles' Walk, not daring to enter the

graveyard – *nothing counts but lifetimes* – and turned into Forty Acre. I stared at the river. My sorrow was to feel drawn to a life I was incapable of sustaining. I was beginning to wonder if the trouble might not be deeper than that. I had not been able to become what I thought I had been called to be. Now I suspected I would not be much good at the other options on offer either. They all required the submission of the individual mind to the mind of the community for the achievement of a common purpose. I could see the point in this. HK had talked about how the independent intelligence could be led, under disciplined direction, to concentrate upon the attainment of a common aim.[44] Working harmoniously together, the most disparate group of people could get things done. That was the secret of Kelham's success. It was the secret of any organisation's success. The trouble was, the timbre of my particular humanity did not seem to lend itself to the shape-shifting required. Back in Glasgow I had already had a collision with my Bishop on the subject.

It wearies me to recall the issue, particularly since things have moved on since then. It has to do with the way churches rate themselves with respect to others. Top of the pinnacle is the Roman Catholic Church. Its self understanding is that it is the only true church on earth and all others are defective in varying degree, some of them so utterly as not to be churches at all. The main focus for this discrimination is access to the Eucharist, the central sacrament of Christianity. The lower down the chain of ecclesiastical being you are placed, according to the high Catholic position, the less Eucharistic integrity you have. To Roman Catholics, no Protestant churches, including Anglicans, have full Eucharistic authenticity. This means we cannot participate in their communions and they will not participate in ours. According to the Anglican tariff, Catholics have a valid Eucharist and so have we, even though they do not recognise it. But at the time of which I speak Catholics were not the only closed Eucharistic game in town. Episcopalians were at it too. The Scottish Episcopal Church did not recognise the Presbyterian Eucharist, and that included the rite celebrated by the Gorbals Group every Thursday evening. This meant we were neither allowed to share our Eucharist with the Group nor participate in theirs. Lilias and I knew the rule and observed it – to begin with. If we went to the Group on Thursday evenings, we did not take communion with them. It was like going to a dinner party and joining in the conversation but refusing to touch the food provided. Religions are full of these separation strategies. Though the expressed rationale behind them varies enormously, fear is a strong factor: fear of ritual or racial pollution; fear of the anger of the jealous god; and the ancient clerical fear of letting their constituents be seduced by rival claimants.

As far as our situation in Gorbals went, after not very long it just seemed silly to maintain the separation, so we started receiving communion along with everyone else. More significantly, I started to take my turn celebrating the Eucharist at Group meetings, using their form of service. This compounded my offence, since all ordained and licensed clergy in the Scottish Episcopal Church had to take an oath to use the prescribed rites *and none other*. After a few months of this Eucharistic outlawry, I felt I ought to inform my Bishop what we were up to. I liked Francis Moncreiff, and I think he liked me. He was a tall, lugubrious, witty man who bore a striking physical resemblance to Lee Van Cleef, the Spaghetti Western actor. He had an endearing impatience with lengthy services, towards the end of which, seated imposingly on his throne in the sanctuary, he could be heard muttering in a loud stage whisper, 'Noooo, not another hymn!' But he was a traditionalist and followed the rules. He told me that what I was doing was wrong, but it was not a sin, a distinction that puzzled me. He then informed me that, while I was guilty of contumacious conduct, he would take no further action. 'And would I like another sherry?' I inferred from this discussion that he, too, thought it was a silly rule, but rules were rules and had to be observed. I continued to break the rule, but I reflected on the situation. I had not really taken this step in any spirit of rebellion, or with much thought at all. It had not created a crisis of conscience for me. It just seemed to be a daft rule, so I ignored it.

I was also ignoring the rule about not marrying the divorced in Church, another matter on which the Bishop hewed to the official line. I did not think of the divorced people who came to me as items in an abstract category called The Divorced, but as individuals with unique stories and therefore exceptions to general rules. Not that I agreed with the rule. It was the same when I performed my first gay marriage ten years later at Old St Paul's in Edinburgh. It was obvious that I could not refuse the sincere request of Peter and Richard to hear them promise to live together till death. I heard their vows in the Lady Chapel one evening after Evensong, using the form of the Prayer Book wedding service: and it took death to separate them, thirty-seven years later. What I did not reflect on at the time was that this untroubled capacity for ignoring rules that struck me as inhumane or silly defined me as an anarchist. I am not using the word in the organised, programmatic sense normally associated with the term. I no more believe in anarchism than I believe in any other kind of ism. I am using it in a temperamental sense, which was probably why I did not think too much about what I was doing at the time. *Anarchic*, in the sense in which I am using the word, means that one treats rules and regulations as having only a relative or provisional status, not as being immutable. Sitting in a car at a red light on a pedestrian crossing on a Sunday morning with not a soul in sight is daft, as are most regulations applied without reference to the context. Yet the minatory power of that red light paralyses us into stupidity and acquiescence. This is one of the faultlines in debates about human value, and it puts the role of institutions and the good of the individuals in unnecessary contention. We need institutions, but they are always *instrumental* goods, good *for* something else. That something else is human flourishing, which is an *intrinsic* good, good in itself. Religions are a famous battleground in this debate, because they imagine their rules and regulations are not just another variant of human arbitrariness, but have immutable transcendental authority behind them, a delusion Jesus challenged. He skewered the issue with a single saying: 'The Sabbath was made for man, not man for the Sabbath.'[45] The saying can be universalised: *The State was made for man, not man for the State. The Law was made for man, not man for the Law. Traffic lights were made for man, not man for traffic lights. Religion was made for man, not man for religion.* Jesus's saying fixes the status of all institutional rules as useful but never absolute.

The trouble with this kind of situational daring is that it undermines the human love of order and continuity. Most people prefer the familiar scales of stability to the jazz of creative morality. However, if everyone followed that preference no moral or social evolution would ever occur and history would be a constant replay of the past. Change comes through two forces that challenge the status quo. All systems have victims who sooner or later challenge the institutions that oppress or discriminate against them. The other agent of change is the defective person who is born without the institutional-loyalty gene. Though I was slow to realise it, I belonged to this group. I am not suggesting that disloyalty is a virtue, only that it is a fact and an occasionally useful one. Nietzsche was intrigued by the beneficial effect the disloyal have on the communities they sat so lightly to.

> It is the individuals who have fewer ties and are much more uncertain and morally weaker upon whom spiritual progress depends in such communities; they are the men who make new and manifold experiments. Innumerable men of this sort perish because of their weakness without any very visible effect; but in general . . . they loosen up and from time to time inflict a wound on the stable element of a community. Precisely in this wounded and weakened spot the whole structure is inoculated, as it were, with something new.[16]

I was far from putting all this together that August afternoon on the banks of the Trent, but I was aware of an inner unease, a dissonance between me and the Church I served. I, an unstable and uncertain man, had been steered into leadership in an institution that laid claim to transcendental levels of stability and certainty. Maybe that was one of the attractions, but it would not have needed a clairvoyant to predict that there would be trouble ahead. I did not know it as I stood gazing into the river that it would be the last time I would witness the old order at Kelham. The circumstances that would lead to its dissolution were even then assembling themselves. Early next morning I got back on my one-brake motorbike, steered it over Kelham bridge and headed north to Glasgow.

Jean Kennedy arrived a week later, and we put her to work. Our holiday scheme was in operation, so she joined me in trips to the country in Lilias's van Jemima, ferrying children to the families who had offered them a break. We fell in love during those journeys, and Jean decided to delay her return to New York from September to December. Should we marry? She, knowing what she wanted from life, thought we should. I was less sure. I wanted to marry *her*, but I did not want to *be married* to anyone. It wasn't just the usual commitment-phobic male thing, though there was that. It was the God thing, the disappointed God thing. As long as I stayed single, there was still a chance I'd make it through to the absolute life – one day. *Make me chaste, but not yet*. Marriage was the gate from which there would be no return. It would commit me to the world of the body, the world of compromise and accommodation. Why she stood it, I don't know. Even when we were out together I would not hold her hand in public, especially if I was wearing a clerical collar. And when we became engaged I was reluctant to admit it. In spite of my behaviour, Jean stuck to her pledge to marry me, and when I drove her to Prestwick in a borrowed car to see her onto the plane for New York, she planned to return the following March for the wedding.

When she came back to Prestwick on a wild March day the following year, I could tell immediately she was troubled. She was twenty-three. Only a few hours ago she had left her family and her homeland to live in a strange country with a man she loved, but who scared her not a little. We did not say much as I drove her into Glasgow. She was to stay with friends till our wedding in April, but I wanted to show her the flat that would be ours when we married. My curacy at St Ninian's would end that summer, and the Bishop was putting me in charge of Maggie Mungo's, the little church in Rutherglen Road that served the Gorbals. The diocese had bought and renovated the flat in number 10 above Lilias to accommodate us, and I wanted Jeannie to see it. Gorbals looked dismal as we drew near, and the close at number 10 was running with damp and as intimidating as hell when we arrived. Jean was upset by this time. She told me she did not think she could go through with it, and she wanted to phone her parents. They were wise in their counsel. There would be no problem about cancelling the wedding. The important thing was for her to be sure what she wanted to do. Take your time. Let us know. Meanwhile, we'll put everything on hold. I too was relieved. Jeannie says my words were, 'I couldn't care less.' That sounds too tactless even for me. But the pressure was off. Meanwhile, I reminded her, I had to furnish this flat. Married or not, I would soon be living in it. Would she help me scramble stuff together?

Next day we started trawling second-hand show rooms for furniture and cheap watercolours, one of which is hanging above this desk as I write. It was fun. We fell in love again. Jean told her parents we wanted the wedding to go ahead, and on a cold April day in 1963 it did. Geoff was my best man, Margaret, Jean's sister, her matron of honour. Jean's father, since he was a Presbyterian Minister and not of the Episcopal elect, was refused permission by the Bishop to take any part in the service other than as father of the bride. While we were exchanging our vows, Joe Bullough, my elderly and forgetful rector, prompted Jean to take me as her wife, to which she responded with a slight emphasis on the word husband. The Bishop celebrated the Nuptial Eucharist. When photographs were taken at the church door afterwards he insisted that he had to stand between us in any shot in which his presence was required. So there we are, the two of us, smiling on the steps at St Ninian's, and between us, wearing a mitre and a fierce expression, stands Lee Van Cleef. *Ya got a problem with that?*

8

THE ABSENCE

It was only a white lie, but it was a lie all the same and I've often wondered where it came from. I was spending a night in a youth hostel in the French Alps on my motorcycle ride to Greece. In the hostel kitchen, where I was frying up something to eat, I ran into a couple of English girls and we struck up a conversation. They asked me what I did and, without hesitation, I told them I was a social worker. It was ninety per cent true, of course, but it was the other ten per cent that made it a lie. Why did I tell it? I was ambivalent not so much about being a priest as about being identified as one, because it made me prey to their expectations about what the role involved. I had discovered that the clerical collar was read by others in ways that did not correspond to my own self-understanding, and I grew weary of trying to explain how they had it wrong. Wearing a dog collar on public transport was an invitation for other passengers to project onto me their own take on my role in ways I wanted to resist. Sometimes it was just annoying, such as the occasion when I travelled on the night train to London and was serenaded by a Glaswegian on the seat opposite who sang hymns at me till he fell into a drunken stupor as the train drew out of Carlisle. Sometimes it was irritating, as when aggressive atheists challenged me to prove the existence of God for them before we got to the next stop. Surely an hour would take care of it? More taxing were the religiously troubled who wanted me to answer their doubts, usually about the latest tragedy to have hit the papers. On one occasion a Muslim taxi driver, after catechising me on my views, told me I was bound for Hell. The most depressing incident, because in many ways the most typical, was when I was visiting parishioners who had a woman and her young son staying with them. Intrigued by my dog collar, the boy asked his mother what I was. He's a churchman. What's a churchman? It means you have to watch your Ps and Qs. My heart sank in the familiar way.

The ordained state seemed to represent for others two forms of certainty I did not possess. Moral certainty was the more embarrassing one to cope with. I hated being thought of as a moral policeman keeping an eye on humanity's Ps and Qs. Part of this was embarrassment at the knowledge of my own weaknesses. Because I was a priest, it was assumed that I was a fully fashioned moral individual of steadfast and immovable rectitude. Maybe clergy ought to be like that. Incorruptible policemen. How could I explain that what attracted me to Jesus was his acceptance of those who saw themselves as failures rather than moral successes? There was a subversive tradition in Christianity that claimed it was sinners who *got* Jesus, people who couldn't mind their Ps and Qs, not the righteous. It was the hopeless prodigal who understood, not his upright and disciplined big brother. Where to start trying to explain all that? But the dissonance went even deeper. It may have been fear of being found out myself, but I actually felt a strong revulsion against the morality-policing aspect of religion that was such a strong element in the Scottish tradition. I was attracted to the prophetic voice of faith that spoke against structural or institutional sin and the way the powerful ordered the world to suit themselves. I hated the prurient kind of religion that pried into personal weaknesses and took pleasure in exposing them. Yet, to the eyes of many, the ordained ministry was freighted with this reputation, which was why people felt they had to guard their reactions when they were around us. No wonder clergy sometimes fell into the trap of over-compensating for this misunderstanding by embarrassing demonstrations of their worldliness and humanity. The whole business was so tainted with false expectations that only the saintly seemed impervious to the treacherous currents that pulled us along. And I was no saint.

If moral expectations were the more painful projections to deal with, theological expectations were intellectually more frustrating to handle. The inner disconnect between the Church's official theology and my own version of Christianity was one I did not fully comprehend at first. As a boy in the Vale, intoxicated by movies and the longings the hills had provoked in me, I had been propelled into religion in search of a great love to which I could give myself away. I was in pursuit of an object ever flying from desire, but I had stumbled into a complex institutional reality whose own relationship with that object was highly ambivalent. The ambivalence lay in the difference between the modes of pursuit and possession. The romantic is always in pursuit, while the realist wants to possess. All institutions over-claim for themselves and end up believing more in their own existence than in the vision that propelled them into existence in the first place. This is particularly true of religious institutions. Religions may begin as vehicles of longing for mysteries beyond description, but they end up claiming exclusive descriptive rights to them. They segue from the ardour and uncertainty of seeking to the confidence and complacence of possession. They shift from poetry to packaging. Which is what people want. They don't want to spend years wandering in the wilderness of doubt. They want the promised land of certainty, and religious realists are quick to provide it for them. The erection of infallible systems of belief is a well-understood device to still humanity's fear of being lost in life's dark wood without a compass. 'Supreme conviction is a self-cure for infestation of doubts.'[47] That is why David Hume noted that, while errors in philosophy were only ridiculous, errors in religion were dangerous. They were dangerous because when supreme conviction is threatened it turns nasty. There would be a time when I would land in that trap myself, but I wasn't there yet. I was with Schweitzer and his escape from words to action. That is why I was moved by Lilias and Geoff. The romance of religion was alive in them – something greater than themselves was pulling them – but it was shown only in love and service. Whatever doubts they had about the claims of Christianity, the need to help the poor was self-evident to them. They were content to be social workers. So was I. Except now I was more than that. I had a church to run. That meant speaking. It meant preaching and teaching as well as action. It also meant opening myself to the projections of those who assumed I was morally and theological sorted, the way any good minister ought to be. Being in charge of a church suggested arrival rather than pursuit, the settler rather than the charismatic drifter.

But it wasn't an immediate problem. There are many aspects of running a church, particularly one as unpretentious as Maggie Mungo's, that are valuable on a purely human level. In the liberal tradition to which I belonged, the church was essentially a pastoral unit, a way of looking after people. However, there was a hidden tension, which was how you gathered the people in the first place in order to look after them. Liberals were better at the looking-after bit than at the gathering, which is why they tended to rely on congregations that had been collected by previous generations. It was Evangelicals who were the great gatherers. The trouble is, to be an effective gatherer you had to be excessive in your beliefs. It takes excessive certainty to convince others and override their doubts. Though liberal Catholics like me were no good at landing converts, we were quite good at keeping them on board once they'd been landed, because we were always living with our own doubts and were therefore reassuring to other doubters. 'If they can stay around maybe I can stick it out as well,' was their thinking. It wasn't all high-octane doubt, anyway. Most people were struggling to get by. They liked the reassurance of a visit to their hospital bed when they were sick or a house call to remind them that they belonged to something bigger than themselves. They liked the way worship on Sundays linked them with something that had been going on for centuries, something they may only hazily have understood, but something that suggested that maybe there was a meaning to things, after all, that Something Cared. And they were joined a couple of times a year, at Christmas and Easter, by many others whose understanding of what was going on was even hazier than theirs. 'But, you know, it just kind of feels right to come, though I'm a bit embarrassed by the impulse. Maybe it's the hymns. You know, the memories they trigger. Who knows? Anyway, we always sit at the back – where we belong.' Cough. Embarrassed laugh.

Apart from looking after the congregation, the church buildings were a resource for helping the neighbourhood. Maggie Mungo's was a box of red brick with a decent hall at the back in which we ran lunch clubs for the elderly during the day and youth clubs for tearaways in the evening. Inside, the church was all treacly brown varnish and a clutter of unused choir stalls. With the help of a well-known local clan I changed all that the week Francis Moncreiff installed me as priest. Alec and Frances had twelve children. I got to know them through their boys, who came to my youth club and called me Doc, after Wyatt Earp's sidekick who stood with him against the Younger clan at the gunfight in the OK corral. They would turn up at my door from time to time to hand in a bag of tinned food that 'fell aff a lorry'. Alec and his two oldest boys were trained decorators and they offered to brighten up Maggie Mungo's drab interior. Within five days the three of them had painted the walls a calm robin's egg blue. I dumped the choir stalls and brought the altar away from the back wall into the middle of the sanctuary. The congregation turned up for my first Sunday to a transformed building. They liked it, but wondered: wasn't there a rule that the diocesan authorities should be consulted about alterations to church fabric? There was. This time the bishop was more amused than exasperated. He informed me that the only other time he'd seen a church transformed with such rapidity was when the Cowley Fathers had taken one over in Edinburgh, *and that they didn't bother getting permission either.*

Our services, though never crowded, were cheerful and we had lots of children. Jean was a trained singer, with a fine soprano voice. Lilias was good, too, and there were others who could hold a tune. There was too much 'Kumbaya' and 'He's Got The Whole World In His Hands', but we deepened our repertoire by singing the psalms in a hot new version. Joseph Gelineau, a French Jesuit and composer, had translated the Hebrew psalms into French in 1953 and set them to music that wasn't exactly plainsong but was reminiscent of it. Cantors sang the verses of the psalm and the congregation responded with a simple antiphon after each verse. Jean and Lilias gave the chanting some class, and the children enjoyed belting out the response. So it was popular religion on Sunday and social work and campaigning during the week. As well as campaigning for better housing, we campaigned against the Bomb. We spent a lot of time on the back of lorries in George Square singing Pete Seeger's songs, 'If I Had A Hammer' and 'Where Have All The Flowers Gone?' We always ended these rallies with a defiant rendering of the international protest anthem, 'We Shall Overcome'. Glasgow had a great folk scene at the time, and CND rallies were the ideal excuse for an open-air concert. Jean, with her true voice, was a great asset here, and spent a lot of her young married life being lifted on and off lorries to help the group belt out the music. But following Jesus up and down Gorbals stairs, and on and off the back of lorries in George Square, was one thing; getting him out of the tomb where they had laid him after his crucifixion was another. One year, as Easter approached, I realised I wasn't going to be able to pull it off this time. It was my first crisis.

I have already referred to the shift in Christian history from poetry to packaging. The journey, from a *movement* that tried to follow the example of Jesus to an *institution* that hardened round a particular interpretation of his meaning, took hundreds of years to complete. The theological shorthand for the shift is called the evolution from the Jesus of History to the Christ of Faith, the move from the man of Nazareth who challenged us to action against principalities and powers to the Godman of Christian orthodoxy who demands our belief. It is the reverse of the Schweitzer journey from word to act, from theology to service. In this doctrinal reversal word is paramount. The right word. Wrong words have to be punished because they threaten to erode the citadel of belief into which we have escaped from the cold winds of an empty universe.

> Joan Bocher, otherwise called Joan of Kent, was burned for holding that Christ was not incarnate of the Virgin Mary, being condemned the year before but kept in hope of conversion; and the 30th of April the Bishop of London and the Bishop of Ely were to persuade her. But she withstood them and reviled the preacher that preached at her death.

That entry in the diary of King Edward VI for 2 May 1550 measures the distance the Church travelled away from Jesus and is still travelling today. The Christian test became words, the right words, the saving words. The biggest of these saving words is Resurrection, the word that captures the foundational belief of organised orthodox Christianity. And that Easter of my first crisis I could not put the Church's meaning upon it. Yet I had to. I had to get into the pulpit of my little church and read the stories of how he had been killed and placed in a tomb. And how they had rolled a stone in front of the tomb. And how, three days later – though the accounts vary – his disciples had come to the tomb and found it empty. And how he had appeared to them over a period of forty days. And how at the end of the forty days they had seen him ascend – literally – into the sky towards heaven. And it was my duty to tell them that this story was true. And not in a poetic sense – I was good at that – but in a factual sense. I couldn't do it.

By this time we had new friends across the street in 3

Abbotsford Place. John and Molly Harvey were at about the same stage in life as ourselves. Molly was a social worker, John was near the end of his studies at Glasgow University for the ministry of the Church of Scotland. It was to John I took my crisis: how can I find something honest to say about the Resurrection in three days' time? We walked the streets of Gorbals thrashing out ideas, and then continued our discussions over a whisky or two in number 3.

We kicked around four ways of looking at the Resurrection before hitting on my get-out-of-gaol-free card. The toughest was the response David Hume would have given. Whatever the motives behind the stories, and no matter how sincere the story-tellers were in believing them, we know that dead bodies do not resuscitate themselves. We also know that humanity is credulous and superstitious, and that history is full of bogus miracle stories. It is therefore more true to our experience of the world to conclude that the disciples were deluded than to believe the Resurrection actually happened.

The second approach was consistent with Hume's scepticism while being sympathetic to the Christian tradition. It was true that bodies do not rise from the dead, but something happened to change the deserters of Good Friday into men of courage and conviction. For this school, the Resurrection was a psychic event in the lives of the followers of Jesus that was later given mythic form. One writer imagined Peter, a year after the crucifixion, back at his job as a fisherman, casting his net into the water and remembering the hope he had in Jesus. Suddenly, he is overwhelmed by the conviction that Jesus's death was not a defeat, but the release into the world of his message of forgiveness and love. That turnaround was the Resurrection.

The third approach was even more sympathetic to the tradition. It could not understand where the stories came from, if there was nothing to them. The only evidence we have is the New Testament, and while there is clearly some embroidery and embellishing going on, there does seem to be a consistent holding to the story of the empty tomb and the series of appearances to the disciples. Anyway, if God can create a universe out of nothing, why can't he raise Jesus from the nothingness of death into a new kind of being?

The fourth approach was not so much a resolution of this irresolvable argument as a way round it. Why not use the Schweitzer approach and move from word to action? Resurrection then becomes a symbol for the possibility of change and renewal at the personal and group level. *Believing* the Resurrection becomes a way of living not a way of speaking. Leave the words to be what they are to those who bother about them, and get on with changing the world.

That's how I made it through what turned out to be a rehearsal for the main event. A few months later a bigger crisis hit. God himself went absent on me, though it would be more honest to say that a presence that often felt like an absence now became an absence that really was an absence. I was well aware that faith in God was not like one of these mutually supportive relationships we aspire to nowadays. I knew you could go for a long time in a relationship with God without getting any response from him at all. God was like those emotionally unavailable Scotsmen who were such a potent part of my heritage. He cared for me – he just wasn't good at showing it. The big difference being, of course, that emotionally unavailable Scotsmen are physically all too available, as a general rule, so those on the receiving end of their inattentiveness are very conscious of their existence. Having an affair with God is a double deprivation, since he is neither emotionally nor physically available. It's hard not to wonder how he got away with it for so long. It's also hard for some of us to stop thinking about him, even if, like Hamm in Beckett's *Endgame*, we are tempted to give up in disgust and say, 'The bastard, he doesn't exist.'

It's no surprise that his absence haunts us. We have been thrown into a universe that offers us no legible account of its origins. It is like a mute amnesiac with no papers: we have to figure out for ourselves where she came from. We have discovered a lot about her physical constitution, including how unimaginably old she is, but we are still stumped about where she came from and why she is at all. So we start hypothesising. In many ways the most attractive response to the question is a reverent agnosticism. In spite of the extraordinary fact that in us the universe has started thinking about itself, and in spite of the equally extraordinary fact of human cleverness and rationality, it seems unlikely that we'll ever be able to push back beyond that originating moment we call the Big Bang. We'll have to settle for a state of unknowing about what came *before* – italicised because there was no 'then' at that point for anything to be before. Strictly speaking, agnosticism should not be described as a hypothesis, because it is not so much positing an answer to the question as learning to live without one. It encourages us to live gratefully with uncertainty and give thanks to we-know-not-what for the gift of being. The risk run by those in this position is that it can lead to intellectual smugness at the expense of those who refuse to, or are incapable of, living with such uncertainty; and it opens itself to accusations of cowardice from the other two positions:

The sense of danger must not disappear:
The way is certainly both short and steep,
However gradual it looks from here;
Look if you like, but you will have to leap.[48]

For those who insist on leaping, there are two options. The first is radical atheism, radical because it has the courage to dig up and burn the roots of belief in God that have grounded the culture and morality of the human community for centuries. For the real atheist, there is no one there and never has been, no one but us. It is from our minds that the idea of the universe has come, as well as the gods and moralities with which we have populated it. There is no author of our being, no giver of laws by which to live, other than the ones we ourselves have created. We are the author of the author, the ruler of the ruler. God is not dead, he never was. He is over, out of it, away. So we must turn away from 'the priest and the doctor in their long coats running over the fields'[49] towards us. Now we are responsible for ourselves, so we should just get on with it. Bracing as that view is, I find it hard to understand how those who take it present it with the same insouciance with which they might observe that the number 23 bus has been cancelled. There is no sense from them of the momentousness of what has happened. Nietzsche understood.

Do we not feel the breath of empty space? Has it not become colder? Is not night continually closing in on us? Do we not need to light lanterns in the morning?[50]

However courageous and cogent the atheist's claim is, it is a hypothesis, a call to live as though it were true and take the leap into emptiness, knowing there are no everlasting arms waiting to receive us, but insisting that we can glide on our own. It is a kind of faith in human strength, the only one available to us.

The other hypothesis also calls for a leap, but in the opposite direction. For those who cannot settle for uncertainty or who cannot find the courage or the conviction to leap into nothingness and fly, there remains the leap toward God. The justification goes like this, and most people still find it persuasive: if everything comes from something, and nothing comes from nothing, where did the universe come from? It is hard to believe it just popped into existence from non-existence. There has to have been some pre-existent condition from which it emerged. One possible circumstance that might explain it is the pre-existence of a reality that brought it into being from its own super-abundance. Since the highest form of life we have encountered so far is self-conscious human intelligence, then the originating reality must, at the very least, be some kind of super-intelligent self-consciousness; maybe even one that it is possible to relate to. Positing the existence of such a reality leads inevitably to the question of *its* existence: who created it? Thus we start spiralling down the groove of an infinite regress. In order not to go mad, therefore, let us create a platform on which to stand by positing a being that is uncreated and uncaused, a self-existent reality dependent on nothing but itself. Terry Eagleton puts it like this: 'God . . . if he does turn out to exist has absolutely no reason for doing so. He is his own reason for being.' [51] The existence of such a being is a possible solution to the riddle of the universe, so let us buy this ticket and start the God game. If you can do that you can start to play. What is the next move?

The obvious thing to notice is that you cannot have a relationship with a hypothesis. The word means foundation, something to build on. It is from this point that the real leap has to be made. So far we have a flat, two-dimensional surface. Next, like watching the latest video game on a screen, if we pop on the 3D spectacles it comes alive and takes on the third dimension of depth. The technical term for this stage of the process is *revelation*, like a cinema screen that bursts into living colour or a curtain in a theatre that opens to reveal the play that is about to begin. In Christianity both parts of this activity are focused on the historical figure of Jesus, a Jew born in Judea 2,000 years ago who lived for about thirty years and was executed by Pontius Pilate, the Roman Governor of the province. In the Christian imagination, Jesus is both the curtain and what lies behind it: he is a character in history, but he is one through whom the Eternal reveals itself. In this life, goes the claim, the *before* is made manifest in time, and that which was *before* 'was' existed shows itself to us through the mediation of a human life.

Christianity is a reverse strip-tease in which a naked figure is gradually clothed in garments of increasing splendour and is finally enthroned at the right hand of God. While we may wonder about the authenticity of the heavenly setting, some of us continue to be provoked by the traces Jesus left in history and we reach back to him through the clouds of theological incense that billow around his memory. I fell in love with this system of mediated encounter with the man of Nazareth. I saw him as a distant figure on the shore of a vast sea. He was tiny to the point of disappearance, yet he irresistibly compelled my attention. Like a medieval knight pledging himself to the service of a beautiful but

unobtainable woman, it was the tantalising inaccessibility of
Jesus that was a strong part of his appeal to me. And unavailable he remained, in spite of attempts on my part to get close.
The Church went to a lot of trouble to get me close. What
it offered me was an ancient device for making the god present
to his worshippers. The idea was that though God himself
was transcendent and unavailable to our senses, his presence
could be mediated to us through a device called a sacrament
that made actual physical contact with him available to our
senses. Just as the Invisible Man in the old Hollywood movies
would put on a coat and hat and pop a pipe into his mouth
to make his presence available to his friends, so the invisible
listener clothed himself in sacramental form to make himself
accessible to me.

At Kelham there was a tiny upstairs oratory, called the
Chapel of the Holy Spirit, where the Sacrament of Holy
Communion was reserved in an ambry, in front of which a
white light perpetually burned. Reserving the Sacrament in
such a wall safe or cupboard began as a practical arrangement
in the Church. In cases of sickness or emergency it meant
the Sacrament could be made immediately available to those
who needed it. A white light was hung in front of the ambry
to mark the presence of the Sacrament. In time it became a
focus for devotion, one that, in Anglicanism, marked off the
Catholics from the Protestants. Anglo-Catholic schoolboys
on church crawls in strange cities would look out for the
telltale sign of the white light, a sure mark of 'sound' practice. Really high churchmen disapproved of the modesty of
a wall cupboard, and preferred the ambition of a Tabernacle
built into the reredos above the altar, preferably flanked with
six candles, one of the signs of the 'full' Catholic position.

Kelham disdained this Eucharistic showmanship and kept the Sacrament tucked away upstairs in this tiny chapel. It became a focus for devotion among more 'advanced' students, a trickle of whom would ascend the stairs after Compline to pray before the white light burning in the darkness. I was one of them. I liked the white light. It was alive and suggested a presence; but it was a presence that also suggested an absence because it reminded me of what was *not* there. *He* was not there. Instead, behind the flickering light there was a box in the wall containing a silver ciborium full of wafers of white bread. I knew how it was done, the making of it; but that was not the problem – as though having seen how the magician did the trick had ruined it for me. The sacramental system, for all its beauty and potency, is based upon the presence of an absence – and the absence had always been more real to me than the presence.

I knelt up there in the Chapel of the Holy Spirit night after night, asking for what I knew was forbidden – a sign that he truly was present in the absence. Signs get a bad press in the New Testament because they are the antithesis of the faith that trusts the absent God as though he were present. The empiricist in me, the doubter, wanted encouragement to keep the gamble going. Not a lot, either; just enough to keep me in the game. No sign was ever given unto me. At Kelham there was a conviction that the only verification of faith on offer was eschatological. It was like a scientific experiment based on a colossal gamble, whose outcome could only be discovered at death, which was why *only lifetimes counted*. Yet, we were also led to believe that waiting on God in prayer could lead to experiences of God on this side of death.

Moments of great calm
Kneeling before the altar
Of wood in a stone church
In summer, waiting for the God
To speak . . . [52]

I was taught many ways of waiting for the God to speak. The method encouraged at Kelham was meditation on the Bible passages we read in chapel. The easiest passages to practise on came from the gospels. One approach encouraged us to try what was called 'composition of place'. I would read the passage and in my mind's eye I would try to imagine the scene, such as Jesus standing on the seashore or sitting on a hill teaching his apostles. I would place myself in the company of his hearers and listen to his words, testing their meaning and import. Finally, I would make a resolution that brought the meditation into the realm of action, resolving to correct a fault or increase a discipline. When I started preaching sermons it proved to be quite a fruitful way of finding something to say about the gospel for the day, but it was pretty useless when trying to meditate on the letters in the New Testament.

I tried the method one sad afternoon in the chapel in Bishop's House, Accra. The Bishop was away on trek and I was holding the fort on my own. Suddenly smitten with a wave of loneliness and homesickness, I went upstairs to the chapel, a sunlit room full of the sound of the sea, and tried to meditate. There were two readings at mass, one from the epistles and one from the gospels. I could make nothing of the gospel for the day, so I tried my hand at the reading for the epistle, which was from the Letter of James.[53] The opening words didn't help, in fact they made matters worse, since they drew attention to my besetting sin.

Let no man say when he is tempted, I am tempted of God: for God cannot be tempted with evil, neither tempteth he any man: but every man is tempted, when he is drawn away of his own lust, and enticed. Then when lust hath conceived, it bringeth forth sin: and sin, when it is finished, bringeth forth death.

That was tough. Here I was, longing for the God to speak, seeking a word of comfort or reassurance, and I get a scolding. OK, I hadn't kept custody of my eyes that morning in the cathedral, filled with those voluptuous Ghanaian women, but it was impossible to do so. I had been sub-deacon at High Mass, a ceremonial role with little to do, except hold the Patten under the chin of the communicant as the celebrant placed the communion wafer onto her tongue – yes, *her,* because it was women I always noticed. I towered above them as they knelt at the altar rail and, try as I might while performing my sacred duty, I found it impossible not to look down Pennsylvania Avenue, Herbert Asquith's code for the female décolletage. So why bring women up this afternoon? They weren't on my mind when I knelt here ten minutes ago, waiting for God to comfort me: now they are, adding lust to loneliness.

I try to move on in the passage.

Do not err, my beloved brethren. Every good and every perfect gift is from above, and cometh down from the Father of lights, with whom is no variableness, neither shadow of turning.

Composition of place does not help here. All I can visualise are Christmas presents being lowered from the gallery in Kelham

Chapel, and I don't get the point of that. I can't do much with 'no variableness, neither shadow of turning' either, except as another reminder of the constant shadows cast by my own endless turning. A judgement, I guess, another judgement. Not what I came for, but probably what I deserve. Why is it that when God does speak he always sounds like my own conscience having another go at me? Uncomforted, I close the Prayer Book and decide to take a long walk along the seashore. I know I'll end up at that popular swimming spot near Christiansborg Castle where the local women bathe, and my lust and loneliness will increase. That's exactly what happens. I come back from my walk repeating one of Gerard Manley Hopkins' so-called 'terrible sonnets':

> . . . my lament
> Is cries countless, cries like dead letters sent
> To dearest him that lives alas! Away . . . [54]

Six years later he seemed farther away than ever. Here I was, pounding the streets of Gorbals rather than a shore in Africa, still shouting at the great Absence. I came close to packing the ministry in at that time. A lot of clergy of that generation did leave, many of them becoming social workers. Years later I encountered one or two who had made that particular journey and ended as Directors of Social Work in some tough cities. Though godless, they could never quite shake off the old sense of demand that had imposed itself upon them in their youth. I thought of taking that escape route too. I made enquiries at the University of Strathclyde, just across the river, about doing a doctorate in the sociology of religion, another lure to unsettled priestly minds of the time. The good thing about that particular exploration was that it put me on to Norman Cohn's book about apocalyptic religion, *The Pursuit of the Millennium,* a study that has grown in relevance since its original publication in 1957. In the event, I took neither of these opportunities for escape, and have regretted it only occasionally. I wanted to hold on to the poetry of religion, even if it meant having to live with some turgid prose as well.

What convinced me to stick it out was not any advice I sought from others. Actually, I did not seek advice. This was partly due to the confident man's certainty he can handle anything that comes at him; but it was also an occupational hazard of the priesthood itself. The trouble with priests is that they know all the ruses to keep people on-side. *He saved others; himself he cannot save.* By this time I was deep into my own mind, pounding ideas as my feet pounded pavements. On one walk through the rain an old Spaniard whispered in my ear. 'You think you come from nothing and it is nothing that awaits you? So what? Perish resisting. And so live that it will be an unjust fate.'[55] With that defiant gesture in the face of impossible odds, my back found its wall. It was the very weakness of the case for religion that kept me loyal. The sight of a beleaguered company trying to hold their tattered banner above the flood that was drowning them gripped my heart – as it still does. Whereas strong super-confident religion, conquering all before it, repelled me – as it still does.

Christianity was on its last legs, so it didn't feel right to desert it. But my rearguard action took me further away from assertive religion. I decided to *act* as though I believed there was a meaning to the universe. And not just any meaning. Love's meaning. In the face of what had happened in the twentieth century, it was hard to prove that love *was* the universe's meaning. But to choose to live as though it were! To commit oneself to the poetry of an everlasting love that is rejected by those it longs after, yet whom it continues to follow on broken feet! I knew that was not what everyone made of the biblical idea of God, but there was enough in scripture to glean it, if only as the hint of a possibility. And were we not all editors of our own gods, anyway? Why not choose *that* idea of God to defend against the last wall? Now and again I had caught glimpses of a tremendous graciousness in people I had known, flawed, tormented souls, who had mediated unconditional love to me. The dispossessed of Israel had caught sight of that graciousness in Jesus, which was why it was they and not the good who had hung on his words. I had groped my way to a wall to stand against. That way I was able to stay.

But it was a vulnerable position. Willing yourself to act as though you believe when you know you don't does not provide you with arguments against confident unbelievers – or confident believers either. It is a gesture many make in order to stay in touch with the poetry and compassion of faith. But it does not equip them for battle on the hustings of religion. That takes the confidence of the true believer, able to defend every line of the party's manifesto against the equal confidence of the opposition. To do that you have to buy the package. I couldn't. Within the religious enclosure, however, I could use my position to some effect, either by instilling the will to remain in other troubled doubters or by softening the impact of harsh religion on those who had become its casualties. I was to spend an increasing amount of time working with people in flight from oppressive religious systems, many of them conflicted by their own sexuality. But I was never able to train myself to become a victorious battler against philosophical atheism, mainly because I myself had never been convinced by philosophical theism. I have had to endure the pain of watching myself in some old television documentaries where I was set up to debate faith with trained philosophers who were convinced and convincing atheists. My poetics were no match for their forensics. And it showed. Sometimes there was even a touch of compassion in their contemptuous demeanour as they watched me floundering. It was like debating with clever Conservative Evangelicals, firm in their mastery of scripture and its certainties, who were equally dismissive of my lack of conviction. Both sides could parrot their contempt of my hesitations: 'If the trumpet give an uncertain sound, who shall prepare themselves to the battle?'[56] Maybe I just wasn't interested in their battles. There seemed to be many more important ones to fight.

III

1968–84

9

THIRTY-THREE STEPS

The assassination of Robert Kennedy and the chaos it symbolised turned me back to the Church as a place of meaning and reconciliation in an ugly world. The fact that I was not far away when it happened only added to its impact on me. At six thirty in the morning of 5 June 1968 I turned on the radio in my bedroom at the Barth Hotel in Denver and heard that Robert Kennedy had been shot in Los Angeles the night before. I left the hotel and boarded the train for San Francisco, where I was due to arrive the following afternoon. When I got there I walked to Grace Cathedral on Nob Hill. In front of the high altar they had placed the Stars and Stripes, draped in black, between two candles. The nave was full of people kneeling in prayer, most of them weeping. I too knelt to pray but no words came. What came was a kind of baffled anguish over the human condition. The good we would we did not; what we hated was what we did. I knew this from my own struggles, but in the cathedral that afternoon it was a world sorrow that overwhelmed me. No wonder the Church talked about the fall of man. No wonder it said he needed redemption. I was weeping too. For Kennedy, but for much more than Kennedy; for all of us and for everything. It was a bloody climax to a strange year.

In 1967 I had been given a fellowship to do a year's

postgraduate study at Union Theological Seminary in New York, where Geoff and Walter had been before me, and where Jean's father had been Secretary. Apart from a chance to do some thinking and reading, it would provide us with an opportunity to spend time with Jean's parents, now retired and living in New Jersey. As a graduation present, my father-in-law gave me a trip across the USA by train, so a few days after Commencement I left Jean and our daughters Ann and Sara – both of whom had been born while we were in Gorbals – with her parents in South Orange and flew to Chicago to get on the train that would take me across America. My plan was to go west through the prairie states to the Rockies, then head south-west through San Francisco and Los Angeles to Flagstaff in Arizona. There I would rent a car, drive to Santa Fe and catch the train back to Chicago. On my drive the place I wanted to get to was Monument Valley, where the south-west border of Utah touches northern Arizona. Like other lovers of John Ford Westerns, I had seen those massive sandstone buttes in *Stagecoach* and *The Searchers* and many other films. No matter how predictable the movie, those amazing formations added grandeur and mystery to it. I wanted to stand there and feel tiny against that startling horizon

Our year in New York had started quietly but ended violently. As well as waging an unjust war abroad in Vietnam, America was fighting a just war at home to give African Americans the civil rights they had been denied for centuries. On 4 April Martin Luther King was assassinated. City after city went up in smoke. The explosion of rioting provoked an eruption in America's universities and colleges, and one of its epicentres was at Columbia. A tamer version of Columbia's sit-in was staged at Union, though it was violent enough to catapult a number of professors into nervous breakdowns. I took part in the debates that convulsed the community, but I was more dismayed than stimulated by what I witnessed. I was surprised at how suddenly sane and rational people could resort to verbal and physical violence. The revolt seemed more like a bout of religious apocalyptic fever than a movement for planned reform. It had the manic energy but none of the poignancy of the Ghost Dance religion that swept American Indian reservations in 1889. The ghost dancers believed that if they danced long and hard enough all white people would be submerged under a deep layer of new earth, the buffalo would return to the great plains, and all the Indians who had ever lived would come back to life, and the land would become a paradise.'' Tragically, the dancers achieved nothing but more sorrow for their suffering people. Just as tragically, the apocalyptic extremists of 1968 only succeeded in stoking up the boilers of hate that are never exactly cool in America anyway. When the protests finally ended, their leader wrote an open letter to the President of Columbia in which he quoted from a piece of graffiti that had been scrawled in the mathematics department during the occupation: 'Up against the wall motherfucker, this is a stick-up!'

My love of the movies had caused me to romanticise American violence. The events of 1968 made me realise how ugly it was, yet how intrinsic to the America way and how quickly Americans turned to the gun to resolve disagreements. I started collecting stories about their love of firearms. One of them haunts me still. Throughout that year the *New York Times* ran a series of stories about the culture wars that were convulsing the nation. In one story they reported how a girl in Arizona had spent a night with a married serviceman at the local airbase. To punish her, her father drove her and her pet dog into the desert.

When they got out of the car, he pulled a shotgun from the trunk and ordered her to shoot the dog through the head. She wept and begged for mercy. She was sorry. She would never do it again. He was without pity. 'Take the gun and shoot the goddamn dog!' She took the gun and blew her own brains out.

The violence that swept America in 1968 provoked a change in Robert Kennedy. A normally combative and divisive politician, he travelled the country calling for a healing of the nation. Wherever he went in his campaign, he recalled how the US had uprooted and corrupted the original inhabitants of the land it had stolen. Quoting from Greek tragedy, he pleaded with his listeners 'to tame the savageness of man and make gentle the life of the world.' It looked like he might win. He took the California Primary. 'On to Chicago,' he cried, as he left the Embassy Room to be led out of the Ambassador Hotel through the kitchen. That's where they shot him. That's why we were weeping in the cathedral that afternoon, weeping for our failure to make gentle the life of the world.

And that's why, sitting on the train drawing out of San Francisco the following morning, I'd had it with the human lust for paradises. Humanity's longing for them was its most dangerous drug. Why couldn't we settle for making the world not perfect, but less savage and more gentle?

I know the things I've lost are so many that I could not
   begin to count them
and that those losses
now, are all I have . . .
Only those who have died are ours, only what we have
   lost is ours . . . There are no paradises other than
   lost paradises.[58]

I settled myself in my seat as the train trundled out of the station. For a while I looked out of the window, enjoying the melancholy reverie train travel always induces in me. Then I picked up one of the books I had brought along for the ride, Arthur Koestler's novel about purges and persecutions in Soviet Russia, *Darkness at Noon*. The epigraph was from Dostoevsky: 'Man, man, one cannot live quite without pity.' I put the book down and looked out of the window again. *One cannot live quite without pity*. Surely that was the key to understanding human hatred. Hatred was an absence of pity. Graham Greene had said something like it. When you looked at other men and women, 'you could always begin to feel pity. When you saw the lines at the corners of the eyes, the shape of the mouth, how the hair grew, it was impossible to hate. Hate was just a failure of imagination'.[19] That is true, but it is pity that does the imagining. Pity is sorrow at another's sorrow, pain at another's pain. To feel another's sorrow! That has to be the way out of the predicament of human hatred. Pity! Yet it is a word some despise. And not just revolutionaries and ideologues for whom pity is always treason, because it blunts the edge of cruelty, their chosen weapon. Pity is despised because it is seen as demeaning to the one pitied. Poor little sufferer! How I pity her! But that is not the tone of real pity. Pity is an identification with the other so profound that you enter her sorrow, even if she is someone you have been taught to despise. It is this that makes pity the antidote to evil. In spite of its colourful reputation, evil is an absence, a deprivation, the lack of something, a great emptiness. What the evil person lacks is the ability to identify with the other's humanity. It *is* a lack of imagination. In order to hurt others we have to rob them of their humanity, refuse to see them as like ourselves, refuse to notice the lines at the corners of the eyes, the shape of the mouth. We have to make them objects not selves, *otherise* them! We have to do the precise opposite of what pity does, which is to humanise them, make us, almost helplessly, feel what they feel, grieve when they grieve, sorrow over their sorrow. Dostoevsky was right. We cannot live without pity. The more I thought about it, the more amazing was the revolutionary energy behind that beautiful little word. It even sounded lovely. I liked the way Hopkins used it: 'My own heart let me more have pity on.'[60]

And that was my second thought. That maybe we had to pity ourselves in order to pity others. Did that follow? Was it another clue? That hatred of others begins in hatred of ourselves? That felt right too. What we hate in others is often what we refuse to pity in ourselves. Was that behind the story of the angry man in the Arizona desert? Wanting to destroy the dog of his own desires, he kills pity instead? I'd noticed this reversal in myself while I lived in Accra. Dismayed by my own sexual longings, ashamed of them, I'd been critical of Africa's relaxed attitude to sex and its humorous indifference to white hang-ups on the subject. Longing for that freedom for myself and lacking the courage to embrace it, I had condemned it in others. That was an old song. One cannot live quite without pity *for ourselves!* There was a theme in the Bible along the same line. It had been quoted to me by gentle confessors to whom I had taken my struggles. They would get me to read Psalm 103:

> The Lord is full of compassion and mercy: long-suffering and of great goodness. He will not always be chiding: neither keepeth he his anger forever.
> For he knoweth whereof we are made: he remembereth that we are but dust.

He remembereth that we are but dust. Those were the words that always got me. Conjured out of nothing, as we are, mere dust, how can we expect much of ourselves? Well, maybe we can, in time, but we must first remember whereof we are made. Dust, but knowing dust, aware of our own complex finitude. It kept coming back to pity, the ability to identify with the other, especially the despised other. There didn't seem to be enough pity in America, I thought, as I looked out of the window. That's probably why they'd been able to settle this vast continent so ruthlessly. Could they have done it any other way? Maybe.

Maybe? That was another disarming word, another word that dampened the kindling of hate. Maybe! It's not a punishing kind of word, like Conviction or Certainty or Right or Wrong or Infidel or Enemy or Truth or Creed or Inquisition or Empire or Revolution or Purge or Motherfucker. People have killed with those words on their lips. In the name of the great demand that has taken possession of their souls, they have descended upon the affections and eccentricities of others and obliterated the frail habitations they sheltered in. Always they have done this through the violence of the word before the violence of the deed. The word has to come first. In the beginning is always the word. The violent word always precedes the violent act. Get the word right and we'll do anything in its name. The fixed and certain word is lethally effective. This is why the people of the Maybe are ineffective. They lack persecutory certainty, because they are too aware of their own weaknesses and confusions to punish others for theirs. Maybe the compulsion to impose their values on others has been undermined by the pity they feel for them, even as they feel it for themselves. And maybe things go wrong with us as often as they do because we try to live quite without pity. Maybe we should try to build our politics and religions on pliant and

179

yielding words not on hard and killing words. Words like pity and maybe. It's a pity the people of the maybe are so few. Pity-maybe-pity-maybe-pity-maybe-pity-maybe went the descant of the wheels as the train rolled on.

I am a reader, especially in trains, but I spent most of that journey looking out of the window in a dazed reverie. Moodily, I got off the train at Flagstaff and into my rented Pontiac. I found my way to Highway 163 and the Navajo Nation Reservation and Monument Valley. I did not intend to take one of the guided tours. Nor did I plan to spend the night in the guest house in the reservation. All I wanted to do was stand and look. I wanted the sense of distance. At the agency office I took the deal that let me drive further into the great space for about fifteen miles. Then I got out of the car and looked across the vivid red emptiness to those spectacular eruptions away in the distance. The startling thing about them is the way they suddenly lift themselves out of the desert as if they've just punched themselves through the surface – yet they look as if they've been there for ever. But they were hard for me to connect with, apart from the images of stage coaches and cavalry forts my Bank Street memories conjured up.

The impossibility of uniting yourself to a landscape was a sorrow I well understood. I had felt it often in the hills of Scotland, though there I could at least move my feet across the mystery and possess it in that way. I knew I could never do that here. It was not the sort of terrain I could ever feel at home in. The dryness. The heat. The hallucinatory power of the distances. The otherness of it all stunned me. I have always loved the American word lonesome. There's more to it than the English lonely. A deeper undertow of sadness to it. I felt lonesome out there at the edge of the trail in Monument Valley.

A beautiful American word for the human condition. I was homesick for Jean and the girls. My train to Chicago was three days away in Santa Fe. I got back in the car and headed for Santa Fe. When I got there, the town was too glossy for my mood, but it gave me the song that still carries the memories of that trip. The night before the train back to Chicago I went to the movies. A nice old-fashioned picture house, the Regal. Steve McQueen and Faye Dunaway in *The Thomas Crown Affair*. It was a slick, enjoyable thriller, but it was the Legrand and Bergman theme song that stayed with me.

> Round,
> Like a circle in a spiral
> Like a wheel within a wheel,
> Never ending or beginning,
> On an ever-spinning reel . . .
> Like the circles that you find
> in the windmills of your mind!

On the train back to Chicago, looking out the window of the elegant Santa Fe Railway car, I was contemplating another departure, making another circle in the windmill of my mind.

Early in 1968, well installed at Union, living with Jean and the girls a block from Broadway in an apartment at 49 Claremont Avenue, with frequent weekend visits to the Kennedys in South Orange in a tough old car Jean's father had bought for us to make the visits easier, I got a letter from Ken Carey, the Bishop of Edinburgh. He wondered if I'd be interested in becoming Rector of Old Saint Paul's in Edinburgh. If so, could I get away for a few days to meet the Vestry, the management committee of the congregation.

I knew Old Saint Paul's a bit. When I was sixteen, at the beginning of one Easter vacation, travelling overnight with Aeneas Mackintosh – my fellow Scot at Kelham – we got off the train at Waverley at seven in the morning. We had a couple of hours to kill before his train to Inverness and mine to the Vale of Leven. There's an interesting church up there, he said, pointing to the cliff of buildings that rose outside the station above platform 11. It's called Old Saint Paul's, and they should be starting the early mass soon. Want to come? We checked our cases at Left Luggage and made our way out of the Market Street exit and walked under North Bridge into Jeffrey Street. Aeneas challenged me to a race up the steep dirty steps of Carrubber's Close. He won. Out of breath, we opened a little side door halfway up the close and stepped into the gloomy building. I'd never been in the church before, but I knew it was a homecoming. It was dark. An expectant darkness, a darkness that held something back even as it welcomed me. I saw seven white lights glinting in the distance, but we turned immediately under a small archway, through a dusty curtain, into a little chapel to the left of the side door. The chapel was in darkness, except for the glow of a golden reredos behind the altar, where a server was lighting the candles for mass. We were in the Lady Chapel, which sat a few steps above the nave of the church like a lifeboat strapped to a liner. A tall white-haired priest celebrated the mass. He invited us back to the rectory for breakfast. Lauder House was just along Jeffrey Street. We had porridge in a dining room shadowed by the tenements that crowded against the side of the house. I said little, but Aeneas charmed Father Lockhart and his curates with stories of Kelham eccentrics. It remained a potent memory in which the colours were smoky grey and black, like the platform scene in *Brief Encounter*.

This was where Ken Carey hoped to establish me on our return from America that autumn. It would mean leaving Gorbals, but the idea of Old Saint Paul's excited me. I flew back from New York for a brief visit that March, and was interviewed by the Vestry in the Clerk's apartment in Chessel's Court. I was offered and accepted the parish. It was agreed that I'd start in September when we were due back in Scotland. The Bishop was happy. We'll have to do something about the house, he said, the worst rectory in the diocese, ice cold, and in the coldest street in the city. They're talking about selling it and finding somewhere else. I didn't say anything. I already liked the house and thought it liked me. I brought some books about Edinburgh back to Jean, who would be coming to a city she did not know and a house she had never inspected, all twenty ice-cold rooms of it.

But that was not all that was going through my mind on the train back to Chicago. I was thinking about writing a book. My scepticism towards the revolutionaries at Columbia, and my dismay at the violence that had disfigured America that summer, had provoked contradictory responses in me. In spite of my threnody on pity and uncertainty on the train between Los Angeles and Flagstaff, the conservative bit of me was reaching back to a more settled and certain theology. The conservative mind believes that the only way to contain the unruly wills and affections of sinful men is through strong, stable and ruthless institutions that are prepared to sacrifice the individual for the greater and more enduring good of the community. And the Church was one of the most important of these restraining structures. Its pessimism about human nature, balanced by the offer of a redeemed and perfected life beyond death which, to a limited but real degree, could be foreshadowed and experienced here and now, gave it a great story to tell a humanity perplexed by its own fears and longings. I began to worry that the liberal theology that had destabilised me and others in the early Sixties would only succeed in dismantling the walls that had been carefully built to protect us against our own inner chaos.

The fundamental difficulty is that all religious systems and the claims they make for themselves are as fragile – and sometimes as beautiful – as the floating villages of the South China Sea. The word faith is the giveaway. The opposite of faith is not doubt, it is certainty. Where you have certainty, you don't need faith. I am certain that 2+2=4. I can do the two-times table on my desk with paper clips. Faith never comes into it. But if I ever require heart surgery I'll need faith to enter the operating theatre, faith in the surgeon who will cut me open and do things to my heart. Inevitably there will be some doubt in me when I submit to the knife. Will I be one of the tiny percentage who do not survive the operation? There's a chance of that, but I'll trust the surgeon to get it right, and I'll go under the anaesthetic expecting to wake up again in a few hours. But I cannot be certain. Ordinary living is full of these acts of faith, and most of them are, to some extent, quantifiable. We can figure the odds by checking the background of the person we are putting our trust in. In the case of the surgeon I must have faith in, I can check his success record for open-heart surgery before submitting to his knife.

Unlike those everyday acts of faith, religious faith is based on a massive, unquantifiable hunch. But it is not the existence of God. You can get somewhere with that hypothesis by thinking about it, as I have already tried to show, and deciding to take the leap or not. Christianity and other revealed religions go much, much further than that. They claim that the God so hypothesised has intervened in history and done things that we are called upon to believe. We have shifted from a probable or improbable hypothesis – the existence of God – to hard historic claims about God's actions in time. The fact that these claims are endlessly disputed within religion itself shows that even believers are far from possessing certainty – which is why they still need faith or trust. Say we decide to make the necessary act of trust: we are still like the man on the trolley being wheeled into the theatre – we cannot be certain. Faith, by definition, always implies doubt. There can be something admirable, some- thing worth doing, in the decision to believe – but it never gives us certainty! And here's the catch. Revealed religions tend to blow a smokescreen round the living reality of the faith–doubt experience and out of the smoke emerges – doctrinal certainty! Behind a great clatter of mirrors and a great fog of smoke they move from faith to certainty. Believers are not encouraged to take the plunge of *faith*, they are invited to swear to the certainty of a series of historic claims that come in propositional form. That is why religious history is so full of disputes over competing interpretations of the certainties contained in the faith package. I have already mentioned the diary of Edward VI who noted the execution of Joan Bocher, precisely because she refused to accept one of these claims – the Virgin Birth – as a historical fact. Once we get to this stage in the evolution of religious institutions we are no longer playing the ancient game of faith. We are no longer saying, let us suppose that God exists and Jesus is his revealed meaning and live in faith *as though it were true*. We cannot know any of this for certain, but there is beauty in the choice and it will give our lives a purpose, and maybe pay the universe a compliment it does not deserve. Care to join the experiment? Care to do the insane and lovely thing? That bracing approach disappears, and is replaced with oaths sworn upon the truth package of absolute religion.

How does such hard and punishing certainty emerge from the existential gamble of faith? Paradoxically, it is lack of faith and fear of doubt that prompt it. What do you do if you can no longer live with the doubt that is co-active with faith? You try to cure yourself. And the best cure for doubt is over-conviction. A well-known mark of the uneasy doubter is over-confidence. It is like the refusal to let pity weaken you in the face of your enemy. Doubt, like pity, erodes certainty. If you are desperate for certainty because you believe only it can hold chaos at bay, including your own inner chaos, then you have to repress your doubt and pump up your convictions. Tone is the giveaway here. If you want to sell something, whether a commercial product or an ideology, hyper-conviction is an essential element in the transaction. Pooling your doubts, sharing your uncertainties, may be humanly more interesting, and may even lead to genuine discoveries that prompt a rueful, modest sort of faith, but it will never persuade multitudes. Or yourself, for that matter, which may be the real name of the game. What persuades or converts others is always dramatic conviction dramatically expressed.

The book I was to write would have all these characteristics, which is why it did well in conservative circles in the Church. It was a facile book, written in a self-consciously epigrammatic style. The publisher insisted on calling it *Let God Arise* when it appeared, and the bombastic title, which I did not like, caught the tone. It does not merit a reading now, but if anyone were to pay it that undeserved compliment, he would find the tell-tale cracks. Adam Phillips says that where there are excessive acts there are excessive uncertainties.[61] They would be easily detected in what I wrote then. Interestingly, another trace element can be found in the book, one that would, in time, overcome the certainty I was clutching at. There was an emphasis on the importance of pity. Dostoevsky's epigram had gone deep. It was the one carry-over from 1968 that was to stay with me in the years ahead. In time it would help to dissolve the certainties I had wrapped round myself at the end of that year. But right then, I needed a place to belong to, an abiding place; the 'glimpsed good place permanent' that I'd longed for in New York.

After Kelham, the closest I got to it was our twelve years at Old Saint Paul's, but even it was a place of parting, another Alexandria. Beloved curates moved on to other positions. Parishioners who had become friends left for work in other places. And always people were dying. The most compelling part of the work of priests is their position as witnesses at the crossroads between life and death. Few other callings are practised in such *chiaroscuro*, proclaiming joy for the birth of those who have come hither and sorrow for the death of those who have gone hence, sometimes in the same hour. At Old Saint Paul's, the shape of the building attached more drama to the ceremony for leaving life than for entering it. The church, built on a steep slope that descended from the Royal Mile to Jeffrey Street, was shouldered between the massive bulk of the Calton Hotel on Carrubber's Close and the gloomy tenements of North Gray's Close. The hall, underneath the church, was entered from a door in Jeffrey Street, which also served as the main way to the church on the level above by means of a theatrical staircase of square, grey, hammer-dressed stone. It was down those thirty-three steps that the dead were led on their last journey. It was the tradition of the parish that the dead were brought to church to lie in their coffins in the chancel the night before their funeral. At the end of the service I would lead the cortège out and down the stairs to the street below, where the hearse was waiting to take the body to graveyard or crematorium, earth back to earth, ashes back to ashes, dust back to dust. I led the dead down those stairs hundreds of times. And sometimes I never wanted to do it again. Apart from the poignancy of all that going down into death, what got to me was the fact that their names were all written down. The Church keeps records of all the exchanges it witnesses at the crossroads between life and death, but it is the naming of the unremembered dead that moves me most.

Buried 10th December 1893: Jane McLeish, 17 Borthwick's Close, aged 5 years.
Buried 16th May 1914: Robert Brown, 111 Pleasance, aged 43 years.
Buried 16th January 1975: Muriel Robson, 10 Warrender Park Terrace, aged 70 years.
Buried 3rd September 2010: James Naylor Wynn-Evans, Priest, 1 Gayfield Place, aged 76 years.

At Old Saint Paul's their names are not only written down, they are read out. One of the most valuable and enduring functions of religion is its role as remembrancer of the unremembered. On the anniversary of their dying, their year's mind, the names of the dead are called out, long after no one is alive who remembers them. Sitting in Old Saint Paul's nowadays, my religion pared away to almost nothing, I can still remember. I wait for the names to be read out. I remember their lives. I remember their dying. And I remember leading them down those stairs to the long black hearse waiting in Jeffrey Street to take them under the North Bridge to the place of their final resting.

Jeffrey Street is a short winding street, built at the end of the nineteenth century by the city's Improvement Trustees. It goes in a semi-circular sweep from the head of the Canongate behind John Knox's House to the southern end of North Bridge, the Scotsman Bridge to locals, because for a hundred years it was the headquarters of the famous Edinburgh newspaper. Always up early, I would watch gigantic rolls of paper being fed into the print shop under the bridge where Jeffrey Street meets Market Street. The city's newspapers were not the only industrial activity in the area. Jeffrey Street was also the city's Fruit Market, and refrigerated lorries would park outside our door in the early hours, engines running, waiting for work to start at four. There were no buildings on the north side of the street, which opened above Waverley Station, looking to the Governor's Palace of the old city prison on Calton Hill and the windowed cliff at the back of Saint Andrew's House, office of the Secretary of State for Scotland. The street is a funnel for the haar, the east-coast fog that sweeps into Edinburgh at all seasons, but is particularly chilling in winter, when it can suddenly wrap the Old Town in mysterious drifting shadows. It was a street of plain tenements till it reached number 39, which was a tall baronial house built in 1886 to house the clergy of Old Saint Paul's. Donated to the parish by Cornelia Dick-Lauder, whose nephew was Rector at the time, Lauder House has a crow-stepped gable and a conical-roofed turret. Were it on a windswept rise of land on the outskirts of Edinburgh, it might double for the house the orphaned David Balfour came to in search of his uncle in Stevenson's *Kidnapped*. Instead, it is set back a few feet from the row of tenements it abuts in Jeffrey Street, and opens onto the sidewalk. There was a small, neglected, overshadowed garden in the back, thrillingly shielded on the west side by Trinity College Apse.

The Collegiate Church of the Holy Trinity had been founded by Mary, Queen of Scotland in 1462 to pray for her ancestors. Situated in the valley between the Old Town and Calton Hill, it was dismantled and the stones carefully numbered when the North British Railway company bought the site for Waverley Station. By the time they moved what was left of them in 1872, a number of the stones had been stolen, so only the apse of the old church was reassembled on a level piece of ground at the bottom of Chalmers Close, before it sloped down into the foetid valley that was being covered in railway lines. When they started redesigning the area ten years later, the apse found itself tucked behind the tenements in Jeffrey Street. Later to become a brass-rubbing centre when the city needed to generate income, in our time it was an Edinburgh Corporation Reading Room, supplied with every conceivable magazine and newspaper, and patronised mainly by elderly homeless men, who dozed their days away in its municipal warmth. I was delighted to have such a resource a minute from my front door, and used it frequently to read the English news-papers and to catch up on ecclesiastical gossip in the *Church Times*.

In spite of the cold in our first five winters in Lauder House – before central heating was installed – we grew to love the house. We filled it with curates and young people in need of a place to live, as well as a stream of waifs and strays. It was a bustling place, and it was Jean who was left to preside over the bustle. I was adept at bringing people into our home, then escaping from them to my study and its coal-burning stove to read and prepare sermons and think great thoughts, while Jean dealt with the turbulent energies I had unleashed into the house. I loved Lauder House, but it was the church along the street that stole my heart.

The site occupied by Old Saint Paul's – old because another Saint Paul's was later built in York Place for the burgeoning middle classes of Edinburgh's New Town – had been in use as a place of worship for rebellious Episcopalians since 1689. Ejected from Saint Giles' Cathedral when the Stuarts were kicked out of Scotland and the Church of Scotland was established on the Presbyterian model, Bishop Rose made a chapel out of an old wool store in Carrubber's Close, where the congregation has remained ever since. When the old building became ruinous, the present church was assembled upon the site, starting in 1880, to a design by William Hay – a pupil of George Gilbert Scott – though the actual building was executed by Hay's partner, George Henderson. The chancel and north part of the nave were built by 1883, the south half by 1890, the Lady Chapel on the side of the nave by 1905. Finally, in 1926, as a memorial to the men from the parish who had died in the Great War, the Warriors' Chapel and the great Calvary Stair were added to the west of the chancel aisle, and the building as we have it today was complete. Given its position, towered over by the hotel on North Bridge that is its immediate neighbour to the west, shouldered by tenements on North Gray's Close to the east, backed up against the tenements on the slope of the Royal Mile to the south, and with its only open face down on Jeffrey Street to the north, Old Saint Paul's is not immediately visible to the casual beholder, which is why people, when they actually come across it by stepping through the little side door on Carrubber's Close, feel they are the first to have happened upon an enchanting secret.

The chances are that when they go in through that little door the lights will be off in the church, so it will take them a while to get accustomed to the tenebrous atmosphere, as weak light filters through the high windows. They will probably sit at the back to let the space introduce itself to them in its own way. What overwhelms me about the building is the sense of watching and remembering it conveys. The eye is drawn to a high stone arch and the iron tracery of an Art Nouveau rood screen beneath it, and then to seven points of light burning in the shade of the distant sanctuary, and to smaller arches and a glimpse of white in a corner, and to the little chapel with the gold reredos over there, like a place made ready for the troubled to creep into and hide in. But there is more happening here than a contrivance of stone and wood and oil and a trace of sweet incense in the air. This is a building that has brooded upon its past and distilled it into a palpable sorrow. It is sorrow for the living as well as for the dead, but first for the dead whose names are written down. In Old Saint Paul's some of these names are written on stone as well as on paper in bound volumes.

Churches as powerful as Old Saint Paul's usually contain the memory of a remarkable figure from the past, recent enough not to have been forgotten like the haar that swirls round the closes of the Old Town on a summer morning only to be evaporated by the sun at high noon. There was such a man here. His name was Albert Ernest Laurie, and he spent most of his life at Old Saint Paul's. He came first as a lay worker to the parish and its teeming slums. He stayed on as Curate after he was ordained, and became Rector in 1893. He died in an armchair in Lauder House before Evensong late on an April afternoon in 1937. The city fathers had to close the streets in the Old Town on the day of his funeral because the poor gathered in their thousands to watch him being carried down the stair he himself had built as a memorial to their own dead. There is one story about him that clutches at my heart. It is not the story about him going down the Canongate at five in the morning to light the fires of bed-ridden old women and make them a pot of tea before opening the church for morning prayer. It is not about the clubs and guilds and schools he opened to ease the lives of the poor in one of the most densely packed slums in Europe, however picturesque it was to the eyes of early twentieth-century visitors to the Royal Mile. Nor is it about the way his sermons drifted lovingly all over the place as he got older, causing the famous Platonist A.E. Taylor, Professor of Moral Philosophy at the University of Edinburgh, and a member of the congregation, to sit at the back of the church groaning audibly, 'No, no, stop, dear man, stop, please stop. Oh no, no!'

The story that overwhelms me concerns the chapel he built at Old Saint Paul's when he came back from the Great War. Hundreds of boys he knew from the parish went off to that catastrophe and never came back. He had followed them into battle as a chaplain, and was awarded the Military Cross for crawling about in No Man's Land between the lines, comforting the wounded and dying as hell was breaking around him. The memory of the boys he lost in the Calvary of the Great War never left him, and he determined that their names would not die with him. After the war he employed Matthew Ochterlony to design a Warriors' Chapel in their memory. Beginning from the Calvary Stairs that mount under a vaulted ceiling from Jeffrey Street to the church, one finds the chapel above the stairs lying alongside the chancel. It is lined in plain stone on which the names of the dead are recorded in bronze Roman letters, with a continuous stone bench beneath running along the wall. High above, regimental flags hang under the oak wagon roof. And nine oil lamps hang in front of the columned names.* On sleepless nights, his mind heavy with memories, Laurie would go along Jeffrey Street and climb the new stairs into the church, where he would kindle a piece of charcoal in a tiny thurible, sprinkle a spoonful of incense on the burning coal and swing the smoking pot before the 149 names recorded there in bronze letters, each one a child from the sleeping streets that lay near his silent church, calling them out softly one by one, remembering them. I have no doubt he believed they had gone on to another life where sorrow and pain were no more, but I am also sure he was in anguish over their loss of this life, and angered by it. And puzzled, perhaps, by his own anger? If he really believed in the resurrection of the dead, why mourn them so? Why build these stairs to tread the Calvary of the trenches again every day? Why build this chapel with its flags and lamps, yet in such a way that it became a place of sorrow rather than a trumpet blast of pride like so many other war memorials? Why make sure their names are all written down here, on this wall, if you know they are already written down in the Book of Life, the record God keeps

---

* The lamps had a particular significance for Laurie. One of his friends in the Great War was another famous army chaplain, Philip Clayton, affectionately known as Tubby because of his Toby Jug build. In Poperinge in Belgium, behind the lines at Ypres, Clayton ran a club where soldiers could meet and relax regardless of rank. A notice was hung by the door: 'All rank abandon, ye who enter here.' Called Talbot House after a young lieutenant who had died at Ypres in 1915, but nicknamed Toc H by the soldiers, one of the features of the chapel in the loft or Upper Room of the house was an Aladdin oil lamp that burned perpetually as a symbol of hope and reconciliation. It was replicas of these bronze Toc H lamps Canon Laurie hung before the names of his remembered dead when the chapel was opened in 1926.

of the 60 billion souls who have peopled his creation and lived their lives and died their deaths and vanished without memorial from the earth? It is because he was not, could not be sure of these confident claims, and was hurt, like Dante, by the knowledge that death had undone so many, and continues, inexorably, to undo them.

That is the pain and the puzzle that lies at the heart of religion, and it is what will keep it going, in some form or other, as long as humans go on being born and living their lives and going down the stairs and under the bridge to join the increasing army of the forgotten dead. Religion names the dead in protest as well as in hope, and God is the object of the protest as well as the hope. It is because the dead do not speak to us and because we cannot know what has become of them that we protest and hope at the same time. But God does not speak to us either, so we are left with our names and our protests and our hopes, and we build places that blend them together, places to which we can speak, but which never speak back to us. Laurie built such a place, a place where he could say the names whose loss haunted him but who never spoke back to him. Another place like this, but on a vaster scale, was built in Washington in 1982. The Vietnam War Memorial is a list of names inscribed on black granite panels, and it too is a place of speaking and withholding. Robert Pogue Harrison talks of:

the solemn gravity of the wall – the encrypted presence of the dead – which seems to turn the deaths of those memorialised into a stubborn question. The silence with which it responds to this question gives the wall's inscribed black granite panels an almost overwhelming power of withholding. The irresistible need many visitors feel to touch a

195

chiselled name, kiss it, talk to it, offer it flowers or gifts, leave it notes or letters, is evidence enough of the dead's private presence in the stone – a presence at once given and denied.[62]

A presence at once given and denied are words that could be applied to the Warriors' Chapel in Old Saint Paul's.* That is why this church speaks to unbelievers with as much power as it does to believers. Indeed, the unbelieving part of me suspects it speaks more eloquently of doubt than of faith, because of the store of sorrow and longing it distils. The hope of religion can be neither proved nor extinguished in this life, and we cannot know whether there is another life in which the matter will be finally resolved. This is why there is so much noise on both sides of the debate about religion, noise being the thickest overcoat available to cover us against the chill of uncertainty. Old Saint Paul's allows itself to be both a stage for the ritual proclamation of belief and, usually when it is empty, a place where we can bring our questions, neither expecting nor wanting them to be answered. Living with the unanswerable question is the key to our humanity. Living with the sense of a presence *at once* given and denied is the genius of a place like Old Saint Paul's. It is not that the presence is sometimes experienced and

---

* It was this tantalising quality that impelled a young Scottish artist to the creation of a great work of art. Alison Watt, like many others before her, found that little side door in Carrubber's Close, stepped inside and was moved by what she found. She sat in the Warriors' Chapel for some time, absorbed by its sadness. In response, she was moved to paint an enormous twelve-foot canvas in four separate squares that now hang above the altar. Called *Still,* the white folds of the mysterious painting suggest 'a presence at once given and denied'. It suggests the presence of a huge absence, the brimming over of a vast emptiness. It glimmers against the grey sorrow of the stone, but does not attempt to subdue it. And the Warriors' Chapel looks as if it has been waiting for it from the beginning.

sometimes withdrawn: it is both at the same time, like a piece of music that consoles and make us grieve in equal measure. Laurie was a man of faith, but he also had to be a man of doubt to build those stairs and that chapel. Faith supreme and unconquerable would not grieve at all that dying, because it would know that death was the gateway to more abundant life. Who could grieve over those whose dwelling was now in the heavenly Jerusalem, where all tears had been wiped away and sighing and sorrow were no more? Laurie hoped for that, but could not know it, might even have doubted it, which is why he had their names all written down. That is the passion that keeps the doubting priest in the place of giving and denying, if only for the sake of those to whom he has been given to stand beside.

COMING THROUGH

O ld Saint Paul's was a potent but dangerous place for someone like me to come to, haunted as I was by the ghost of my failure to give myself away utterly to God. I was the first married priest to have been appointed Rector of Old Saint Paul's, and there were people, myself included, who wondered if they had not been given spoiled goods. Monogamy was hard enough, so it was absurd to mourn my failure to be celibate, but the romance of the given-away life tugged at me still. This was a parish where priests were called Father and were expected to be available at all hours of the day and night. There were early masses every morning, as well as Matins and Evensong said in church every day. And there was a complex routine of elaborate services to preside at on high and holy days, with beady-eyed acolytes around to remark on my rusty ceremonial skills. The church belonged to the Anglo-Catholic tradition, the stream in the Anglican Church that had reclaimed many of the practices and beliefs of the Pre-Reformation Church. Though many of the reclaimed practices were later inventions of Roman Catholicism, including the practice of addressing priests as Father, there was a lot to be said for restoring the colour and beauty that had been lost at the Reformation. Old Saint Paul's gave back to me what I had most loved about Kelham, which was the sense of living completely within the Church's Year, with its rhythm of feast and fast, light and shade, joy and sorrow. So my new position thrilled me, especially the sooty old church along the street which I enjoyed opening every morning for early mass. I liked going up Laurie's stairs into its brooding silence, and always sat at the back for a bit to let it gather round me.

I responded to my new role in two predictable but unhelpful ways. A married man with three children – Mark was born the year after our arrival at Old Saint Paul's – and a house full of often needy people, I determined to show the parish that I could be as dedicated and on-call as any celibate. This is a not-unfamiliar tension in the life of the priest who feels that the needy of the world have a more immediate call on him than his own family. I was in church when the children were getting ready for school and out visiting when they were being made ready for bed. And when the doorbell or the telephone went, no matter what was happening with the family, the caller took precedence. I could not bring myself to leave the person at the door or on the phone to their own lives and get back to mine, because I felt I had to be the man for them, the man for others, the totally available man, available to everyone except his own family. This became a particular problem during the evening meal. The rectory was a port-of-call for lonely or homeless people who usually came to the door when we were eating. I would bring the caller into my study and hear his story – always *his* – and either offer him a meal or a voucher for a bed down the road at the Salvation Army Hostel in the Cowgate. I was rarely able to bring the encounter to an end soon enough to get back to the family round the table in the big kitchen at the back of Lauder House, because my duty was to the man in front of me, angry at the turn his life had taken, not to my own children wondering where their father had got to.

The second response to my new situation was a reversion to monastic authoritarianism. I usually had two curates whom I ran like an elite military unit. At one point I took this as far as supplying a uniform for the three of us and an identical form of transport. I got a job lot of blue donkey jackets and heavy serge firemen's trousers, ideal for hard-working clergy battling cold winds and the Edinburgh haar. Martin Shaw, one of my curates, told me that his father, a Glasgow businessman, had access to a load of police bikes and wondered if I'd be interested in getting three for the team. I was. They were old-fashioned, single-gear, sit-up-and-beg bicycles, heavy, robust, and hell to pedal up Edinburgh's hilly streets – but pedal them we did, in our donkey jackets and firemen's trousers and Doc Marten boots. When we were not taking services or visiting the sick or presiding at youth clubs or taking classes, we were out on those bikes in all weathers visiting parishioners. It was not as grim as it sounds, though there was too much intensity of purpose in me and not enough sense that there was more to life than work. To recompense them for the rigours of the high seasons, I always took my curates to the current hot movie on Boxing Day and Easter Monday, as long as they were prepared to cope with the Burmese cheroots I smoked at festive seasons, bought from an old-fashioned tobacconist on George IV Bridge.

Parish work could be exciting, especially when we went into campaigning mode in the community. We responded to the homeless callers and rough sleepers in the district by starting a soup kitchen. There were a number of hostels and lodging houses in the Cowgate and Grassmarket that catered for a large population of unsettled and homeless people, many of them men with a drink problem. A shop in the area exploited this clientele by selling them industrial quantities of a cheap hairspray to drink. They called it Bel Air. We called it instant cirrhosis. We acquired an empty shop next door to them at the bottom of Blackfriars Street and opened a soup kitchen called the Ritz. Under the leadership of Betty Strang from Jeffrey Street, it became the cheapest café in Scotland. Tuppence got the customers a cup of tea and a sandwich, another penny got them a plate of home-made soup. It was staffed by volunteers from the congregation, and soon we were feeding fifty a day, most of them homeless and without means. At first we opened it five mornings a week from ten to noon, then the young people of the congregation volunteered to open it on Saturdays as well. The labour was free, so we were able to meet the running costs easily. We got bones for nothing from local butchers and vegetables at cut prices from local grocers. Soon it became a community as well as a café, and men would sit for hours playing cards and dominoes.

Occasionally there was trouble, but nothing we couldn't handle. The heartbreak of the work was listening to the stories of men who had lost everything. The prominent solicitor with the gambling demon who lost his family and his big house in Glasgow's West End; the former soldiers who could not hack it in Civvy Street when their service was up; and always there was Scotland's oldest regiment, the drinkers, men and women who had abandoned everything in their dedication to the bottle. There was something almost holy in their dereliction, their lives stripped away to nothing. Sitting with them over a bowl of soup, out would come the press-cuttings, the honourable discharge papers, the grubby photographs, reminders of the now of then that they were powerless to bring back again.

A lot of homelessness was the consequence of personal

tragedy, but much of it was systemic, a consequence of the way society was organised, so we prepared a more strategic attack on homelessness in Lauder House, where the Scottish inauguration of the charity Shelter was planned. A number of factors coalesced to create the momentum behind its creation. Jeremy Sandford's television play *Cathy Come Home* revealed the plight of the homeless to a mass audience for the first time. It was followed by a series of articles about landlords who got rich by factory farming the homeless at the nation's expense, a phenomenon I knew well from Gorbals. Churches responded to the crisis by forming housing associations, like the one we had started in Glasgow. We formed Castle Rock in Edinburgh shortly after I arrived in the city, and it is still a massive provider of social housing in the east of Scotland. As well as campaigning for political change, Shelter was invented to take over fund-raising for housing associations so that they could concentrate their efforts on supplying homes. Working for Shelter became the idealistic thing to do, and the London and Edinburgh offices were soon filled with young women with long hair and short skirts, dedicating their lives to making a better Britain.

So there was a lot of excitement around the place, but the heart of our work remained that brooding building on Carrubber's Close and the elusive mystery it represented, the presence at once given and denied that lies at the heart of religion. Like everything else in human affairs, it was subject to the pressures of change and the eruption of fashionable trends. There are fads in religion, as in everything else, inventions and rediscoveries, aimed at titillating the jaded palate or stirring up the moribund conscience. At Old Saint Paul's we were not immune to the surrounding religious environment, though it might be more honest to say that I was far from immune to it. A crisis I had after my fortieth birthday precipitated me into my next attempt at finding a resolution to my inner turbulence. At Kelham we called it 'the Doom', this mood of despair and aridity that haunts the religious person trying to make sense of his commitment to a presence both given and denied. Maintaining a good relationship with a living, breathing person is hard enough: think how tough it is to maintain a passionate commitment to the Silent Invisible One who is at the heart of the religious relationship. Clergy do it by techniques of prayer and by going into periods of retreat, like marriage enrichment courses designed to rekindle their early ardour. And sometimes new spiritual crazes erupt onto the scene, claiming to be able to set the dead embers of faith ablaze with new heat and intensity. The one that hit the Seventies was the Neo-Pentecostal movement, and I wondered if it might be the answer to my own prayers.

The sexual analogy is inevitable in trying to talk about this, or inevitable to me. And there is precedent for it. The mystics often use erotic language in describing their experience of God. And since sex is as notorious for what it fails to deliver as for what it does, it is a suitable analogy. The search for personal completion through the discovery of our 'other half' is as ancient a theme as Plato's Symposium, and its corniness only emphasises its enduring power. We feel ourselves incomplete and we try to assuage the lack through sex, hoping to find the one who will make us whole not just for tonight but for ever. That ancient transaction is easily transposed into religion, which can be defined as the need to join ourselves to One whose love will never fail to satisfy. Sadly, it does fail. As with erotic longing in general, religious longing promises much but delivers little. And it is not hard to diagnose the problem. It is the unavailability of the Great Lover. If sex with an available person can be problematic, it is infinitely more problematic with the Great Absence. I have already discussed the devices religion uses to compensate for that absence, the different forms of prayer, the sacramental practices, all designed to fill the emptiness and compensate for the lack of response from God. One that particularly appealed to me during an arid phase at Old Saint Paul's was the ancient craft of collecting beautiful prayers. The Christian tradition is full of these exquisite miniatures of longing. I filled my notebook with them and read them as compulsively as I read poetry, but it was my own poet who defined their limitations:

> . . . cries countless, cries like dead letters sent
> To dearest him that lives alas! away.[63]

Was there no way of bringing 'him that lives alas! away' nearer, so near that I could experience him personally rather than imagining him or writing to him or reading about him? Was there no way of getting out of myself and into Him? Did religion have to be confined to the mind and the heart? Was there a way it could involve my body and make me feel something like the ecstasy of good sex? Some claimed to have had such an experience. Paul talked about being caught up into heaven. And in the Acts of the Apostles there was an account of the community of Christians going into an ecstatic rave in Jerusalem as the spirit of God fell upon them. Such ecstasy is a well-known characteristic of fervent religion. As the word implies, it takes the worshipper out of herself. Getting out of ourselves is something we all need from time to time, whether or not we are religious. It is why we use euphoric and psychoactive substances. It happens at raves and rock concerts as well as at evangelical rallies, all designed to take us out of ourselves and give us a break.

That's what the Pentecostal or Charismatic movement did for its practitioners in the Seventies. The inspiration came from that incident in the Acts of Apostles when the disciples of Jesus gathered in Jerusalem on the feast of Pentecost fifty days after Passover. Saint Luke, the author of Acts, says the Holy Spirit fell on the disciples and they all began to speak in foreign tongues, to the amazement of foreigners who heard their own languages in this outbreak of ecstatic utterance. The phenomenon is called 'speaking in tongues', and it comes in two forms, *glossolalia* and *xenolalia*. *Glossolalia* is easier to explain. It means to babble with the tongue, make mouth music. You only have to try it, if you are uninhibited enough, to know what fun it can be, and how psychologically releasing. More problematic is what they call *xenolalia*. The claim here is that, under the inspiration of the Spirit, people don't just babble ecstatically, they actually speak languages they do not know. Acts claims that this is what happened in Jerusalem on the day of Pentecost. Charismatics believe God prompts this activity, sometimes in real languages, sometimes in joyful noises. What then happens is that interpreters, also under the inspiration of the Spirit, claim to understand what has been uttered, in either mode, and provide a convenient translation. A lot of this went on in the young Church and Saint Paul was dubious about it. He saw it as a way of letting off steam with very little consequence for anything, apart from having a good time. His hymn to love in 1 Corinthians 13 was his most considered response to the phenomenon:

Though I speak with the tongues of men and of angels, and have not love, I am become as sounding brass or a tinkling cymbal.[64]

In 1970s Christianity a lot of brass-sounding and cymbal-tinkling went on, some of it in Old Saint Paul's. It hit Carrubber's Close because I wondered if it might be the answer to my own need for direct experience of God. I started reading about it. I was sceptical about the claims to *xenolalia*, though I knew odd things went on in the world, but I thought *glossolalia* was interesting. An American guru of the movement, Graham Pulkingham, had brought his group to live in England. Called the Community of Celebration, it seemed to be cheering people up with its brand of expository preaching and upbeat new music, written and performed by their own choir, the Fisher Folk. I phoned Pulkingham, and asked if he would see me. We arranged to meet in London, in one of the rooms at All Saints, Margaret Street. I made a special trip to see him, going down on the early train and coming back in the evening. When we met, after gentle questioning, he asked what he could do for me. I told him I was spiritually empty and wanted a shot of energy to revive my wilting faith: would he pray with me? He put his hands on my head and started to pray for me in American English, which soon morphed into a stream of pure sound with no meaning I could discern. I experienced a joyful surge of energy, and soon I too was making strange noises – the difference being that I thought mine sounded like Chinese. One of the books I'd read claimed that this had happened at a prayer meeting in the presence of a woman from Shanghai, who said that one of the participants had just chanted the Lord's Prayer in Mandarin. Had this happened to me? The competitive bit of me thought that *xenolalia* would be a cut above *glossolalia*. Whatever it was, it was enormously releasing and I couldn't stop when I walked out of All Saints for the train back to Scotland. Which was a problem. How could I sit silent for six hours on my journey back to Edinburgh? When the urge over-took me I resolved the difficulty by slipping into the lavatory where the clatter of the wheels disguised the sound of my mouth music. The train wasn't busy, so no one banged at the door when I was in there for hours, pouring my heart out in meaningless ecstasy or speaking words of wisdom in pure Chinese, an idea that was growing on me. I still had that wee man perched on my shoulder, observing my performance with appreciation. I could get quite good at this, I was thinking. When I got off the train at Waverley I spied a young woman who looked Chinese, so I decided to test my theory. Going over to her, I unleashed a burst of what I had been chanting in the train lavatory. She fled up the exit to Waverley Bridge into the city. Unperturbed, I made my way into Market Street, under the bridge and into Jeffrey Street. Though I was no holier after my day in London, I was back with a lavatory-seat-shaped halo round my arse. In Lauder House Jean waited my return with growing apprehension. She was afraid I would come home with yet another call to pursue, yet another will o' the wisp to blunder after. What I was thinking about meant staying where we were and expanding our already expanded family even further, but before that could happen there was this new enthu-siasm to spread.

Paul was right about praying in tongues. Love *was* more important, but it was also harder. *Glossolalia* was easy, and it was also more fun. The history of religion is full of revivals like this, attempts to experience the god in new ways and whip up enthusiasm and inspiration among his followers. The word *enthusiasm* means to be possessed by the god. The word *inspire* means to be blown into by a transcendent force. Behind this longing for experience of the god is the frustration that is intrinsic to all religion. The mystery that beckons us is both given and denied, but denial is the more common experience. Small wonder that we seek ways to pump the god into ourselves, so that, if only for a few hours, we can get out of ourselves and into the god or get the god into us. Compare video clips of pop concerts and revival meetings. It's the same phenomenon, *afflatus,* the god blowing joy into its devotees. Watch those shining faces. Observe those arms in the air, waving, reaching up, trying to lift themselves off the ground and out of their earth-bound lives for an hour or two. Most of it is harmless, and some of it is therapeutic, releasing tension, loosening clenched muscles, giving ourselves a break. Paul did not deny that praying in tongues was a gift of the Spirit, he just said it was a trivial gift, an escape – but people like to escape.

This is something the severely rational person neither understands nor approves. Understandably, because escape into ecstasy can be demonic as well as benign. There can be ecstatic destruction and genocide as well as ecstatic joy and release. We may claim to be rational animals, thinking, calculating animals, but beneath our capacity for reason other forces are at work in us. Psychically, we are not that far away from our evolutionary forerunners whose emerging consciousness must have been frightening as they looked out on a dangerous and unpredictable world and tried to make sense of it. No wonder they posited angry forces Out There. No wonder they invented ways to propitiate them. And no wonder they sought occasional release from the tyranny of consciousness. The positing of a tremendous Other was humanity's response to its own bafflement. It put a kind of meaning on life and gave form to longings we only ever partly understood. That is why we should be slow to condemn those who find religion a help in making it through the maze of life. My heart won't let me condemn it, though I am stunned by the cruelty that is never far beneath its surface. Part of me is still moved but part of me is offended by multitudes of weeping worshippers, eyes closed, arms in the air, reaching, reaching beyond themselves to the tremendous lover in the sky. Religious ecstasy is a potent source of escape, even if it is only into an imagined meaning. But it has a dark side. A side that conjures memories of traumatised children going under the knife and bawling animals whose blood is daubed on doorposts to keep the angel of death from destroying those within. All of that is in there, hiding behind the pillars of memory, waiting to release itself in ecstasies of disapproval and destruction. It did not take long for the enjoyable ecstasy of the Charismatic Movement to morph into something darker.

If giving lukewarm believers a sufficiently powerful experience of God has always been the Church's biggest pastoral challenge, its biggest theological challenge has been to keep them believing in a God who saves the world, in spite of powerful evidence to the contrary. From the beginning, Christianity claimed to be a religion of redemption from the forces of evil and suffering. Theologies like this are common among oppressed people, as the Ghost Dance movement among Plains Indians in nineteenth-century America reminded us. The unbearable sorrow and anger of an oppressed people transposes itself into a conviction that God is about to act. He won't delay much longer. Things have gone too far. His children are being ground into the dust. Soon, soon, he will come soon. The New Testament suggests that Jesus saw himself as such an instrument of eschatological hope, the agent through whom God would transform the world into a kingdom of justice. The first Christians expected this supernatural transformation to happen in their lifetime, which was why Paul spent a lot of time in his letters to these expectant communities, cautioning them not to give up their worldly responsibilities – such as working for a living – because no one knew the day or the hour. But this kind of eschatological hope dies hard and human history is full of poignant longing for supernatural rescue from the tragedies of time. It did not happen in Paul's time and it has not happened since. But that does not stop the longing from welling up to such an unbearable degree in the hearts of believers that it metamorphoses into a certainty that the time, at last, is near.

That's what happened to the Neo-Pentecostal movement of the Seventies. What began as a movement to cheer up bored believers stranded in the departure lounge of history, ended as a full-blown eschatological movement convinced that the Second Coming was at hand. He was coming back, and it would be soon! I never did believe in a Second Coming in history, so this twist in the story of the Neo-Pentecostal movement did not convince me. But it worried me. Bad religion can be comforting, a blanket that protects us against the chilly winds of an empty universe, but it can be dangerous too. Belief in the imminence of the Second Coming became the preserve of the Christian Right in America, where it fed the growth of a conspiracy theory that became one of the most powerful weapons in America's culture wars. One of its leaders is a writer who is hardly known outside the US, Tim LaHaye. LaHaye has been named as the most influential Christian leader of the last quarter century, more influential even than Billy Graham. He is the co-author of the *Left Behind* series of novels about the end-time, which have sold more than 30 million copies through outlets such as Walmart. LaHaye sees all around him a conspiracy of humanists, liberals and feminists, who are out to destroy the family and eliminate Christian values from the US. The dangerous thing about the movement is that, rather than looking for ways to address the problems that beset the world, the apocalyptic mind-set welcomes them as signs that the end is accelerating towards us. The late Jerry Falwell, a co-conspirator of LaHaye's, when asked about the growing degradation of the planet said it did not concern him. Jesus would be back soon to end the world, so we should use it before we lose it.[65] I spent a lot of time agonising over God's failure to rescue us from the pains and sorrows of time, and worked my way to a kind of resolution, but before looking at it I want to say more about the Spirit's swoop through Old Saint Paul's.

A regular visitor during my years there was a saintly ascetic called Neil Russell. Neil had found his way through that little door in Carrubber's Close, and it had changed his life. After years working in Africa, he was made Bishop of Zanzibar, but because the poverty in which he chose to live became a reproach to the ostentation of the local ruler, he was expelled and returned to his native Edinburgh. He became a member of a small religious community that lived in intense simplicity at Roslin near the famous chapel, and was made honorary assistant Bishop of Edinburgh. Not long after his return he came to the door of Lauder House. I thought he was a tramp I hadn't met before, and was about to go into the kitchen to get him something to eat when he introduced himself. When the Spirit blew noisily into Old Saint Paul's, Neil desperately wanted the refreshment of the gift of tongues, but it wouldn't come. This was a man who lived like a desert father; a man who had given away everything he possessed; a man who lived on hand-outs and wore only second-hand clothes, including a pair of desert boots of mine, abandoned because the soft suede revealed the ugly shape of my knobbly toes; a man who spent two hours every morning in silent prayer; a man who was so manifestly holy he scarcely seemed to be of the earth at all. Yet no matter how hard he tried he could not pray in tongues. I watched him being counselled by callow university students who could switch tongues on and off like electric guitars, he sitting at their feet like a novice before advanced practitioners.

In the tongues business, getting the gift was referred to as *coming through*. Imagine my excitement, when devouring the recently published *Oxford Book of Twentieth-Century Verse* edited by Philip Larkin, I came across a poem by D.H. Lawrence, 'The Song of a Man Who Has Come Through'.

> Not I, not I, but the wind that blows through me!
> A fine wind is blowing the new direction of Time,
> If only I let it bear me, carry me, if only it carry me!
> If only I am sensitive, subtle, oh, delicate, a winged gift!
> If only, most lovely of all, I yield myself and am
>   borrowed
> By the fine, fine wind that takes its course through the
>   chaos of the
> World . . .[66]

Neil never did come through, in spite of the ministrations of his youthful mentors. Observing that irony was for me the beginning of the end of the experience, it did leave a little gift behind. One evening my daughter Sara couldn't get to sleep. She had a sore stomach that nothing would soothe. I knelt beside her bed. I put my hands upon her head, closed my eyes, and prayed in tongues over her. Sara giggled. The pain left. She went to sleep. Christianity was a funny business, outsiders could see that. But it was also poignant, I could see that.

The tongues gradually fell silent, but the wind hadn't yet finished blowing through me. There was something else I had to try. An interesting aspect of the Neo-Pentecostal movement was its rediscovery of early Christian communism. The leaders of the movement, including Graham Pulkingham, pointed out that the first Christians held everything in common, which was why Pulkingham had founded the Community of Celebration. If you were serious about Christianity you had to abandon the nuclear family, get out of the rat race, and start living in communities that held all things in common. It was the answer to the problems of gross inequality that disfigured capitalist economies. If Christianity became a network of these communities, they could absorb the victims of the world's greed and cruelty into their own lives and bring them healing. It was a message that touched the old monastic nerve in me. I had put my hand to that plough as a boy, but I had looked back. I had caught a glimpse of the way of self-denial in community and had forsaken it. Was this a way to recoup my spiritual losses, a second chance at the common life? By this time Lauder House had been divided, and a new curate's apartment provided on the upper floors. Martin Shaw and his wife Elspeth and their son Ben lived there. We had the rest of the house, with plenty of room for people who needed a place to stay for longer or shorter periods. David, the other curate, was in a flat in Jeffrey Street. I broached the idea of binding us all into a single economic community. They went along with it. Jean did too. A few weeks later I wrote these words in the parish magazine.

Shortly after Easter the Shaw and Holloway families and David Boag entered into a commitment to live together in community. There is no elaborate constitution. We pray

213

together twice a day and study the Bible (which is why the daily offices are now said in Lauder House), and we have pooled all our money and have a common purse. We eat the main meal of the day together, at 5.45 in the evening (and we are always happy to see members of the congregation at the meal, as long as they let us know they're coming).

Our reasons for doing this are quite simple: we felt that God had called us to do it, in order to learn more about loving each other the better to love others.

Neil Russell came to Lauder House to hear our vows. The event did not have the solemnity of the religious professions I had witnessed at Kelham, where the novice spent the night alone in the great chapel before giving himself utterly away to God at mass the following morning. In my heart I still felt I had failed the call of God to follow him with absolute abandonment. I was a muddled, compromised, divided man who had let God down. Was this a chance to regain his approval, prove I had the right stuff? It wasn't Kelham Chapel, with the shadows gathering round me as I sacrificed my life on the long grey altar under the looming Rood, it was only the kitchen of Lauder House. But it was something, was it not? And I did try to inject a little drama into our promises. Neil began:

Following the example and command of our Lord Jesus Christ, the holy Apostle Paul summons us to grow together in unity and love so that we may become a temple of the Lord and a visible expression of Christ's presence in the world. And we read in the Acts of the Holy Apostles how the first believers held all in common and were united daily in prayer and the breaking of bread.

You are gathered together here because you believe God is calling you to follow the example of the holy Apostles, by joining yourselves together in a household of faith in order the better to praise God and be his witnesses in the midst of the world.

Then we made two simple promises, pledging ourselves to live in the community with all lowliness and meekness, with patience, forbearing one another in love, eager to maintain the unity of the spirit in the bond of peace. I had a joiner screw an enormous slab of compressed wood onto our already huge kitchen table, so that up to twenty people could sit round it for our evening meal. Jean told me much later that her heart sank when Elspeth Shaw said to her son Ben, now you have a second mummy. I didn't notice. I was launched on a new adventure.

It lasted six months. It's hard to say exactly what collapsed it, but I suspect it was exhaustion – as well as creeping self-knowledge on my part. In addition to the core community, we always had one or two people with mental health or addiction problems staying with us, and they took their toll. One was brought to us from the stage of the Traverse Theatre, where he had gone mad during a one man show he was doing. It had taken the management time to realise that what was happening wasn't in the script and was, in fact, the beginning of the manic phase of a bipolar swing. They brought him to our door just after ten in the evening and we took him in for the night. Though we put him to bed, we discovered next morning that he had not slept; instead, he had spent the night going through our cupboards and drawers, not with any malicious intent but compulsively, manically. At breakfast our children were electrified to see him at the table wearing Sara's Brownie uniform, singing snatches of opera to himself, with the family cutlery and dish supply arranged in symmetrical patterns all round the kitchen. I took him to the Royal Edinburgh Hospital where they managed to bring him down. He spent the rest of his life creatively, though he was to die in the first phase of Edinburgh's AIDS epidemic in the Eighties. And he was not the only visitor whom we tried to absorb into the quasi-monastic flow of our new life.

The chaplain of a prison in the south of England phoned and asked me to look after a man they were about to release. He had been gaoled for a clever fraud, and his advisers recommended a complete change of scene for his own safety and the possibility it might afford of a fresh start. A brilliant accountant, his catastrophic alcohol problem had not only led him to prison, it had lost him his wife and children; and his own brothers had been forced to distance themselves from the chaos of his life. I met him on platform 11 in Waverley Station and took him under North Bridge and along Jeffrey Street to Lauder House. He was dapper, bowler-hatted, charming, animated, full of plans. Grateful for our hospitality, he said that once he had found a place to stay he would set up as a tax accountant. As long as he stayed off the bottle, all would be well. He was not able to stay off the bottle, and things turned out badly for him, but the ride he took us on was hilarious as well as tragic. He did make money as a tax consultant, but after a week or two of sobriety he would hit the bottle. Then he would come back to Lauder House to detox or do cold turkey on a bed in my study, helped by our GP who was always prepared to come at a moment's notice to inject him with Largactil, an anti-psychotic drug that brought him down lightly. During one of his sober spells I got him to write down some of his memories. Apart from an addiction to semicolons, his writing voice captured his rather stately style of utterance. He called one of his essays 'The Carriage Room', and I published it in the magazine.

That winter of 1968 in London was a hard, cold and bleak one. I had been living rough most of the time since I had taken my discharge from hospital earlier on in the year and I had so far failed completely to get back into the mainstream of life. That week, before Christmas, I had managed a bed in a hostel for a few nights, but the final blow came the day before Christmas when I was told at 'the Ministry' that my benefits could not be paid until after Christmas; all my protests were of no avail and I had no one I felt I could turn to, so I spent the night of Christmas Eve on the Embankment, waiting for the day to come.

I pondered long, feeling deeply alone, rejected and despondent. Finally my mind became resolute. I spruced up, the best I could, in a public washroom, and approaching Christmas dinnertime I made my way to the Carriage Room.

The Carriage Room was a new and rather elegant restaurant in a large hotel in the Strand; I knew it from outside, and from the bill of fare encased in glass at the door, knew that it offered something special, albeit expensive, for Christmas dinner; I had no money, but I buried that knowledge away deep down; somehow an answer would be provided, and even if not and I finished up in the cells, at least I should have warmth and shelter and human contact again. In my hunger and longing I did not think too far ahead, anyway; my compelling need was to sustain a tradition and belief which I had treasured all my life.

Bracing myself and bringing out my old bonhomie and self-assurance, I entered the Carriage Room; asked for, and was given, a well sited table for one; and proceeded to go through the card as though all was well in the best of worlds. I ate slowly and carefully, not to put too sudden a task on a stomach grown unused to food; drank moderately but enjoyably, savouring the warmth of a good wine. Little by little I mellowed and expanded, noticing people at tables about me, smiling with them and exchanging Christmas greetings with warmth, cordiality and great friendliness.

He enjoyed a five-course dinner, followed by coffee, a liqueur and a cigar. For that passing hour he 'was taken up, caught up and carried away in it, with all the happiness of Christmases past brought back and remembered again'.

The waiter, who had looked after me with great attentiveness and cordiality, brought the bill to me, proffering it on a plate. I smiled at him with my most winning smile, regretting that I had seemingly omitted to bring any cash with me and suggesting that, no doubt, the hotel would accept my signature on the bill?

The house detective, 'a man of great good nature and some cordiality', invited him to his private room. There Geoffrey told him the story of his breakdown, his years in hospital, loss of position, family, friends and everything else that had gone to make up his life. Was there no one to whom he could turn? He mentioned his brothers 'in the North country' who had broken off relationships with him long before. Pressed, he gave the detective their addresses and phone numbers.

Without asking me further, he picked up the telephone, asked for numbers, and finally contacted one of my brothers; they were all enjoying Christmas Day together at one of their homes. He spoke at some length to my brother; I sat, half listening, but thinking more of what once was and now seemed had gone for ever.

The house detective replaced the phone and sat in silence.

Your brothers, he said, will pay the bill, and I am to give you a couple of pounds for yourself; they hope that you have had a good Christmas Day and that all will go well for you.

Silently, I rose and took his hand. He pushed two notes into the breast-pocket of my jacket, escorted me back to the Carriage Room, to the cloakroom where I was helped into my overcoat, scarf and gloves; then escorted from the hotel with every courtesy and well wishing from all, into the cold crisp air which flew steadily up from the Thames into the Strand.

I stood for a moment on the pavement, catching the elusive, fleeting, yet eternal feel and sense of it all; Christmas Day had come, was here, and always would be.

Christmas might always be there, but he wouldn't be. After a few tumultuous winters in Edinburgh, he died. He outlived the Lauder House community, however, and might even have helped deliver it the *coup de grâce*. We were all stressed by the routine we had imposed upon ourselves, and I was becoming increasingly aware that, far from being a sociable creature who liked a lot of people around him, I preferred solitude to society, a good book in my study to a noisy crowd in the kitchen. Even worse, I was discovering that I had the kind of personality that resented interruptions to the purposes I had set for myself, and life in Jeffrey Street had become one long interruption. I talked piously about living in the now of life, went on about the sacrament of the present moment and how it disclosed God's presence – mainly to myself, because the others were all better at coping with interruptions than I was. I went on about meeting whoever came to the door as a divine visitor, no matter what else we might be doing at the time. Whenever the bell went – and it went a lot – we would joke that Jesus was at the door again. I grew to resent the frequency of his visits. I began to wish we could render the house invisible several days a week, so that we could get on with our own lives unharassed by the sacred wanderer. And it was tough on our children, who rarely got us to themselves. How much of their father did the married monk thing leave for them?

One night, after a particularly crazy meal when we had a heavier atmosphere than usual round the table, with a number of people groaning into their hands and the children understandably fractious, I knew it could not go on – or I could not go on. The following morning at the weekly staff meeting I suggested throwing in the towel on the community. David was moving to another post, anyway, and it might be better if the

Shaws and Holloways got a bit more time to themselves, just to be families in their own right. There was relief all round. We voted for immediate disbandment. I had the top off the big table by lunchtime. That evening, for the first time in ages, there were only five of us round the table. There continued to be a lot of traffic through the house, and it was always a busy place, but we had removed a crucial element of extra strain. And I had learnt that I was not cut out to be a guru with a colossal extended family around me.

I also discovered that my relationship with God had changed. Far from seeking to justify myself to God for my constant failures, I began to feel that he should occasionally justify himself to me. As the creator of all things, ultimate responsibility for everything had to rest with him, especially for the pains and sorrows of the admittedly weak but not entirely wicked children of the earth whose unanswered cries had been beating against his gate for centuries. My wrestling with my own compulsions, as well as my experience of the tragedies of others, did not demonstrate any discernible improvement in the human condition as a result of the death of Jesus – allegedly decreed by God for our salvation. Except in one way of reading the story. I became obsessed with the question put to Jesus by John the Baptist: 'Art thou he that should come, or do we look for another?'[67] After listing a series of miracles he had performed, including the raising of the dead, Jesus added a mysterious coda 'blessed is he, whosoever shall not be offended in me'.[68] Well, I was increasingly offended in him. In my parish I saw no dead rising, no lame leaping, no blind seeing. Again and again I led the dead down those stairs and under that bridge. The lame continued to stumble and the blind to feel their way with a stick. In spite of the claims of Revivalists, the world did not seem any more redeemed after than before Christ. What I started preaching was not that tragedy could be overcome by the action of God, but that in responding to tragedy *meaning could be imposed upon it*. It was at this time I first read André Schwarz-Bart's novel, *The Last of the Just*. It was the story of Ernie Levy who died in Auschwitz in 1943, another victim of unredeemed history. At the end of the novel, Ernie is on a train to Auschwitz and the gas chambers. He is surrounded by children, one of whom is dead.

Ernie said, clearly and emphatically, so that there would be no mistaking him, '*He's asleep* . . .' Then he picked up the child's corpse and with infinite gentleness laid it on the growing heap of Jewish men, Jewish women, Jewish children, joggled in their last sleep by the jolting of the train.

'He was my brother,' a little girl said hesitantly, anxiously, as though she had not decided what attitude it would be best to take in front of Ernie.

He sat down next her and set her on his knees. 'He'll wake up too, in a little while, with all the others, when we reach the Kingdom of Israel. There, children can find their parents, and everybody is happy. Because the country we're going to, that's our kingdom you know . . .'

'*There*,' a child interrupted happily, repeating the words rhythmically as though he had already said, or thought, or heard, them several times, '*there, we'll be able to get warm day and night.*'

'Yes,' Ernie nodded, 'that is how it will be.'

'*There*,' said a second voice in the gloom, '*there are no Germans or railway-trucks or anything that hurts.*'

'No, not you,' an enervated little girl interrupted, 'let the rabbi talk, it's better when he does.'

Still cradling the dead boy's sister on his knees, Ernie went on . . .

But a woman digs her fingernails into Ernie's shoulder . . .

'How can you tell them it's only a dream?' she breathed, with hate in her voice.

Rocking the child mechanically, Ernie gave way to dry sobs. 'Madame,' he said at last, 'there is no room for truth here.'[69]

There is no room for truth here. Like Ernie's story to the doomed children, was religion a consoling fiction – necessary, but still a fiction? Was I called to preach it not because it was true, but because there was no room for truth in a world so desperate for hope? Did I really believe it myself, or was I just trying to pump hope into myself? I knew we could help to *ameliorate* the human condition. Christianity, in spite of its flaws, had been good at that, was still good at it. That's why those people came to our door and were insistent on being helped. This, they seemed to be saying, is what you are for. We know it, you know it, so open up and get on with it. And we did. We fed the hungry and visited those in prison and clothed the naked and tried to share our goods with the poor. But the dead did not rise, the lame did not walk, the blind did not see. We could help the poor of the world but we could not heal the woe of the world that made them poor and would go on making them poor for ever. Woe was for keeps. What I was left with was a version of Ernie's story, the beauty of which became its own meaning and justification. I became lyrical in reaching into tragedy to find the answer not beyond but within the sorrow.

What I came up with was a naming of the fact: *ye now therefore have sorrow.* That was the human condition. There was no escape from it, but naming the fact without cringing before it offered a kind of transcendence. But it was not theology that brought me to this point. Theology had ceased to help. Its abstractions rarely illuminated the tragedy of life, and there was something demeaning about its attempts to justify God. God needed to be accused not excused, challenged not crawled to on bended knee. Fiction helped in this. So did poetry. Neither sought to explain, only to express, to give voice to the earth's anger and sorrow. Maybe religion was best understood not as a science that explained why there was suffering, but as a way of gathering people round the mystery of suffering itself and sitting with them before it. And sometimes that gathering was on a death train where only the consoling, necessary lie had any right to speak. That or silence. What if God was on the train, too, and was the child on Ernie's lap and her brother on the heap of Jewish corpses? There either had to be no God or a dying God. Not *dead*, dying, always dying. Was that what the story of the dying Jewish carpenter was about? Not about magical rescue and redemption from tragedy, but a picture of tragedy itself, a fiction that gave us the power to endure and not be defeated. In another great holocaust novel, Elie Wiesel's *Night*, a child is hanging on a gallows in Auschwitz.

And so he remained for more than half an hour, lingering between life and death, writhing before our eyes. And we were forced to look at him at close range. He was still alive when I passed him. His tongue was still red, his eyes not yet extinguished.

Behind me, I heard the same man asking:

'For God's sake, where is God?'

And from within me, I heard a voice answer:

'Where He is? This is where — hanging here from this gallows . . .'[70]

That could mean either of two things. In Auschwitz God is dead — God is over — and we are alone in a pitiless universe. Or in Auschwitz God is dying, dying beside us on all our calvaries. Dead or dying. Which God was it? Whatever my answer, dead or dying, he was no longer the God I had started out with.

I I

A DOUBLE-MINDED MAN

I began the journey of this book weeping in a graveyard. I stood there mourning the loss of my youth and its ideals. But there was more to it than that. I was also mourning the passing of a way of life which had filled that place with laughter and aspiration and disappointment for three quarters of a century. But there was more to it than that. I was mourning time itself and the way it steals everything from us, and I was confronting the way I had disappointed myself. Certain phrases from the New Testament can still overwhelm me with something that is not despair but is close to it. I have already referred to Paul's lament, 'Demas hath forsaken me, having loved this present world', and the way it summons up a whole complex of regret in me. Part of the regret is over things I have done and things I have failed to do. Any normal human heart feels the knife edge of regret at moments of retrospection and self-examination. But there is another kind of regret that is more difficult to explain. It is sorrow not over what we have done but over what we *are*. It may even be sorrow over what we are *not*. And I don't mean not handsome or rich or charming. One of the lessons a long life teaches is how formed we were by characteristics and circumstances that were entirely beyond our control. Being

226

who we were, we were bound to act the way we did. To have acted differently we would have had to be a different person. Maybe a better person, because, tragic as it may appear, even unfair, there are good people, not so good people, and bad people. And the big discovery we make in life is the person we have been *revealed* to be. We don't have that knowledge when we start out. We imagine there's a list of characteristics we can acquire if we fancy them, whereas the main lines of our personality were cast before we knew it. This does not mean that we have no control over our decisions and choices. It does mean that we will have little control over them till we acknowledge who we are and accept the reality of the hand we have been dealt to play.

There was another New Testament phrase that made me realise I had been trying to wear the wrong clothes. They come from the Epistle to James: 'A double-minded man is unstable in all his ways.'[71] It took me a while to realise that I was double-minded and unstable, if not in all my ways, then certainly in many of my attitudes and opinions. Janus-like, I seemed able to look two ways at once, be in two minds about things. Melancholy was one of my two minds, and melancholy is a conservative disposition. If we lament the constant flow of time and how it carries everything away, we will be disposed to the work of preserving or conserving what we can from the flood. We will be committed to institutions not only because they help to protect us against our own capacity for destruction, but also because they are good at keeping the past around us as long as possible. Old buildings, in particular, are important to this kind of mind. Kelham Hall is no longer the home of the Society of the Sacred Mission and the hundreds of boys who spent their formative years there, but the fact that it remains as a physical entity gives it enormous potency for those who go back to it sorrowing over lost time. It evokes what it no longer contains. Old Saint Paul's in Edinburgh is also a sorrowing building, but the fact that it remains in continuity with its own past makes its evocative power stronger and more disturbing. One of the unsettling aspects of the place for me was the way it continued to evoke Albert Laurie's presence long after he was dead and buried.

Shortly after I arrived in Lauder House, Laurie's niece died. I had not realised that she was still alive, probably because she had not attended Old Saint Paul's for decades. She had lived in Findhorn Place in the Grange area of Edinburgh for over thirty years, since Laurie's death. I was asked by her executors if I would like any of the books in the house, most of which had once belonged to Laurie himself. I spent an afternoon going through what remained of his library, but I took none of his religious books. Instead, I asked for his collection of the novels of Anthony Trollope, some of them in the Oxford World Classics edition, some of them in the Collins Classics edition. They bore the pencilled autograph, A.E. Laurie, Lauder House. That winter I sat on Sunday evenings after Evensong reading them, conscious that I was in the same room, before the same fireplace, reading the same novels, possibly smoking the same tobacco, as my predecessor. This was about the time the skids were being put beneath the wheels of British Christianity and its demise was being confidently predicted, so that those of us in the ordained ministry were beginning to think we might be the last generation of an endangered species. This concerned me in two ways. There was a selfish anxiety. This was how I earned my living and supported my family. It was a meagre wage, to be sure, but it was more than many had to live on, and there were privileges attached, one of which was living in an interesting house that was heavy with memories. Less selfishly, I was moved by what looked like the passing of a way of life that had its own culture and charm. Reading Trollope before an open fire in Lauder House amplified the mood. Was this way of life something else that was soon to pass from the earth? I started getting books out of the library about the English Country Parson, partly to stoke my melancholy, partly to recapture remembrances of a way of life that was as dead as steam trains and horse-drawn carriages.

This instinct for elegy was fortified by the ecclesiastical tradition to which I belonged. I had been initiated as a boy into the glamour of Anglo-Catholic religion. Though I did not know it at the time, Anglo-Catholicism was a conservative, restorationist movement, intent on bringing back to the Anglican Church, in Kathleen Raine's words, 'the now of then'.

> If I could turn
> Upon my finger the bright ring of time
> The now of then
> I would bring back again.[72]

What it wanted to bring back were many of the practices of the Catholic tradition that had been abandoned at the Reformation. There was more to it than vestments and candles and incense and processions and acolytes, though these became the badges of the movement. Trivial they may have been, but they had captured my young imagination at Saint Mungo's Alexandria and drawn me after them into the sanctuary.

> . . . under the Travers baroque, in a limewashed
> whiteness,
> The fiddle-back vestments a-glitter with morning rays,
> Our Lady's image, in multiple-candled brightness,
> The bells and banners – those were the waking days
> When Faith was taught and fanned to a golden blaze.[73]

Behind the theatricality of Betjeman's golden blaze there lay a serious moral purpose: an attempt to reclaim the heroic side of Christianity. Ango-Catholicism was not all gin and lace. Beneath the pomp of the processions there was a call to a serious and holy life. Though it made me shiver with apprehension, self-sacrifice was the term that encapsulated the underlying idea. It had been a strong theme at Kelham. It had also marked Canon Laurie's style. In fact, it had been a profound aspect of the Anglo-Catholic revival since the beginning. John Henry Newman, the poet and first genius of the movement in its early Oxford days, left the Church of England in 1845 because, among more theological reasons, he thought it had ceased to be a heroic church. In his obituary of Newman in *The Times*, Richard Church, Dean of Saint Paul's, said that Newman had always sought to return to the ardour and self-surrender of early Christianity.

> What was there like the New Testament or even the first ages now? . . . there was nothing completely like them, but of all unlike things the Church of England with its 'smug parsons' and pony carriages for their wives and daughters seemed to him the most unlike; more unlike than the great unreformed Roman Church with its strange, unscriptural doctrines and its undeniable crimes and alliances, whenever

it could, with the world. But at least the Roman Church had not only preserved but also maintained at full strength through the centuries to our day two things of which the New Testament was full, and which are characteristic of it – devotion and self-sacrifice. The crowds at a pilgrimage, a shrine or a 'pardon' were much more like the multitudes who followed our Lord about the hills of Galilee – like them probably in their imperfect faith which we call superstition – than anything that could be seen in the English Church.

It was what happened after Newman's departure for Rome that gave the movement its finest moment and its most heroic phase. The second generation of the Anglo-Catholic revival did not stay in the university debating theology. Instead:

> it plunged into the dark places of our awful cities. It spent itself, with sacrificial ardour, in the service of the Poor. It shirked nothing. it feared nothing. It took blows and insults with a smile. It went ahead, in spite of menace and persecution. It . . . wore poverty as a cloak, and lived the life of the suffering and destitute.[74]

When the Anglo-Catholic movement went into what Canon Scott Holland described in that passage as 'the dark places of our awful cities' it chose unfashionable addresses in which to establish itself, places like Carrubber's Close in Edinburgh or Paradise Row in Saint John's New Brunswick. Paradise Row was an unpaved alley near the docks. The church was built at the tram terminus, and locals called it 'the last stop before Rome'. But whether it was Old Saint Paul's Edinburgh, Saint

James Vancouver or Saint Peter's London Docks, the spirit and purpose were the same. In the grimmest areas they built churches of great beauty and numinous power where they gathered the poor round them and fanned their 'faith into a golden blaze' by the use of colour and ceremony. This was what had captured me as a boy, this sense of a mystery both given and withheld, within reach yet always eluding my grasp. What the second phase of the Anglo-Catholic movement achieved, the phase that moved it from the university to the slum, was to tie worship and social action inextricably together. At Old Saint Paul's, the Ritz was as important as High Mass. What happened in the soup kitchen validated what happened in the sanctuary. How could we claim to encounter Jesus in the Eucharist if we refused to encounter him in the poor? How could we lift him high in the sanctuary if we did not also work to lift the oppressed out of the conditions that held them down? But from the beginning there was a tension in Anglo-Catholicism that would lead to its fragmentation. It was the gravitational pull of the past and the way it distorted our efforts to respond to the future.

The yearning in Anglo-Catholicism for 'the now of then' cast a long shadow. Its love of the past, when faith was fanned into a golden blaze, its nostalgic journey back to the way things were, had two flaws – one of which was, in time, to prove fatal. The less damaging flaw was self-conscious attitudinising. People who live in a truly traditional society tend not to reflect upon their situation. They take it for granted as the way things have always been and always will be. But when people from a later generation reach back into history to restore its practices and values, they cannot do so without being self-consciously aware of what they are doing. This inevitably lends a studied

retro-chic air to the process. This was why in the upper reaches
of the Anglo-Catholic movement a lot of play-acting and
costume-changing went on. We all did it, especially if we were
candidates for the priesthood and our ordination approached.
Clergy had to acquire a uniform before embarking on their
calling, though it was fairly simple for priests. Coloured stoles
were usually provided as gifts from family and friends, the
tradition being that the mother of the young priest provided
his white stole. The big items were the cassock and surplice,
and we usually bought these ourselves. But what kind would
we go for? The traditional Anglican cassock was a double-
breasted garment that buttoned at the side. It was sometimes
called a Sarum cassock, because it was held to have been worn
at Salisbury Cathedral from the eleventh century till the Reformation. The other option was the Latin or Roman cassock, a
single-breasted item with a lot of buttons down the front from
neck to shoe. It came in a more elaborate, caped version, called
a soutane, which was favoured by really flashy dressers. Catholic-
minded ordinands on limited budgets, like me, usually opted
for the Latin version of the cassock, eschewing the flamboyance
of the cape. On the other hand, I did opt for the Sarum version
of the white surplice that was worn over the cassock. The
Sarum surplice was a voluminous garment like a Victorian
nightie, which almost reached to the floor. It had capacious
sleeves that encouraged dramatic gesturing in the pulpit at
Evensong. Ecclesiastical tailors sent their agents round theological colleges at ordination seasons to drum up business,
though there were only two options in my day, Wippell or
Vanpoulles, the latter being considered more Catholic than the
former. Both were tucked away in Tufton Street behind West-
minster Abbey, and pale young curates could be seen gazing

longingly into their windows at displays of mitres, copes and chasubles – and the dazzling futures they promised. There was little harm in any of this, though it did demonstrate the mysterious weakness of the human male for dressing up in elaborate uniforms and insignia. Though it was not a fatal vanity, it could be silly and precious; when it was done mischievously, archly, it could have charm and humour; but it was never without self-consciousness.

If reaching into the past to ransack its wardrobe and props department was relatively harmless, the second flaw in the Anglo-Catholic movement was more serious. This was its lack of interest in the future as a source of new inspiration, and an absolute refusal to believe any good could come from it. 'No man having drunk old wine desireth new: for he saith, The old is better.'[75] The entirely conservative mind mistrusts change. It believes that what has survived from the past into the present must have had what John Henry Newman called 'chronic vigour', so why risk losing it for something never tried or tested that may turn out to be worse? The trouble with philosophies of repetition like this is that they go on repeating the bad as well as the good, since both inevitably co-exist in any human tradition. The pain of unstoppable time is felt most keenly by the conservative mind at those moments of transition when the bad elements of the past are being challenged and have to be let go if the tradition itself, cleansed and renewed, is to be carried into the future. As usual, it was a poet who captured the essence of the dilemma:

> If there has been no spiritual change of kind
> Within our species since Cro-Magnon Man
> And none is looked for now while the millennia cool,

Yet each of us has known mutations in the mind
When the world jumped and what had been a plan
Dissolved and rivers gushed from what had seemed a
    pool.

For every static world that you or I impose
Upon the real one must crack at times and new
Patterns from new disorders open like a rose
And old assumptions yield to new sensation;
The Stranger in the wings is waiting for his cue,
The fuse is always laid to some annunciation.[76]

There was too much melancholy in my make-up to make me unconcerned about whatever the Stranger in the wings had in mind for us. Change could make me sad, but it did not make me afraid. More importantly, it never made me angry. Anger at new annunciations is the mark of the invincibly conservative mind; and it is futile, because we can no more stop history than we can hold back the sea. Though I could not know it at the time, my instability or capacity for change, my ability to look both ways, was to provoke a deep seam of anger in the leadership of the Anglo-Catholic movement. I began to gauge the power of its resistance to change at my first encounter with its institutional life.

A few years after the Pentecostal wind had blown in one door at Old Saint Paul's and blown out through another, and things had settled down again, a different excitement asserted itself, one that was more congruent with the traditions of the place. In 1978 an attempt was made to revive Anglo-Catholicism as an organised movement in Anglicanism. For those who wanted to maintain it as a separate tradition within the Anglican

Church, its own success had become the biggest threat to its survival. What had started in Oxford in 1833, as a conservative protest against the British government's efforts to curtail the privileged position of the Established Church of England, had broadened into a movement that contained many strands, some of which would have been anathema to the Oxford fathers. In addition to restoring a social and political dimension to the ministry of the Church, it had completely changed its liturgical aesthetic by bringing back a lot of the colour and pageantry that had been lost at the Reformation. As with other reform movements in history, many of the things it had championed against the odds in its early years became, in time, the practice of the majority. It could have been said that its work had been accomplished. It had radically altered both the ceremonial style and the theological self-understanding of Anglicanism. However, the first law of institutions is their own survival. They rarely dissolve themselves when they have accomplished what they set out to achieve. When it looks as if their significance is fading, they go into revival mode. Anglo-Catholicism tried to stage a comeback as the sesquicentennial of the Oxford Movement in 1983 drew near. Inevitably, the first gesture towards revival was a conference, held to mark the launch of what was to be called Catholic Renewal. It met at Loughborough University in the spring of 1978, and I was invited to be one of the keynote speakers. We had a new brace of curates at Old Saint Paul's by this time, Alan Moses and Graham Forbes. Graham was too busy working with disaffected youngsters in the Canongate to be bothered, but Alan was interested, so he joined me on the jaunt to Loughborough.

The best way to describe the ecclesiastical scene in the late Seventies is as the phoney war before the real one broke out.

Just as nothing much happened in the first six months of World War II, so not much happened immediately after the Loughborough conference of 1978, but the ensigns had been hoisted aloft and the forces were preparing themselves for battle. There was the usual mixture of workshops and lectures. And there were some enormous set-piece liturgies, not unreminiscent of National Socialist rallies, in which hundreds of priests in white chasubles concelebrated High Mass, an emerging trend at the time. I wasn't sure what to make of it. In my own lecture I anticipated the issues that would soon divide us, but I did so indirectly. My Janus-headed mind was looking both ways, I suppose. I was coming to realise that I felt little loyalty to the movement as such – or to any other organisation for that matter – which is why I was destined to disappoint those who had seen me as a leader-in-the-making whom they might follow. The conservative part of my mind well understood why traditional institutions, including the Church, tried to protect humanity from the destructive floods of time. But I was also coming to recognise that I could not privilege any institution above the individuals who composed it. When it came to a choice between them – which was usually when it meant applying the rules against them – I noticed that I usually came down on the side of the individual. I had never put E.M. Forster's challenge to myself in the precise way he did – that if it came to a choice between betraying his country and betraying his friends, he hoped he'd have the courage to betray his country – but in practice that is what I had been doing. I had gone the other way, on occasions, in favour of the institution instead of the individual, and had always regretted it. At Loughborough I did not tackle the issues head-on that were soon to convulse the Anglican Communion, but I did tilt at a few windmills. I talked about the way some priests were not much good at respecting the authority of the ecclesiastical wood because they knew, loved and lamented over so many of the individual trees. I went on:

> For instance, homosexuality is not a moral *issue* for them – it is Jim and Harry, their confusion, frailty and search for love. The marriage of the divorced is not an ecclesiastical issue for them – it is a succession of people they know, often stunned by failure and desperate to redeem it in a new future. Maybe even the ordination of women is not an issue so much as a person, quiet, pacific, unaggressively but surely aware of her vocation.[77]

The words I spoke at Loughborough were to prove predictive. The wood did rise against the trees, but that was still a few years away. For me and my family, the main, if indirect, outcome of the Loughborough Conference was to be another major upheaval. Present at the conference was the warden of the Anglican Institute in Chicago, and he invited me and Graham Leonard, then Bishop of Truro and titular head of Catholic Renewal, to come to America to lecture and preach the following spring. The Institute turned out to be a ramshackle affair, but my visit to it occasioned the next big change in my life.

I arrived in Chicago in March 1979, weeks after one of the biggest blizzards in the history of America. Every street was lined with buried cars, still covered in the dirty snow that had been blasted over them when the ploughs had cleared the city weeks before. The Institute was in a rickety old mansion in the Hyde Park district, and I travelled from it to preach and lecture. To accompany me on these trips by train and airplane, I bought the thirteen-volume paperback edition of Anthony Powell's novel sequence, *A Dance to the Music of Time*, and managed to get through it all before my return to Scotland. Anthony Powell turned out to be a more congenial companion than Graham Leonard. My difficulty with the Bishop of Truro had nothing to do with any unpleasantness in his personality. He was warm and friendly and an entertaining gossip. Among many other titbits, he told me that he had recently sat at a dinner beside Harold Wilson, the former Prime Minister. Like Graham Leonard himself, Wilson was a professional pipe-smoker. Leonard said he was amazed at how filthy Wilson's hands were, presumably from too much fussing with his pipes. What I came to realise in my discussions and debates with Graham Leonard was the role non-theological factors played in theological debate. In particular, we are all experts at finding intellectual arguments for decisions we have actually taken on temperamental or emotional grounds. I soon realised that Graham Leonard had a unipolar mind, and it was fixed undeviatingly on the past. He did not swivel or swither like me, tugged between the now of then and the now of now. He was a profoundly conservative human being, and his conservatism was a part of his not inconsiderable charm. But it baffled me. We spent a lot of time speaking to groups about the ordination of women, a change that had already been accomplished in the American Episcopal Church. He was implacably opposed, as I well knew, but I became increasingly aware of a submerged iceberg in his thinking that demonstrated how temperamentally different we were. On the surface he presented the familiar arguments. Most opposition to social change in Church and Society follows a familiar trajectory. At first there is opposition to the proposed reform on instinctive rather than rational grounds, and an attempt is made to halt it for allegedly rational reasons. In the case of women's ordination, Graham Leonard paraded the supposedly theological objection, which was as simple as it was crass. Jesus was a man. At the altar the priest represents Jesus. Therefore the priest has to be a man. A number of rejoinders were possible to this. Jesus was a Jew. At the altar the priest represents Jesus. Therefore the priest must be a Jew. Jesus was circumcised. At the altar the priest . . . and so on. He would have none of it. But he was embarrassed by the arbitrariness of his own logic. It was then the tip of the iceberg bobbed above the surface, and it revealed the anxious nature of the conservative mind as it negotiates change and contemplates doing something for the first time.

What he really believed was that, whether desirable or not, the Anglican Church did not have the authority to make such a change. It was a broken-off branch of the universal Catholic Church and did not have the right to take such a momentous decision on its own. Only if the Pope decreed the change could it be made. For him the issue was not about justice or injustice, it was about obedience to appropriate authority. It was the institution that defined and guarded value. Right and wrong were what it said they were, which is why a Jesuit once drily remarked that in Rome everything is forbidden till it is made compulsory. I saw things the other way round. If the Pope *could* command it, couldn't he see that it was already the right thing to do, because not even the Pope could make a wrong thing right simply by fiat. If he *could* say it was all right to do it, even though he had not yet said so and might never say it, then it must already be right in principle. If it is not principle or truth that delays it, but only the time it will take to change one man's mind, then it is unjust to delay. I was rating justice for trees as a higher value than the wood's authority to manage their lives for them, while Graham Leonard believed the opposite.

I do not want to moralise the difference between us, to claim my view was virtuous and his was vicious. The issue was much deeper than that. It showed that he was *au fond* a believer in a way that I never had been. He, a decent and kindly man, obeyed the Church, even if it meant acting unkindly, because he believed in the Church as God's Kingdom on earth with the Pope as God's Vicar. I knew I had never believed this. If I had, would I have disobeyed the Church's rule on marrying divorced people, as I had consistently all my ministry? Would I have officiated at my first gay wedding in the Lady Chapel at Old Saint Paul's in 1972, in spite of centuries of opposition in Christianity to homosexuality? As I have already observed, I did not perform these actions in any spirit of revolt or rebellion. I did not announce them, parade my own rebelliousness. It just seemed impossible not to respond to the people in front of me, confused about their own failures, needing a kind of mercy. It takes a lot of belief, a lot of divine assurance, to deny people mercy, to turn away from the woman quietly seeking to serve the church, the person with a broken marriage behind them, the gay couple wanting acceptance and stability. I did not have that assurance of belief. The ultimate test of belief is obedience, particularly when it goes against your human grain. Had I read the signs, I would have recognised that I had never possessed that capacity. *Au fond,* I was *not* a believer. Or one of my minds wasn't. I could see the beauty of the great institution of faith and the security it gave those who could obey it against the protests of their own heart. Lacking that capacity for obedience, I also lacked the fundamental capacity for faith that is its essential concomitant. I did not figure out all the possible consequences of this uncomfortable knowledge, but it would prove to be a solvent that would burn away much of what I thought I believed. But here in Chicago in these debates with the Bishop of Truro, it had already marked me as suspect in the eyes of the leadership of Catholic Renewal.

Towards the end of my time in Chicago I preached in one of the Episcopal churches in the city. After the service I was approached by a distinguished-looking man in a three-piece suit. He introduced himself as Roger Moore, Senior Warden of the Church of the Advent in Boston, and he wondered if I could spare him thirty minutes. We found a café. He took out a packet of fragrant, moist Edgeworth tobacco, from which he packed and lit his pipe. He was an unhurried man of serious demeanour. A lawyer. Would I be prepared to fly to Boston next week to meet the search committee of the Church of the Advent, which was looking for a new rector? They had heard about me, hence his flight to Chicago to hear me preach. They wondered if I would at least meet them to help them in their search. At the most it would take twenty-four hours out of my life. And I would get to see Beacon Hill for the first time. He told me it was certainly worth a visit. Intrigued, I agreed. I flew to Boston a few days later. I had, in fact, seen Beacon Hill before, without realising it. When I'd gone to a movie in Santa Fe in June 1968 during my visit to the South-West, I had seen Steve McQueen in *The Thomas Crown Affair*. I had noticed the elegant red brick terrace, the old-fashioned gas lamps, the Maple trees that lined the street on which Thomas Crown lived, and I had liked what I had seen, not knowing that it was Beacon Hill in Boston. I had admired the old-fashioned graciousness of the streets I had seen in the movie. I liked it even more now that I was here in its midst. They put me up in the Somerset

Club on Beacon Street, facing Boston Common, and it was there I met the search committee. It was the beginning of a period of painful uncertainty in my life. Maybe the soundtrack of the movie and its song about the windmills of the mind had been auspicious.

They did not formally offer me the post on that day, nor did I say I was interested in applying for it, but they were obviously giving me the once-over, and seeds of unrest were sown in my restless mind. I got back to Edinburgh the following week. Jean met me at the airport. On our way back to Lauder House I mentioned the quick visit to Boston. It hoisted a flag of unease in her mind. She did not want to move back to America. Fine. I wasn't really interested either. They were only picking my brains.

But they did not go away. Roger Moore came to see me in Edinburgh, and claimed afterwards that he nearly froze to death in our guest room. The overtures unsettled me, but I was unsettled, anyway. I had been at Old Saint Paul's for twelve years. One of my minds loved it and could never imagine leaving it. Where would I be without these hours in this mysterious building that confronted me with a presence both given and withheld? My other mind was restless, ambitious, excited by the prospect of a return to America and an unpredictable future. I think it was the unpredictability that got to me. In Scotland I could pretty much see what lay ahead. Laurie had stayed his whole life at Old Saint Paul's. He was married to the place and only death had separated them. One of my minds longed for that level of stability and commitment. Faithful unto death. But my other questing, restless mind wanted adventure, the new, the unexpected. More strangely, it wanted the unknown. A move to Boston would tear up the script and I'd have to improvise a new one. A new movie to star in! A future presentation! Later that summer of 1979 they invited me and Jean over to see them. It was hot and humid in Boston. Jean disliked it. I was intrigued, but still uncertain. So it went on for the rest of that year. It was not till the following March, when I made my third visit, that the deal was struck, and I decided to accept the position that had by now been offered to me several times. I announced my departure to Old Saint Paul's, and immediately felt heart-sick.

After our farewell from Jeffrey Street at the end of June in 1980, we spent the summer at our cottage near Dollar in Clackmannanshire, before our move to Boston in late August. Jean's parents had helped us buy Pathend Cottage in 1970, and it became as indelibly imprinted on my heart as Kelham and Old Saint Paul's. It was 200 years old, on the lovely tree-lined lane that led down to Muckhart Mill. The cottage faced away from the lane, and sat comfortably in its own garden high above the River Devon. A huge cypress tree at the back door gave it dignity and grace. Tall as the steep old house, on a windy day the tree flickered and ruffled and rejoiced. There was something of the sentinel about that tree. I loved coming over the hill above the cottage with the children after a walk and seeing it guarding the entrance. We would play a wayfarers game. I wonder if good people live in that white house beside the green tree, I'd ask. I wonder if they'd be kind to wandering strangers like us. Let us go down and see. We'd make our way down the hill, through the field, over the fence and into the cottage, where the woman of the house would have tea and home-made scones ready for us, with pots of her own wild raspberry jam waiting on the table. We spent part of every summer at Pathend, and the children often brought schoolfriends to stay. The parishioners also made constant use of the place, and it became something of a country annexe to Jeffrey Street. We swam in the river, hiked in the hills, cycled the country roads, picked wild raspberries, and read books and played games in the evening. I particularly loved it in autumn when we would snatch a few days while the leaves were falling and the rosebay willow herb's flowers were turning to silver wisps. Jean's father loved it, too, and wrote a poem about it.

> After the city streets, a country lane,
> After the noisy world, the quiet hills.
> Instead of tramping feet, a running stream:
> Instead of troubled hearts, the gift of peace.
> Beyond the paths that wander without end,
> I turn to you – my hearth, my home, my friend.

But we were going to lose it, too. We did not know whether our move to America would be for ever, but we knew it would be for years, and there was no way we could manage the cottage from across the Atlantic. So we sold it, but we arranged to stay in it for that final wistful summer. Soon enough, everything was for the last time. The last visit to the Pow Mill Milk Bar for their famous bacon rolls. The last visit to the butcher in Dollar who made his own haggis. The last walk down past Muckhart Mill and up the hill beyond. The last stroll along the edge of the river in the field next to Pathend. The last swim in the river itself at our favourite place, where you could do about twenty strokes before hitting the rocks. The last supper. The last drive up the lane into a new future.

The new owners were due to move in on the morning of our departure. Our remaining pieces of furniture in the cottage had all been claimed by friends and parishioners, and they were to be collected that same morning. Hours before our departure there was a flash flood of rain, and water poured through the back door down the narrow passageway into the kitchen. We used all our towels to soak up the water. The new owners turned up with their furniture while we were still carrying our furniture out of the cottage into the garden where it waited in the rain, covered in tarpaulins, to be picked up by those who wanted it later that day. Somehow, thanks to Jean's genius for planning, we got through it all. Along with Kip our dog and Tizer our cat, we loaded ourselves into the car that was to take us back to Edinburgh for the weekend before our Monday afternoon flight to Boston. No one spoke as I negotiated the car up the lane. We got to the huge beech tree where the lane bent towards the road. That was the beech tree we'd slung a rope over for a swing years ago. It was hanging there as we passed. Under that beech tree was the barbed wire fence on which Sara had impaled herself one summer afternoon when she was very young. We were nearly at the road when Mark, in the back seat with his sisters, tried to stifle a sob. That set us off. We all wept uncontrollably. I was leaving Alexandria again, and this time I was dragging my family with me.

BOSTON COMMON

Beacon Hill in Boston is one of America's oldest urban neighbourhoods. It lies immediately north of Boston Common and Boston Public Garden. It is bounded on the south by Beacon Street, on the north by Cambridge Street, on the east by Somerset Street, and on the west by Storrow Drive, close to the Church of the Advent itself, where it sits on what is called 'the flat of the Hill' close to the Charles River. Maybe it is significant that I never properly oriented myself in my new abode. Because Lauder House faced north in Edinburgh, I could never rid myself of the feeling that 135 Mount Vernon Street faced the same way, when it was exactly the other way round. Though I spent four years resolutely facing the wrong way in Beacon Hill, I liked the feel and touch of the old neighbourhood from the very beginning. And it *was* old. Around 1800 a group of entrepreneurs known as the Mount Vernon Proprietors undertook to subdivide the south slope of Beacon Hill for mansion houses set on parcels of land of an acre or more. Not many of these were built, however, and in the following years developers covered the rest of the Hill in attached Federal-style row houses or terraces that opened straight onto the sidewalk.[78] They give Beacon Hill a cosy yet elegant feel, and the brick sidewalks and flickering gas lamps add to the charm of the neighbourhood.

It was under lamplight and along those brick sidewalks I led Kip on her evening walk the warm and sticky August night of our arrival in Boston in 1980. Outside our new front door I turned right and headed down Mount Vernon to Brimmer Street, where the roots of the maple and flowering pear trees caused weird undulations in the sidewalk. The Advent filled the corner of Mount Vernon and Brimmer Street, a dignified rather than a dominating presence. While Kip sniffed the railings, I stood back and looked at the church I had been called to serve. It looked comfortably at home where it sat on the flat of the hill. We continued along Brimmer to Pinckney Street and back along Charles Street, the main drag of the neighbourhood, packed with interesting shops and restaurants and fast-food joints, such as the famous Paramount, which was just round the corner from the Rectory. Charles Street on its way out of Beacon Hill goes between Boston Common on its east side and the Public Gardens on the west. Smelling grass and what it promised, Kip dragged me into the gardens, the scene of the children's picture book, *Make Way for Ducklings* by Robert McCloskey, the story of a pair of mallard ducks who decide to raise their family on an island in the lagoon in the gardens. After that first exploratory turn round the gardens on the evening of our arrival, it became a favourite walk for me and Kip in the brief time that was left to her. I did not imagine during our walk that night that she would not survive her first winter in Boston, or that I would almost immediately begin to regret the restless mind that had taken us away from Scotland.

There were layers to the regret I fell into. The most obvious was straightforward homesickness, and it was felt by all of us.

I found Mark in tears one day. What's wrong, son? 'I just want to go round to Chessel's Court to play wi' ma pals,' he said. But it was Jean's homesickness that was deepest and most despairing. In spite of the joy of being near her sister Margaret and her nephew Steve, who lived in Boston, she ached to be back in Edinburgh. So did I. But I was also excited by the challenge of finding my way in a new parish, and I did not anticipate any great difficulty in doing so. Like Old Saint Paul's, the Church of the Advent was a historic Anglo-Catholic parish, so how difficult could it be to move from one to the other? As different as America is from Scotland, and then some, as I was soon to discover. What I had not reckoned on was the enormous cultural divide between Scotland and America, a divide that only becomes obvious when one emigrates.

Apart from relatively trivial differences in the way we use a common language, the substantial difference between us is captured by the paradox of American social culture. It was, I was to discover, an intensely political culture that opened the leaders of every institution to constant challenge from its members. This meant that almost anything could become a source of dispute, as the rights of challenge and disagreement were asserted. This is what makes American institutions at every level profoundly democratic and self-adjusting, at the price of constant confrontation and discontent. At the parish level, this often leads to situations of strife and breakdown in the relationship between pastors and their congregations, the flipside of which is the eagerness with which Americans participate in group life at every level. Americans believe in belonging as passionately as they believe in believing. The shadows on this astonishing democratic energy are the conformism and outbreaks of group-thinking that regularly afflict the nation.

Some of these viral social epidemics are more irritating than dangerous, but American history is also dark with witch hunts and lynch mobs, and its soundtrack is loud with the hectoring tones of demagoguery and its humourless cousin political correctness. It is as if America suffers from an auto-immune deficiency disorder that attacks the antibodies of scepticism and irony, which are there to protect us from the toxins of social hysteria and group-rage. Studying in America, vacationing in America, marrying an American, all of which I had done, had not prepared me for the shock of difference I felt when I moved there to live and work. At forty-six I was too old to make the transition easily, but it might have helped had someone prepared me for the jolt and disorientation of the move. As it was, under my confident exterior, I felt as if I were walking in a fog through which I could not quite discern the measure and proportion of things. Or it was like moving underwater, with all the distortions and delays that medium imposes. To find myself, with little in the way of preparation, responsible for a large and significant institution like the Church of the Advent, in what I was slowly coming to recognise was a very foreign country, was something I only gradually realised had disturbed and unsettled me at a deep level. Looking back, I am grateful to the Advent for the scene shifting that went on in me, but at the time it was disorienting.

Though the congregation was established in 1844, eleven years after the beginning of the Oxford Movement, the church itself was not completed on its present site in Brimmer Street till 1894. It is a glorious Victorian Gothic building whose architect was John Hubbard Sturgis. Though much larger in scale and less florid in decoration, it is physically reminiscent of William Butterfield's All Saints Margaret Street in London. It

is built on hundreds of wooden piles driven through the land-
fill of Back Bay down into the clay bed beneath, and capped
with granite to form the bearing stratum.[79] Architecturally, it
feels completely at home in its place on the flat of Beacon Hill,
where 'it broods beautifully beside its brick neighbors, hardly
noticeable until one arrives a block or so away, although the
graceful broach spire is a landmark from the top of the Hill
or across the river'.[80] Much as I admired it, I did not fall in love
with it. I was like a man who had left one woman for a more
handsome and wealthier rival, only to discover that he was still
in thrall to the one he had deserted. I recognised objectively
that the Advent was a wonderful building, though I always
preferred the exterior to the interior. I was particularly moved
by the way it lifted itself straight out of the brick sidewalk on
Mount Vernon Street before opening onto the garden on the
corner with Brimmer Street. When I go to movies set in Boston
I still eagerly watch to see if I can catch a glimpse from the
Cambridge side of the Charles River of that beautiful spire
standing above the warm cluster of terraced brick houses on
the flat of the Hill. I was not so moved by the interior of the
church, though I recognised that it was a magnificent setting
for great liturgies. The sanctuary is dominated by an enormous
reredos in pale Caen stone, which I found chilly after the warm
gold of Old Saint Paul's, though it was rendered vivid at
Christmas when it was decorated with banks of scarlet poinset-
tias. The Advent was a building that delivered itself completely
and proudly to the beholder and held nothing of itself back.
It was at its best when it was full of worshippers, and the choir
and sanctuary were alive with robed choristers, acolytes and
clergy, as the high mass was celebrated. I slowly began to realise
that the difference between the church on the elegant level of

Brimmer Street in Boston and the church on the dingy slope of Carrubber's Close in Edinburgh was that the Advent's power lay in withholding nothing, while Old Saint Paul's power lay in the fact that it withheld so much.

And it was what was withheld that I began to miss. I had loved Old Saint Paul's most when it was empty. I loved the Advent most when it was full. Empty, the Beacon Hill church was like a theatre waiting for the stalls to fill and the curtain to lift and the performance to begin so that it could come to life and be itself again, like an actor who is only at peace with himself on the stage. Old Saint Paul's was most itself when it was empty, most alive to me when nothing was going on in it except its own brooding and remembering. The contrast may have something to do with the fact that Old Saint Paul's has always been kept open so that people can drift in, sit awhile with the building and its memories, and drift out again. Churches that stay open unclose themselves to the sorrows of humanity and alchemise them into consolation. And not a cheap consolation. Just as artists reconcile us to our ills by the way they notice and record them, so open churches console us by the way they accept the unreconciled aspects of our natures. This is a mystery the godless poet Philip Larkin acknowledged in his poem, *Church Going.*[81] Almost in spite of himself, he recognised that 'the ghostly silt' of a church can exercise a strange power over those who visit it. Silt is the perfect word. It suggests the slow silent accumulation of pain and regret, and their distillation into memory and mercy. Because they have heard it all, these serious houses on serious earth. Into their 'blent air' generations of the wretched have whispered their compulsions, and not always in hope of having them removed, but simply to experience the relief of naming them. Churches not only bear the memory of our dyings, they also carry the knowledge of the helplessness of our failings. They are a haven for the homeless woman whose destitution is obvious, muttering to herself over there in the back pew; but they also accept the moral destitution of the confident man sitting in the dark chapel, gazing at the white star of the sanctuary lamp, heavy with the knowledge of the compulsions that have dominated his life and refuse to leave him. Here both are accepted in their helplessness. There is no reproach. Churches do not speak; they listen. Clergy speak, unstoppably. They are 'randy' to change, challenge or shame people into successful living. Church buildings that stay open to all know better. They understand helplessness and the weariness of failure, and have for centuries absorbed them into the mercy of their silence. This is grace. Unearned undeserved unconditional acceptance of unchanging failure, including biological failure, our last failure, our dying. The unclosed church is the home of the destitute and the dead. And since we will go on failing and dying, some of us will go on gravitating to these places that do not shut themselves against our need.

The Advent was kept locked for security reasons, though visitors could be buzzed into the building by the parish secretary. Though I understood the policy that kept the church closed, I always felt it deprived it of a life of its own where it could have gathered memories into itself and opened itself to the sorrows of humanity. It closed itself against those who needed to slip in quietly and unseen to sit in the dark with their own hopelessness. It takes confidence to ring a buzzer and invite yourself into a building to look around. And the confident did it, many of them. But what happens to the unconfident who want to hide themselves away for a while, unseen?

. . . creep,

Wretch, under a comfort serves in a whirlwind . . .[82]

I see now that all the time I was at the Advent I was grieving
the loss of Old Saint Paul's, so I do not think I allowed myself
to see the Advent for what it was in itself, a beautiful and
generous building that had attracted an astonishingly varied and
creative congregation from all over Boston. Most of the
misjudgements I made were attempts to impose the pattern we
had evolved at Old Saint Paul's over my twelve years there onto
the Advent almost overnight. The symbol for my grieving
tactlessness was what happened to the seven sanctuary lamps.
The lamps in Old Saint Paul's were genuine oil lamps. Restrained
and elegant, each showed not a flame, but a small white star
of light. The Advent also had seven lamps in the sanctuary.
They had the confident handsomeness of all the furnishings
of the church in Brimmer Street, but they were no longer oil
lamps. For convenience, each held a nightlight in a little glass,
which was regularly changed by the sexton. And they were red.
I sat in the nave when I first arrived, trying to bond with the
building, but those red lights held me at bay. They were in my
face. They were too assertive. There seemed to be no sorrow
in the place, no sense of uncertainty, no sense of absence and
loss. I pined for the seven white dots of light I knew were
burning quietly in the shadows of Old Saint Paul's. I asked the
sexton to replace the red nightlights with white. He did so, but
they looked even less numinous than the ones he replaced. You
could see they were candles burning in small tumblers, whereas
the dark red glasses, to be fair to them, revealed only the flames.
We went back to the red lights. There were other changes I
made, mainly to the liturgy, all aimed at conforming the usage

to what went on at Old Saint Paul's. I offered solid reasons for my changes, because reasons were demanded by the congregation, as befitted its American suspicion of autocrats who knew what was good for other people. Most of the changes worked and were, in time, integrated into the life of the Advent, but I can see now what I was up to: rather than patiently letting the new place disclose itself to me, I was intent on making it as like the old place as I could get away with. If I had understood myself better, and acknowledged what was going on in my heart, I wonder what would have happened had I said to them: I am heartbroken over what I have left behind. It will help me if I make this place look more like the place I came from, so please bear with me. They argued and challenged with that assertive democratic ease that is the cultural hallmark of America, and I got away with most of it because I argued back. But what was increasingly obvious to me was that I had the psychology of a visitor not a settler. In my heart I hoped to go back to Scotland one day.

But meanwhile I had a fine team of clergy and many hard-working lay leaders and a lot of good work was done. The only enduring legacy of my four years at the Advent was the Community Dinner we started for the homeless. Boston had a large population of street people, victims both of their own demons and the tough reality of America's ethic of personal responsibility. An Irish writer, Timothy O'Grady, who also loves America, was as troubled as I was by this harshness. Talking of what he found on his return to Ireland, he observes:

> I found something else there that I'd seen little of in America
> – the idea that chaos and helplessness are never far away
> from anyone, that they just take you as a strong wind takes

a tree, and that their victims are to be commiserated with
rather than scorned.[83]

I did not see much of that relaxed Hibernian tolerance in the
US. You either swam or you sank, and there wasn't much life-
saving equipment available on the riverbanks of America other
than what was provided by private enterprises, including the
churches. The Boston churches were supporters of the Walk
for Hunger, the proceeds from which went to support a dinner
programme and other services for street people. We joined with
the Old West Church in providing a dinner on Tuesday nights
for 150 guests, the whole thing cooked in the Advent's well-
appointed kitchen, and served by volunteers from the parish.
There was rarely any trouble from our guests, but I sometimes
wondered what our well-heeled neighbours made of the queue
of survivors that started to form outside the Advent on Tuesday
evenings, especially when the deep New England cold settled
over the city. We got to know the regulars and to miss them
when they did not turn up. They seemed to me to be American
versions of the characters I'd met at the Ritz in Edinburgh.
The difference was that everything seemed heightened and
enlarged over here, the destitution more extreme, the violence
more frightening, the hopelessness more intractable. And there
was a stronger sexual theme. One of our regulars was a flam-
boyant character who drenched himself in eau de Cologne and
sometimes drank it. A priest on the staff told me that he was
reputed to give the best head in Boston, occasionally as a favour
but usually for a small fee. I hadn't heard that way of putting
it before, but I had noticed the unembarrassed openness of
the Boston gay scene.

Before I arrived at the Advent someone sent me a copy of

the glossy magazine, *Boston,* and pointed me to a particular entry. It was one of those filler columns magazine editors love: best cup of coffee in the Hub, best place for oysters, best Irish pub, and so on. My eye was drawn to the item circled in red by my anonymous correspondent: 'best place for a gay pickup: coffee hour after High Mass at Beacon Hill's Church of the Advent'. So I was not surprised to find that many if not most of the men, young and old, in my new congregation were gay. Most of them were Out and proud of it, some of them were married and in the closet, with the door slightly ajar. Aware of the more camouflaged nature of the gay scene in Britain, I was at first disconcerted by the openness of the Advent, but I soon grew to welcome it. I got used to gay couples coming to me to discuss their flagging sex lives, though I doubt if I was ever much help at restoring their early ardour for one another. Boston was a city of refuge for gays, and it attracted hundreds of refugees from the disapproving atmosphere of the American heartland. And the Advent was a magnet. This was partly because a gay priest had been on the staff of the parish for decades before my time and had mentored generations of gay men during the long winter of persecution that was the story of their lives.

Not that there was anything unusual in that. Anglo-Catholicism has had a strongly homophile if not exactly homosexual ethos from its beginnings. Indeed, Geoffrey Faber, in his controversial book *Oxford Apostles,* published on the centenary of the movement in 1933, explored the homoerotic atmosphere of Newman's Oxford circle in the 1820s and '30s.[84] Faber pushed his homoerotic angle too far, but there is no doubt of the homophile energy in Newman's friendships and the communities in which he enclosed himself, both before and after his conversion to Roman

Catholicism. The nature of the early founders aside, there is no doubt that Anglo-Catholicism, as it evolved, became attractive to gay men, though the reasons for this are probably more theologically rooted than is commonly understood. The high camp aesthetic of the more florid wings of the movement was clearly attractive to a certain kind of gay sensibility, as anyone who has had to negotiate a high mass in one of the more fashionable outposts of Anglo-Catholicism will testify. This is surface attraction, however, and there is usually a certain amount of self-parody going on. At a deeper level something more interesting and more moving is happening.

Even in societies that have stopped persecuting homosexuals, gays remain a minority community, and minorities are always under some kind of threat from the surrounding majority, even if it is only from their curiosity about or incomprehension over their sex lives. Gays will always be outsiders in straight communities, and it is their status as outsiders that draws some of them to Christianity and, in particular, to its Anglo-Catholic variant. I have known many gay priests over the years. What has moved me most about their persistence in remaining within a Church that at best only grudgingly accepts them, and at worst actively persecutes them, is their identification not with campery and high jinks in the sanctuary, but with the figure of Jesus, the great Outsider. Many of them intuit that Jesus was himself probably gay, but whether or not that was the case, there is no doubt of his appeal to the rejected and discarded in ancient Israel, an appeal that is still strong today. This meant that, at its best, Anglo-Catholicism was a form of Christianity that was hospitable to the unrespectable, to people who were not good at bringing their desires to heel, people who knew their need of mercy and forgiveness because they were never going to qualify morally for entrance into the members' enclosure of the more respectable religions. Gays may have been drawn to Anglo-Catholicism for complex reasons, but they informed the tradition with their own experience of the search for acceptance, which is why the churches they served often became havens for people who would not have survived in the thinner atmosphere of congregations of the disciplined and the good. In a world that judged and outlawed them, it was a relief to find communities that did not make them feel bad about themselves. That tenderness towards human frailty meant that other outsiders were drawn in. It was a gay priest with a drink problem who drew me into the Church and set me on my path in life, and he was a priest whose brokenness led to his expulsion from the ministry. It was gay priests who helped me understand that not everything can be fixed and some things just have to be lived with. 'If you can't fix it, you gotta stand it,' as the gay cowboy put it in the film *Brokeback Mountain*. It was that kind of courage the Church needed when its gay children started going through their great ordeal in the Eighties.

It started slowly. My first encounter with what was happening was an urgent call to visit a dying parishioner in Massachusetts General Hospital, the famous MGH, which lay at the other end of Charles Street on the northern boundary of Beacon Hill. I did not know him well, and he had disappeared from the Advent a year earlier. This was not unusual in a shifting urban population. I recalled the name, however, because it conjured up the image of the tall, handsome young man who bore it – and the Latin number III tagged to the end of it. A smart-suited lawyer, he was a refugee from a small town in Texas. Devoted to his wealthy parents, intimidated by his father but close to his mother, he had been unable to tell either of them that he was

259

gay. When I arrived at the hospital I was told he was in a special isolation unit and I would have to wear protective clothing to visit him. I was shocked by the change in him. He was emaciated and covered in purple lesions I would soon learn to identify as Kaposi's sarcoma. The closest I had seen to his present state was a photograph of Matthias Grünewald's *Altarpiece* in the hospice for plague victims at Isenheim, an image that would soon be famously associated with the disease Clyde was dying from. They put me in white overalls and made me wear discardable rubber gloves when ministering to him, a stricture I would soon learn to resist, though I swallowed slightly when placing a tiny fragment of the communion wafer onto his ulcerated tongue. He died that night. His heartbroken parents took his body back to Texas for his funeral. For them, he had died of a cancer that had nothing to do with the deadly disease that was beginning to afflict gay men. Their inability to accept the truth about their son distanced them from his Boston friends, whose grief at his death might have helped console them for their own terrible loss.

It was a pattern I was to see repeated on both sides of the Atlantic in the coming years. It measured the depth of hatred in traditional Christian opinion towards gay people, a minority that was no longer prepared to submit to such entrenched cruelty. This was my first encounter with the AIDS epidemic. The papers had labelled the mystery disease *the gay plague,* because it seemed to be mainly gay men who were dying of cancers and infections that had not been seen by beleaguered doctors for centuries. Cruel jokes were made by conservative commentators, thrilled that the Fag community was finally getting its dues. One writer, unable to conceal his glee at the emergence of the epidemic, suggested that gay men should have their backsides compulsorily tattooed with the tag from Dante: 'Abandon hope all ye who enter here.' Evangelical preachers announced the disease as God's punishment for a sin He particularly abhorred. God had gone to extraordinary lengths to concoct a virus that targeted the auto-immune system of people he disapproved of. Many of us wondered, if He was so clever, where He had been during the Holocaust or Stalin's great purges, only to be reminded that it was not genocide that hacked off the Almighty, it was sex. AIDS brought out the worst in human beings, but it also brought out the best, not least in the gay community itself.

Even after the virus was identified, and it was understood how it attacked the immune system and opened the body to a devastating siege from infections normally repelled with ease, there was considerable uncertainty about how it was transmitted, other than through unprotected sex. Could it be picked up from saliva? One parishioner with full-blown AIDS who came to lunch with us was suffering from oral candidiasis or thrush. He asked for an extra tumbler and kept spitting into it throughout the meal to relieve the terrible discomfort. We tried to show no anxiety while he was at our table, but when he had gone I put on rubber gloves and carefully put the tumbler and its contents into a plastic bag to dispose of safely. We soon learned to modify the more extreme protective responses to the situation, guided by the medical community who rose to the challenge with compassion and intelligence. People are able to live indefinitely with the virus today, if properly treated, but then its diagnosis was a death sentence of a particularly grim sort. At the time one New York doctor at the forefront of the campaign not only against the virus, but against the ignorance and cruelty of responses to it, quoted Camus' novel *La Peste*:

to state quite simply what we learn in times of pestilence: that there are more things to admire in men than to despise. The story could not be one of final victory. It could only be the record of what had to be done, and assuredly would have to be done again by all, who while unable to be saints but refusing to bow to pestilences, strive their utmost to be healers.[85]

I certainly found much to admire in the way some groups responded to this new pestilence. The medical profession purged the epidemic of the taint of shame that hung around the disease, especially in some religious circles. The response of the gay community was also heroic and compassionate, and it helped to steady the nerves of the rest of us. The funerals of those who had died of AIDS became acts of defiance and solidarity as well as acts of mourning, and we refused to bow to pestilence and strove our utmost to be healers.

If the gay community of Boston taught me much about grace in the face of tragedy, it was the women of the Advent who opened my eyes to the limitations of the Church's traditional language about God and its attitude towards women. All language about God is necessarily metaphorical and analogical. When they are discussing the limitations of language, philosophers talk about the problem of *equivalence*: because of the special position language holds in our culture, we think we can put everything into words – we think that if we can say it we will get it – but there is no exact verbal equivalence to even the most prosaic item. Words are the names we give things, the signs we create to point to them, but the things themselves are not what we say they are. Writers who work with language as their chosen medium know these limitations better than anyone.

All the time they are trying to get beyond the words to communicate the experience that lies behind them. That's why the guiding mantra for writers is 'show, don't tell': show me your hero is charming, don't *tell* me he is; demonstrate the courage of your heroine, don't *tell* me she's brave. Get as close as you can to giving the reader the experience you are trying to describe. Go beyond the words, get through them to the reality of the experience you are trying to communicate.

If language is difficult at the immanent level, the level that is available to our senses, then it is infinitely more difficult at the transcendent level, the level beyond the physical where we locate the possibility of the mystery we call God. I was to reach a point where I would find any language about God impossible to use without a level of qualification that rendered it almost futile, but it was the women of the Advent who taught me that even the metaphors and analogies we wielded to talk about God were divisive. Their question was: why the exclusive use of male metaphors? I came to believe that it was more to do with historic male dominance of human institutions than with any virtue and coherence in the metaphors themselves. The hard thing was to find elegant substitutes for traditional masculine language. In my own writing, rather than adopting formations like he/she and his/hers in talking about human abstractions, I have preferred to alternate the gender of the pronouns, but this is more awkward when talking about God. In this book I have reverted to describing God in masculine pronouns, because that is the God to whom I have been drawn and from whom I have been in flight since my boyhood.

The women who challenged me at the Advent did more than complicate my thinking about the limitations of religious language, however; they also stiffened my resolve to campaign for the ordination of women. Their education of me began with a humorous dispute over hymns. 'Rise Up, O Men of God', went one of our hymns. Did this mean women should remain seated? Groan . . . OK, but could I not understand how they felt about the almost exclusive use of male personal pronouns in our worship? Just imagine the effect it would have on me if week after week I was forced to use only female pronouns in the liturgy. Could I not drill below the surface of this apparently slight and superficial issue to see what was really going on here: an explicit and implicit relegation of women to a subsidiary role in Church and Society?

The penny did finally drop, and the ordination of women switched from being a change to which I could see no objection, to one I now believed was essential if the Church was to be a just institution. But it would be easier said than done to achieve it everywhere. The debate over women's ordination illustrates the peculiar difficulty religious institutions have in negotiating the changes in human understanding and organisation that are such a pronounced mark of our history. I remember how opposed my mother was to the appointment of a woman to her GP practice in Alexandria. At first she insisted on always seeing Doctor Macaulay when she went on one of her many visits to the practice, but she mellowed in time and by the end of her life preferred to be seen by a woman. But she had never claimed that a woman could not *be* a doctor, only that she preferred men. This is normal social conservatism of an everyday variety. It is not rooted in sweeping ontological claims. It is a preference; something we are used to and prefer not to change. What bedevilled religious debate about women in the ordained ministry was that it was not just conducted on the basis of ordinary human resistance to change; opponents

claimed that the difference between men and women was onto-
logically so profound that it rendered women incapable of being
priests. Women could manifestly *do* priestly things, but they
could not *be* priests, any more than men could bear children. It
followed that female priestly acts would be spiritually fraudulent,
and the people they ministered to would be receiving not the
grace from God that only men had the power to impart but
its counterfeit. I'll look at the sources of this magical thinking
later in this book, but I want to notice here that its influence
hung around me for longer than I care to admit, and it was the
scornful incredulity of theologically sophisticated American
women who finally laughed it out of the court of my mind.
What they showed me was that beneath the proud theological
language of the opponents of women's ordination there lay a
deep, unacknowledged layer of hatred and mistrust of women
that was rooted in ancient religious taboos. Yet the opponents
of women were not intrinsically cruel men, carelessly given to
the hurting of others. Their cruelty was not personal; it was a
consequence of their faith. Was it true, then, that it took religion
to make good men act badly?

In spite of its hallowed place in the religious canon, I had
always been troubled by the story of Abraham's willingness,
however reluctantly, to kill his son in obedience to God's
command in the book of Genesis. I had been taught to see
the story as a shining example of absolute submission to God,
even against the dictates of Abraham's love for his own son.
But how could obedience to God make an evil act good?
Disputes about the ordination of women and homosexuals
were a world away from arguing about child sacrifice; but were
they not in the same ballpark? Was their something about religion itself that clouded our ability to act justly? I wasn't quite

sure at that point, but in 1984 I arrived back in Britain with a faint but fundamental unease lurking in the back of my mind on the subject. Disputes over the place of women and gays in the Church had not yet broken out over here, but anyone could see that the battle lines were being drawn. I got back in time to witness the first skirmishes in what would be a protracted war, and one in which I would be closely involved.

IV

1986–2000

13

NEW CLOTH

My father occasionally stole from his employer, the United Turkey Red, in whose freezing and dilapidated factory on the banks of the River Leven he laboured much of his life away. I say stole, but it did not feel like that to him or to us. It was more like a covert form of redistribution, a way of evening the odds that were heavily stacked against the workers who earned the owners their profits. He would occasionally wrap round his small wiry body the discarded tail-end of a batch of cloth he had been dyeing, and walk through the factory gates at the end of the working day with his raincoat on to disguise his added bulk. Most of it was given away. The contraband would reappear in our neighbours' houses as curtains or cushion covers or cheerful dresses for the women. It helped to brighten our street, with the added spice that it was also an act of subversion.

Another thing that surprised me about my father was that, in his quiet way, he was a social organiser, someone who got things done. Admittedly, they were usually contrived round activities in which he was himself engaged. For example, there was a small gambling school he ran that met on Sundays on a disused railway line in the countryside above Jamestown. I went with him once but was so bored standing around while the men gambled that I

269

never went back. Sundays in Scotland were heavy and lifeless, and if you did not go to Church there was not much else to do. My father sought to banish the blues in several ways, and the most regular was the gambling. Men would go out for an innocent walk on Sunday mornings, picking up the *Sunday Post* on the way, and would end up on what was called 'the Bogie Line', far into the hills and well beyond the prying eyes of the Law. There they would gamble in a fairly crude and immediate way. The game was called 'Banker', and it involved betting on the highest card, the winner taking the bank. No notes, only coins. My father enjoyed gambling. He did the football pools as well, and there was always excitement in the house on Saturday evenings as he jotted down his scores. Apart from the immediate thrill of the bet, his gambling kept hope alive for us. We were not miserable people trapped in grinding poverty, desperate to make a break for it, but we *were* poor, and it was exciting to sit round the fire on a Saturday night as the results came in on the wireless, dreaming that this might be the moment our luck changed. Hope is always worth a gamble. He did the horses, too, with occasional success. But it was with the gang up the Bogie Line on Sunday mornings that he achieved his most frequent successes, however modest. Whenever he won the bank he would come home in great good humour and empty his pockets onto the kitchen table, allowing his children to divvy the coppers and thruppenny pieces between them. It meant more McCowan's Highland Toffee for us on the way to school on Monday mornings.

Another of his anti-Sabbath ruses was the drinkers' bus run. Pubs did not open on Sundays, nor did off-licences, so it was a hard day for seasoned imbibers, made worse by the sullen silence that hung like a cloud over the Vale. The one loophole available was the fact that hotels could serve alcohol to '*bona fide* travellers', and it was through this gap that my father sent the occasional omnibus. They were all-male affairs. He would hire a bus and advertise an outing to scenic spots in the surrounding countryside. Men would pile onto the bus at the Fountain at the top of Bank Street and they would head up the east side of Loch Lomond to Drymen, which had a nice hotel. As *bona fide* travellers the hotel bar was open to them, and they would experience the Absolution of the first pint and the Amen of the dram that followed. So went the day. Aberfoyle, Callander, Stirling, Kilsyth, Kirkintilloch, Duntocher for last orders, and back to Alexandria, where they staggered out of the bus, loud and happy at the huge fast one they had pulled on the powers that be.

I wonder now if my father had a deeper effect on me than I realised at the time. Did I get from him a sense not that laws were made for other people, but an implicit recognition that most of them were arbitrary, many of them were stupid and some of them were unjust? *The Sabbath was made for man, not man for the Sabbath.* No wonder I came to believe that Jesus's most subversive claim rendered all social and religious law provisional, and not just because he said it, but because it was manifestly true. Had I really grasped the force of my innate scepticism towards institutions would I still have agreed to become a bishop in 1986? Probably, but I would have known that it was more vanity and ambition that prompted me than the wisdom of self-knowledge. To be fair to the person I was then, I did not yet know myself. We live ourselves forward and understand ourselves backward, but I had not lived long or reflectively enough to know who I was. In particular, I had not unravelled the complexity of my attitude towards religion. I knew I was not an atheist. The invincible thing about atheists and what gives them coherence is that they refuse to accept any explanation for the riddle of existence that comes from *outside* the universe. For them there is no Outside. There is the universe and only the universe. It alone is available to our explorations. And no god has been discovered within it. What I did not know then was that I was not quite a theist either. The invincible thing about theists and what gives them coherence is that they take their search for explanations for the riddle of existence right outside the universe, and that is where they find the solution they are looking for. It is their confidence that makes these apparently opposing positions so interchangeable, with a stream of thinkers switching from one position to the other with equal conviction. I am used to theists who once were atheists and atheists who once were theists challenging my uncertainties. Confidently sure of themselves, they tell me they sorted the issue years ago: 'We called the chess-board white – we call it black.'[86] At that time I had not yet discovered I could not settle permanently on either square. I knew I was religious. With Emily Dickinson, I felt this world was not conclusion. With Ludwig Wittgenstein, I accepted that to be religious 'is to know that the facts of the world are not the end of the matter',[87] and that 'even when all *possible* scientific questions have been answered, the problems of life have still not been touched at all'.[88] And I thought I had a god I believed in. He was the father in Jesus's Parable of the Prodigal Son, the patriarch who abandoned all standards of proper behaviour and rushed like an insane lover to embrace his delinquent son. He was the god A.S.J. Tessimond called X in his poem 'Heaven'.

> . . . X is never annoyed
> Or shocked; has read his Jung and knows his Freud,

He gives you time in heaven to do as you please,
To climb love's gradual ladder by slow degrees
Gently to rise from soul to soul, to ascend
To a world of timeless joy, world without end.

Here on the gates of pearl there hangs no sign
Limiting cakes and ale, forbidding wine . . .

And X, of whom no coward is afraid,
Who's friend consulted, not fierce king obeyed;
Who hears the unspoken thought, the prayer unprayed;
Who expects not even the learned to understand
His universe, extends a prodigal hand,
Full of forgiveness, over his promised land.[89]

So I was comfortable with my religious position when the call
came. Besides, I wanted to get back to Scotland, preferably to
Edinburgh. If I knew anything about myself by this time, it
was that I loved that city above all other places. Saying 'Yes' to
my election as Bishop of Edinburgh in 1986 was to come home.
But it was a twisting road I took to get there.

In the spring of 1984 John Macquarrie, one of my professors at Union, then Canon of Christ Church and Lady Margaret
Professor of Divinity in the University of Oxford, wrote to
me in Boston to ask if I would be interested in becoming vicar
of Saint Mary Magdalen's in Oxford, Christ Church having
been patrons of the living since the Reformation. It was a
church I knew, a church I was fond of. I had spent part of my
last summer before leaving for America leading a preaching
mission in the parish. I had come to associate it with the duality
that I realised was part of my make-up, though it was the sense

273

of geographical dislocation that marked my consciousness that summer. Oxford was lovely that June, and between my engagements in the mission I walked in Christ Church Meadows and Port Meadow reflecting on my situation. I was suspended between two realities, the one I had just left in Edinburgh and the other across the Atlantic I would soon travel to. Oxford was a good place for such a mood. As I walked through those sunlit days, I asked myself where I belonged. I was uprooted from one spot and not yet planted in another. I wondered if I had settled anywhere since leaving Alexandria. I had rooted myself in Kelham and been snatched away. Since then it was as though a bit of me was always poised for flight, with my rucksack packed, ready to leave at a moment's notice while everyone else was sleeping. Mary Mags, sometimes just Mags to her members, was tender to my mood. She was a kindly church, softened by the light that filtered through her windows, evoking a mood of quiet English tolerance.

She had been on her plot at the foot of Saint Giles in Oxford since Hugh of Lincoln rebuilt her in 1194 to replace a wooden church burned down by Viking raiders, and she had lived through many changes. In 1841 the young architect who would go on to build Kelham Hall in Nottinghamshire was employed to 'improve' her while he was working on the Martyrs' Memorial immediately north of the church. Her most radical change had occurred in the 1950s, during the incumbency of Colin Stephenson, who had revved up her already Anglo-Catholic style into a liturgy that made pontifical celebrations in Saint Peter's Rome look like Calvinist funerals. Even in her improved state, there was something unassumingly medieval about Mags. It was a building that seemed to me to be more tolerant of than committed to the antics of its Anglo-Catholic inhabitants, probably because it had long memories. Its closest memories, however, were of generations of students, John Betjeman among them, whose faith had been fanned into life by the colourful extravagance of its liturgy.

> Those were the days when that divine baroque
> Transformed our English altars and our ways.
> Fiddle-back chasuble in mid-Lent pink
> Scandalized Rome and Protestants alike . . .[90]

I made lifelong friends at Mags, but the unease I had experienced in my debates with Graham Leonard in Chicago in 1979 resurfaced with new urgency. Mary Mags had become the bell-weather of extreme reactions to the ordination of women among Anglo-Catholics, an issue that was now well and truly confronting the Church. My predecessor as vicar of Mags had gone to Rome over it, and my successor was to do the same, along with a significant group of parishioners who relocated themselves to Saint Aloysius Catholic Church just along the Woodstock Road. I was not in Oxford long enough to make any lasting impression on the congregation or to influence its thinking on the issue of women's ordination that was so obsessing the Anglo-Catholic wing of the Church. It was my successor's successor who helped Mags through this painful time and guided it into a more inclusive type of Anglican Catholicism. But brief as they were, I began to confirm something about myself during those two years in Oxford, something that would become a source of anger and disappointment to others not only in Anglo-Catholicism, but, ultimately, in the wider Church.

Its outward sign was an increasing passion for long-distance walking. One of the reasons I was glad to be back in Britain was that I was now able to do the kind of hiking I needed. New England was intensely wooded and walks were invariably between trees till one got to the bald summit of the hill and could see the view. I loved being back in open country, and I soon got to know the walks near Oxford in long treks on my days off and during holidays. I was a fast walker, intent on covering the territory, rarely looking round me as I moved, always in my head. This need to push on and eat up the miles is why I prefer to walk alone. It was the writing of Bruce Chatwin that helped me understand that as a man walks so he lives. Chatwin loved nomads. He believed that most of the ills we suffer from are the result of settling down, not moving on; of trying to possess and exploit creation, instead of treating it with the courtesy of passing guests. I began to realise that my walking was symbolic, the sign of a nomadic nature, a non-settler, yet my other mind longed for a place of abiding. And with this divided nature I had found myself as a leader of the wing of an institution that thought of itself as possessing fixed and unalterable truth. At this stage I hadn't made the moves that would find me out, hadn't even found myself out. It was the next move that would do it, the bishop's move. Bishops are supposed to be defenders of the Faith. Like the medieval knight sworn to defend the chastity of his lady against all assaults, the bishop was supposed to be the protector of the integrity of Christian doctrine. History contradicts the perfection of the theory, of course, as it contradicts all perfect theories. The record shows that bishops are as prone to dispute and disagreement as any other species. But the theory had the magnetic attraction of all shining delusions, and bishops had to pledge it their allegiance. The Diocese of Edinburgh elected me as their Bishop on a March Saturday in 1986, and I accepted the call. They set 11 June, the Feast of Saint Barnabas, for my consecration, the same day I had been ordained a priest by Francis Moncreiff in Glasgow in 1960.

But first I had to prepare myself. It was the night vigil in Kelham Chapel all over again, a time for self-examination and resolution. I went from Oxford into a silent retreat in Kent, where the past ambushed me with an old loss. When I rolled up at the convent at the beginning of the week I was to spend there, the Guest Mistress informed me that they had a temporary chaplain in residence, someone who knew me. At Evensong I recognised the black cowl and red girdle of the Society of the Sacred Mission. And I remembered him who was wearing it. How could I not? We spoke to each other briefly that evening before I went into silence. I discovered that he was back in England after thirty years in South Africa. He was seeking release from his vows to the Society, vows pledged under the great dome that softened the jagged silhouette I always searched for above the distant trees as the train rushed through Newark. He was another leaver. He looked tougher, more weathered, both within and without, but he was much as I remembered him. We did not reminisce about the holiday we had taken together in Devon and Cornwall many summers ago. On my last evening I made my confession to him in the convent chapel. As I expected, he was gentle. He knew whereof I was made, remembered I was but dust. And as Father Stanton used to say to the poor of late nineteenth-century London from the pulpit of Saint Alban's Holborn, 'You can't always expect dust to be up to the mark.' I wasn't up to the mark either, but I experienced absolution's rush as my old companion spoke the familiar words over me.

He came out to see me into my car the next morning, the morning of my departure. I was about to turn the key in the ignition when I remembered the rosebay willowherb flaming at the roadside that long ago summer. I mentioned it, recalled the vacation we had taken together.

'We were in love,' he said.

'Yes,' I replied. A quiet disturbance threaded my mind, *an invisible procession going by.* 'Can I do anything for you, help in any way?'

'A radio,' he said. 'I'd like a transistor radio for the flat I'm moving into.'

'Is that all I can do?'

'That's all.'

I promised to send him one (and did) and drove off to take my vows in Edinburgh. The disturbance came with me, carrying the memory of an old disappointment. My emotion on the day of my consecration had nothing to do with defending Christian Orthodoxy; it was all about not disappointing God again. Would it be different this time?

Scotland had changed a lot in the years I had been away, as it moved inexorably towards the restoration of its own parliament after 300 years, but Edinburgh was the same. I made my promises in Saint Mary's Cathedral on a shining June day. Though I had always admired Saint Mary's, she was another magnificent building I had never been able to love. I was proud of the way she dominated the Edinburgh skyline from many perspectives, particularly the view from Calton Hill, well tramped by me and my dog Kip in our Old Saint Paul's days. From there you looked the length of Princes Street to the West End where the three great towers of Saint Mary's sat confidently on the horizon. Bishops don't run their cathedrals, but they spend more time around them than in the other churches in their dioceses, so I was able to get to know Saint Mary's intimately over the next fourteen years. She was another Gilbert Scott Victorian Gothic spectacular, completed in 1879. I grew fond of her, but my affection never deepened into helpless love. But one corner moved me and touched that old regret. The diocese of Edinburgh had been established by King Charles I in 1633, and there was a little chapel in the north transept of the cathedral dedicated to the royal martyr, as loyal Episcopalians described him. It wasn't used a lot, but I liked it when I was at the Eucharist there early on a winter morning, the wind howling outside, the cathedral hushed as the surrounding city began to wake in the dark. I thought of the king's last days of freedom at Kelham Hall before his arrest in 1647. I pictured his disconsolate walk there, a walk I knew well. I remembered the twelve yew trees, the hidden graveyard, as another circle closed. But Saint Mary's moved me most on late October afternoons when shadows peopled the nave and the chancel was bright with red-cassocked choristers singing Evensong.

> In the stillness of autumn quiet,
> We have heard the still, small voice.
> We have sung *Oh where is wisdom?*
> Thick paper, folio, Boyce.[91]

Apart from lurking round cathedrals, what do bishops do? As is inevitable in an institution that takes itself very seriously and robes even its most straightforward activities in transcendental garments, the meaning of *episcopos* has been mystified by the Church over the centuries. The word means 'overseer', which suggests bossing, but can also be translated as 'looking after'.

In particular, the bishop looks after those who look after others, the clergy. *He saved others, himself he cannot save.* Those words had haunted me since my years in Gorbals. They capture the spiritual loneliness of clergy. They look after others, themselves they cannot look after. And the bishop is supposed to fill the gap.

The bishop is the *pastor pastorum,* pastor of the pastors, and it's the best thing about the role. It means keeping in touch with clergy and their families, who are far from immune to the problems that afflict the rest of humanity, but may be disposed to pretend they don't happen to them because of the expectations that are imposed upon them by their parishioners. It was this that most troubled me as a young priest, this sense people had that I must be purer and more rarefied than they because of the strip of plastic round my neck, when I knew that the opposite was the case. There are few jobs in the world in which perfection is part of the person spec, but it is implicit in the case of clergy, which is why it is often hard for them to handle the messy stuff that comes with being human. Not that every priest trusts their bishop with the ills that beset them. Some of them may not like you. Some of them may be afraid of how you might handle compromising knowledge about them. Some of them resent the fact that you got the job they wanted for themselves or for some other candidate more in tune with their opinions. Coming into a diocese as its bishop is not unlike the position priests find themselves in when they take over a new parish. If their predecessor has been greatly loved, or had a strong rapport with particular segments of the congregation, it can take the new pastor time to win their confidence and trust. I knew about this. Both at Old Saint Paul's and the Church of the Advent I had encountered a lot of transitional grief in parishioners who saw me as a supplanter of better men. These are deep waters. So it takes time. Over the years, being alongside clergy through their sorrows and losses – the death of children, the grave illness of a spouse, heart attacks and cancer scares, drink problems, messy affairs, fractious congregations, bullying parishioners – the bishop can build up trust and maybe even earn some love. But never from everyone. So rejection also comes with the territory. But looking after the clergy, caring for the carers, was the best part of the job, the bit I liked most.

The other part I enjoyed was the queenly role, the visits to parishes in the diocese for Confirmations and Special Occasions. Edinburgh was a wonderfully varied diocese to wander in. It included vibrant city and suburban churches, as well as struggling congregations in housing schemes and small towns. And there were the lovely Border towns to visit, each with its own proud history. Since you have to do a lot of speaking and preaching as a bishop, it helps if you can string words together. Even the ability to act the fool can be useful. I learnt that from Desmond Tutu, who can't leave a church after a service without dancing down the aisle, especially if there's a good lively hymn to do it to. It wasn't everywhere I got away with that, but there were one or two places in the diocese that liked the service to rock a bit, and I was always game for a bit of jiving down the nave.

But it was not all fun and rolling in the aisles. The Church is a bureaucracy and bishops are bureaucrats who spend a lot of time in meetings, which come in layers of ever-deepening complexity. There is the diocesan administration, making sure that parishes deliver their quota – *ecclesiastese* for taxation – and keep their property in good repair. This involves the manufacture of many committees, the universally practised displacement activity for people who are not quite sure what they are supposed

281

to be doing. Next, there is the provincial bureaucracy, because bishops operate as a board of directors to oversee the work of the Church at the national level. The third tier, which you get sentenced to if you become a Primate or first bishop of a province, is the international meeting of Primates, a self-aggrandising outfit I'll return to later. It was the bureaucratic side of the job I enjoyed least, and the bit I regret most. Jesus told us in his Parable of the Prodigal Son that the young man in question wasted his substance in riotous living. He had something to show for it, however, even if it was only the moral bankruptcy that brought him home again. The Church wastes its substance in prolonged meetings to discuss and refine and endlessly reorganise itself, the mark of institutions in crisis throughout history. Those were the years the locust has eaten, barren years. I wish I could have them back.

That said, I enjoyed my time as a Scottish bishop – much more than as an Anglican Primate – but even at the diocesan level I encountered tensions with the clergy, some of which presaged more serious challenges to come. Apart from pastoring clergy and cheering up congregations, the bishop is often described as the focus of unity in the diocese. A good analogy would be the conductor who gets a large group of musicians to function as a single instrument, an *ensemble,* an orchestra. Behind the image is the fact that the Anglican Church is a coalition of diverse theologies, ranging from Romanists who only recognise the Pope's authority all the way over to Conservative Evangelicals who accord an exclusive authority to their own way of interpreting the Bible. This turbulent continuum of competing views was less pronounced in the Scottish Episcopal Church when I became a priest than when I became a bishop. The Scottish Church had been a narrow continuum throughout most of its history, ranging from middle of the road to moderately Catholic. That changed in the Eighties with the Evangelical revival and the Church Growth Movement. When I returned to Edinburgh in 1986 I discovered that a vivid new hue had been woven into the Episcopalian tartan, an electric evangelical blue.

Until this point my attitude to evangelicals was not unlike the attitude of many people to homosexuals. I knew they existed but didn't think I knew any. I came back to a diocese in which evangelicals were increasingly prominent. In my role as conductor of the diocesan orchestra I enjoyed my visits to the vibrant evangelical churches that had sprung up in the city. One in particular, on the eastern edge of the New Town, was making waves. It had been a famous and flourishing church, whose architecture was modelled on the Chapel of King's College in Cambridge, but it had fallen on hard times. The congregation was reduced to a few elderly people, faithful to the sere traditions of Scottish Episcopalianism. To revive it, my predecessor as Bishop had organised what is called a 'church-plant'. From a flourishing evangelical congregation in the west of the city a large contingent of parishioners had been infused into the dying congregation at the east end. The immigrants quickly transformed the place, and by the time I arrived in 1986 it had one of the largest congregations in the diocese, many of them students. This was because its theology had received the coveted seal of approval from the Christian Union, the evangelical association that policed the spiritual life of university students and told them which churches were safe to attend and which were to be avoided because they were doctrinally unsound. Not that I was aware of this at the time. I can't say that the pop-concert style of worship did much for me, but they clearly enjoyed it, so I was happy to join them as often as I could. In fact, I preached there more than I preached anywhere else in the diocese, because it was one of the few churches in the city that maintained evening worship on a Sunday, a favourite time for students. It was the reaction to a sermon I preached to them about the Good Samaritan in Jesus's most famous parable that alerted me to the fact that there might be trouble ahead. Appropriately, it's a parable about something that happened on a long and twisting road. I thought I was talking about the four characters in the story, but maybe I was on that twisting road myself.

Scholars vary enormously in the way they interpret the four gospels. We know they are heavily edited documents, powerfully influenced by the early Church, which read many of its own experiences back into the narratives about Jesus. This is why some scholars are sceptical about the words that have been put into his mouth by the gospel writers. But even the most sceptical scholars are convinced that in the parable of the Good Samaritan we hear the authentic voice of Jesus, and a radical and surprising voice it is. The conventional reading of the parable understands it as a condemnation of religious hypocrisy. Instead of following their religion's code of compassion, the Priest and the Levite take a wide swerve past the man who had fallen among thieves. In fact, this little story is not about the dangers of insincere religion; it is about the dangers of sincere religion. It is not about religious hypocrisy; it is about religious fidelity. That's the kick in the story, the surprise. The Priest and the Levite followed their religious code to the letter, a code that forbade them to touch foreigners or dead bodies, and the naked man by the roadside was probably both. Their heart prompted compassion, their religion prompted caution, and they followed their religion. But in the Samaritan, bound by the same code, compassion overcomes the strictures of his religion and he goes to the aid of the dangerous stranger.

The story encapsulates Jesus's attitude to the danger we are in when we allow our moral codes and religious traditions to assume absolute authority over us. We need moral and religious systems to protect us from the chaos of our passions; but if we give them absolute authority they become a greater danger to us than the unfettered passions they are supposed to curb. By this parable, and by his dismissive attitude to the rigidities of law and custom, Jesus rendered every code provisional and discardable when confronted with real human need. The meaning of the parable of the Good Samaritan was that compassion was a powerful dissolvent of inherited prejudices.[92] I advised my hearers to be alert to appropriate challenges to their unswerving convictions. Something might be waiting for them round the next bend that required the abandonment of old traditions in order to respond to a new reality.

My evangelical listeners strongly disagreed with what they took, correctly, to be the implications of my reading of the parable. Code was important to them – and a rigid code it turned out to be – with no deviation permitted from the prohibitions of traditional morality. The scriptural package was inviolable – as interpreted by them. Puzzled at first, I quickly came to realise that the source of the difficulty was the absolute authority they accorded to the words of the Bible. For them the Bible's ancient codes were non-negotiable *because they came from outside*. We couldn't handle scripture the way we would handle any other text *because it wasn't like any other text*. We couldn't negotiate the standards of the Bible the way we negotiate other conflicting opinions. Conservative Evangelicals, I discovered, did not negotiate. They asserted what had come to them from above, from *Outside. It was written,* so the matter was closed. If human history could be at least partly understood as a journey into new knowledge, then to go on that journey convinced you already knew everything there was to know about human relations foreclosed the future entirely. There could be no stranger waiting round the next bend offering you a new annunciation. Everything that needed to be known was already known. Apart from anything else, it struck me as a very unexciting way to live. But, then, I mused, some people did not like excitement, while I probably liked it too much. No major rupture followed between us after my sermon, but it hoisted a warning flag in their minds. There was something not quite sound about the Bishop's theology, particularly his ethics, or the way he thinks about ethics. We'd better keep an eye on him. On my side, a distant alarm sounded. There's potential for turbulence here. Is this something we can agree to disagree about or is it a deal-breaker? Time alone would tell. Interpreting the Bible was clearly a minefield. I'd better be careful. That was going to be difficult, because I knew I was genetically deficient in the carefulness gene.

And another warning flag was flying above the field. This one was not about bibles, but about bishops and other clergy. Specifically, it was about the attempt by women to breach these callings that had been shut against them for so long. They had won their battle for inclusion just about everywhere else. Surely it was only a matter of time before the Church gave way and admitted them to ordination. I knew from my debates with Graham Leonard that this was not going to be easy. It was the *Outside* dimension again. As far as the Church saw it, the Ministry was not a calling like any other, it was a transcendental vocation, so normal negotiating processes did not apply. I first encountered the height of the difficulty in a conversation I had with the Bishop of Accra when I was with him in Ghana in the Fifties. In a casual conversation over dinner one night I demonstrated a functional approach to the office of bishop as the best way to manage the pastoral and administrative needs of the Church. Coming from Scotland, I was aware that the Kirk had a different, more collegial system of church governance, called Presbyterianism. It never occurred to me that, whatever the dissimilarities in the two systems, they could be anything other than different ways of doing the same job. I was solemnly corrected by the Bishop. He pointed out to me that the Order of Bishops in the Anglican Communion was not a functional convenience, not even an anciently hallowed functional convenience, but a divinely mandated succession through which the authority of the original apostles was passed on to the Church. And it had a physical aspect to it. The first apostles handed on their authority to their successors by laying their hands on them; their successors did the same thing to the next generation; and so on right down the centuries, creating an unbroken pipeline of authority called Apostolic Succession. Break the line or go for a new supplier and you lose the original *mana*.

It is this theory, based on little in the way of historical evidence, which is the biggest source of division among Christians. You can call yourself a bishop; you can wear the gear and strut your stuff under a three-decker mitre; you can swing your crozier with a drum major's dexterity; but if you did not receive your authority through that official pipeline of grace, then you are a deceiver and not a true bishop. One of the most passionately played board games in Christianity is *Who's On and Who's Off the Pipeline?* The Roman Catholic Church claims exclusive ownership of it and either invalidates or qualifies the orders of all other Churches. It claims, for instance, that the Anglican Church switched to a rogue supplier at the Reformation and therefore has no valid ministers. But that's only how the game begins. Anglicans claim that their orders are intact, because they did not switch suppliers at the Reformation but merely added a new branch to the pipeline. Calvinists, on the other hand, are not only proud to have switched suppliers, they claim that the Catholic pipeline had been degraded from the beginning and was never connected to Christ *but to SOMEONE ELSE*. Enough! I am becoming sarcastic. Suffice it to say that a new move was being proposed in the pipeline game, and I need to mention it before moving on, because how it was played had an important effect on my own thinking about the Church. Suppose you went along with the pipeline theory of ordination out of respect for tradition or because of its symbolic value or because you thought it guaranteed some kind of professional accreditation for ministry: what would happen if a woman's head were put under the pipe and what, if anything, was to stop us doing it? Those questions were being asked with increasing urgency, and the opposing battalions were already lining up their theological artillery against each other.

A moment of further thought on these ecclesiastical disputes brings the recognition that this heightening and abstracting of professional roles is by no means confined to religion, and is, in fact, an aspect of the male dominance of all institutions throughout most of history. This was the point that had been repeatedly put to me in my office at the Advent by the women who had challenged me to think more deeply about the matter. Patriarchal religion may add a transcendental spin to male assertiveness and apply an extra coat of brightly coloured enamel to male vanity, but it is essentially a subgenre of the universal power game among men, the only difference being that its pretensions extend the action into the next world as well as controlling it in this one. It was women who really understood what was going on here, and it was women who helped to open the eyes of men to the games they were playing. Apart from my female Advent parishioners, another woman who helped to open my eyes was Virginia Woolf. In her tract *Three Guineas* she contrasts *the private house*, woman's sphere, with *public life*, man's sphere.

> Your world, then, the world of professional, of public life, seen from this angle undoubtedly looks queer. At first sight it is enormously impressive. Within a small space are crowded together St Paul's, the Bank of England, the Mansion House, the massive if funereal battlements of the Law Courts; and on the other side, Westminster Abbey and the Houses of Parliament. There we say to ourselves, pausing, in this moment of transition on the bridge, our fathers and brothers have spent their lives. All these hundreds of years they have been mounting those steps, passing in and out of those doors, ascending those pulpits, preaching, money-making, administering justice. It is from this world that the private house . . . has derived its creeds, its laws, its clothes and carpets, its beef and mutton. And then, as is now permissible, cautiously pushing aside the swing doors of one of these temples, we enter on tiptoe and survey the scene in greater detail. The first sensation of colossal size, of majestic masonry is broken up into a myriad points of amazement mixed with interrogation. Your clothes in the first place make us gape with astonishment. How many, how splendid, how

extremely ornate they are – the clothes worn by the educated man in his public capacity! Now you dress in violet; a jewelled crucifix swings on your breast; now your shoulders are covered with lace; now furred with ermine; now slung with many linked chains set with precious stones. Now you wear wigs on your heads; rows of graduated curls descend your necks. Now your hats are boat-shaped, or cocked; now they mount in cones of black fur; now they are made of brass and scuttle shaped; now plumes of red, now of blue hair surmount them. Sometimes gowns cover your legs; sometimes gaiters.* Tabards embroidered with lions and unicorns swing from your shoulders; metal objects cut in star shapes or in circles glitter and twinkle upon your breasts. Ribbons of all colours – blue, purple, crimson – cross from shoulder to shoulder.

Even stranger, however, than the symbolic splendour of your clothes are the ceremonies that take place when you wear them. Here you kneel; there you bow; here you advance in procession behind a man carrying a silver poker; here you mount a carved chair; here you appear to do homage to a piece of painted wood; here you abase yourselves before tables covered with richly worked tapestry. And whatever these ceremonies may mean you perform them always together, always in step, always in the uniform proper to the man and the occasion.[93]

Woolf makes two observations about this male exhibitionism, this parade of peacock's feathers. It is, she believes,

---

* Anglican bishops used to wear gaiters, but not any longer.

a way of demonstrating superiority over other people; more significantly, it encourages a disposition towards war. She meant the observation literally – she was writing in 1938 as the clouds of war gathered over Europe – but there are different kinds of warfare, and theological warfare is one of the most petty and pernicious. She might have said to the garishly uniformed executives of the Church, 'You pride yourselves on being men of peace and concord, but your finely graduated distinctions of dress, with their heavenly justifications, are but the religious manifestation of the power game men have been playing for centuries. If you must go on playing it, at least have the courage of Nietzsche to admit your power lust and spare us your pieties.' She wasn't around to make those points when the game reached a new intensity in the Eighties and Nineties. I was, and it would change my life.

14

DRIFTING

It would be wrong to give the impression that the life of a bishop, or the life of the Church for that matter, is one of constant struggle and controversy. Religion is certainly a vexatious subject, and it gives rise to a lot of disagreement, as the history of splits and schisms in Christianity clearly indicates. But if conflict is a constant in Christian history, so is consolation, and the Church's ancient ministry of comfort to the afflicted goes a long way towards mitigating its record for discord and intolerance. Even bishops can be useful here. If not by rolling up their purple sleeves and getting themselves stuck in, certainly by identifying areas of need in their community and finding the right people to tackle them. I had already encountered HIV/AIDS in Boston and seen it scything remorselessly through the gay community. I had heard the hatred the epidemic had prompted from some sections of the Christian community. I had also seen other sections of the Church organise itself to respond with love to people who were HIV-positive and to those with full-blown AIDS. I had seen the crisis bring out the best and the worst in people, but it was the best that prevailed and, in the end, it silenced the taunting voices of the Christian Right. It was to prevail in Edinburgh as well.

Catching up with the press on my return to Scotland, I was

surprised to see that Edinburgh had been labelled 'The AIDS Capital of Europe'. The demography of the epidemic was different to the one in Boston, however. It was certainly taking its toll of gay men, but the biggest risk group were intravenous drug users, and dirty needles were identified as the culprits. This new twist in the story of the virus, now an irresistible combination of sex and drugs, was a delicious mix for the puritan mind to obsess about. We heard all the traditional anthems that identified HIV as God's judgement on sin, but they were more muted than in the States, and we did not waste much energy opposing them. I was already clear that there was no point in negotiating with fundamentalists. By definition, they did not negotiate. You had to accept them as an inevitable part of the *dramatis personae* of the human comedy, like the old man who for years had been walking Princes Street wearing a sandwich board announcing that The End of the World is Nigh. We didn't argue; we organised. As was the case in the US, the medical profession was in the forefront. Soon free needle-exchanges were set up and free condoms were handed out in clinics and health centres. A hospice for the dying, Milestone House, named after an old Roman milestone found near the site, was opened in 1991 by Princess Diana, who continued to support its work till her own death.

The churches of Edinburgh across the ecumenical spectrum weren't far behind the doctors in rising to the challenge, and a host of imaginative ventures was established. One, conceived and administered by Helen Mein, the wife of a priest in the diocese, was called Positive Help. As the label suggested, its large team of volunteers provided help and support to people with HIV and AIDS, such as driving them from Edinburgh's most afflicted housing scheme on the north side of the capital for treatment at the City Hospital and Milestone House, miles away on the south side. Jeannie did her share of ferrying. Like many of the clergy, I gave my support to a lot of these activities. I sat on committees and spoke at events, but the biggest contribution I made was to identify the unusual gifts of a woman in the diocese, whom I appointed as our chaplain to people affected by HIV/AIDS. She was an example of the hidden work of love that goes on everywhere behind Christianity's bluster and posturing, and helps to redeem them. She possessed in abundance a gift I conspicuously lacked. It was the gift I had already noticed and envied in Lilias and Geoff back in our Gorbals days, the capacity to abandon their own interests and preferences and, as Hugh MacDiarmid put it in the poem I have already quoted, sink:

> . . . without another care
> To that dread level of nothing but life itself.

MacDiarmid went on to describe it as the capacity for 'mere being', and he thought it was more common in women than in men. It is the ability to wait beside someone when the waiting is all that can be done or ought to be done. I have been too driven and purposeful in my life to be good at this, and that failure is now one of my deepest regrets. I have, of course, screwed myself up to do it when I had to. I have waited by bedsides of the sick and dying, but I have always been conscious of the meter whirring away inside my impatient soul, calling me to the next thing and the next. Jane Millard had the capacity for waiting, the ability to sink to the level of nothing but life itself, and she had it to an unimaginable degree. During the heavy early years of the epidemic in Edinburgh, before doctors developed combined drug therapies that kept people alive, AIDS was still a death sentence, and a grim one. This meant that Jane's was a parish of the dying and the grieving. It meant waiting, again and again, beside men and women whose young lives were being stolen from them by the virus. It took its toll on her, the way war takes its toll on soldiers who live with relentless grief. At the height of the crisis she was involved in two hundred funerals. An aspect of the art of her ministry was to craft services that gave expression to anger as well as grief. Above all, it was an art that celebrated the courage and humour of those she had accompanied to the end. Of enormous cost to her were sixty long vigils she kept by the bedsides of dying friends, as she helped them slip their moorings and drift from life. During these vigils she kept notes scribbled on the backs of envelopes or any other scraps of paper she could lay her hands on at the time. She called her scraps 'Fragments of the Watch'. In one of our regular meetings to find out how she was coping, she told me about them, and I asked to see them. The next time we met she brought them in a plastic bag. Scraps of torn envelopes, pages from old notebooks, anything she could lay her hands on at the time to record the going out of another life. They were more moving to me than the famous 'AIDS Quilt' that was touring the world at the time. In 1987 a group in San Francisco had started the Names Project, in which three-by-six foot quilted panels, memorialising those who had died of AIDS in America, were stitched into a quilt. As the toll mounted, the quilt kept growing till it could have filled hundreds of football pitches. Part of it came to Edinburgh, and I went to see it. It was hard not to be stunned by the loss of these thousands of young lives, each represented by the tender art of the quilter. It reminded me of how hurt I felt at Old Saint

Paul's when, after leading them down the stairs and under the bridge to their final resting place, I had to come back and write the names of the dead in that heavy old book in the sacristy. Death had undone so many, *and I had to write down their names*. Jane's fragments brought back that sorrow. To sift through them was to touch worlds of grief. I asked her to let me publish them, but she refused. They were sacred to her and she wanted to keep them secret. More than twenty years later, she has allowed me to include four of them here in their raw state.

> How do you think dying is?
> I think I will fly
> Bird or plane?
> Bird, eagle or something
> My mind fills with passages – Isaiah, psalms, already on
>   my way to making his service of celebration and
>   thanksgiving.
> But he is very close to death now. An eye flutters open.
> 'Going by boat,' he says distinctly.
> Upsetting my plans.
> So at his service I read the story where Peter walks on
>   the water, and Our Lord catches him, and then gets
>   into the boat to go the rest of the journey with him
> . . . just to make sure he gets there.

I only had one conversation with you, and only because I knew you had been a jockey, could discern it was something about horses. Your Mum and Dad had been sent for as you had taken another dip in your laboured breathing. I wanted you to know that you could just slip away, or wait for them to arrive, so I offered a journey.

It's a crisp summer afternoon – a real Scottish summer – and you are riding down a path in a wood. The path is covered in forest debris, and the hooves make that muted thud of a measured stride. You are bareback, and can feel the warmth of his skin against yours, feel the power from his rippling muscles in the springy step of his keen walk.

It's up to you when you move on a pace. Remember that you are bareback and will come to the point when you are losing control, his heaving, sweaty sides like glass. If you want to wait for them, keep him back under your control.

If you are ready, let the reins go slack and get the rush from the exhilarating gallop.

At the bottom of the track is a high gate. Jumping that is your transformation. Remember you are the one to urge him on or hold him back. You are in control.

Your Mum and Dad are on their way, and can be with you as you jump that gate if that's what you want. He's a wonderful horse, you are well matched. Ride well.

Days from dying, he insisted that he teach me to fish, and we made a precarious journey to Flotterstone so he could talk fishy tactics. In his day, he could catch fish with his hands.

When he was dying, he began to bleed heavily from most orifices, but the nurses graciously allowed me to accompany him undisturbed by clean bedding. The warmth of the blood on his thighs became the numbness of water on wading boots as I used his teaching from those few days before to take him fishing. I had in my mind's eye that the scooping of the fish from the water in a rainbow of droplets would be his leaving. But it wasn't like that. He began to gulp air like a fish, he became that fish, and I couldn't put him back in the water.

She was very afraid of dying. 'I don't want to die. Him upstairs will get a big stick and shout at me, tell me to go to hell. I'm frightened. I don't want to be shouted at.'

And I hugged her, bereft of anything theological to say that sounded real, and she snuggled in.

'Talk to me,' she whimpered.

'There was a man who had two sons . . .' and I told her the story of the prodigal son and loving father.

'Will you be with me when I die? Be sure and tell me that story.'

So I did, about an hour ago, now we are waiting for the undertakers.[94]

At the height of the American epidemic a Manhattan doctor had reminded me of Camus' words about another plague, that 'there are more things to admire in men than to despise'.[95] Holding Jane's 'Fragments of the Watch' in my hands, I wondered if Camus' words could be applied to the Church. I tried it: *there are more things to admire in the Church than to despise.* Not a bad fit, I thought. Not perfect, but good enough. And people don't always hear it. They hear the scary voices. Sadly, there seemed to be a lot of Christians who liked making the scary voices. The congregations that were growing, the ones good at evangelising, were the scary ones, the ones that spoke with absolute conviction about everything. Conviction sells. Did that mean that uncertain, unjudging Christianity was on the way out? Or was there something we could do about it? Was liberal evangelism an oxymoron? Can there be an evangelism of uncertainty, if what seems to attract people to the churches that are growing is their hard-edged certainty? I felt there was something unhealthy about an approach to Church growth that worked by persuading people they were suffering from a terminal disease called Sin for which only their Church had the cure. I liked neither the message nor the effect it had on the people it persuaded. It hardened them and gave them a sense of their exceptionalism. *And they didn't negotiate!* How could you engage with people who did not negotiate?

I was musing in this way because there was no doubt the Church was shrinking in Britain – except among Evangelicals, although there was even some doubt about the nature of their success. Some analysts thought they were only recycling other Christians into their own swimming pool, rather than recruiting absolute outsiders. I gave them the benefit of the doubt and thought they probably were bringing in fresh blood. I just didn't much care for what they did with the new blood when they got it. Bishops at the time, no matter the discomfort they felt about the subject, were supposed to be leading their dioceses in an aspiration called the Decade of Evangelism, designed to turn back the tide of faith from Matthew Arnold's 'melancholy, long, withdrawing roar'.[96] We were to reverse the statistics of decline. Christianity was a missionary religion, we were told. It did not grow by osmosis; it grew by selling itself, which was difficult if your theology did not easily lend itself to the kind of packaging that seemed to work in today's religious market-place. But where was there to turn?

I was intrigued to find a little book by John Saxbee, called *Liberal Evangelism*. Maybe it isn't an oxymoron after all, I thought. What I liked about Saxbee's book was what he called the Parable of the Two Tunes. He referred to the American modernist composer Charles Ives, who discovered as a boy that he could hear two tunes in his head at the same time and follow them both faithfully. That, said Saxbee, is what liberal Christians do. They listen to the Christian tradition, but they also listen to the best tunes of the time in which they live, its science and philosophy and ethics and its struggles with human change and discovery. Living that way, being faithful to two tunes at the same time, produces tension, but it is an honest tension, a creative tension. It is more honest than only listening to the past and ostentatiously turning off your hearing device when the present intrudes, which is what the more conservative traditions do. Shortly after receiving that insight, I was in Arkansas speaking at a conference. My co-presenter was a young American priest called Alice Mann, who was talking about how to make the Church more inviting, how to draw people by its beauty of caring, by its warmth and welcome, and by its openness to the future. Bingo, I thought, she's what we are looking for, if this Decade of Evangelism thing is to reflect the ethos of the Scottish Church. Back home, the Scottish bishops agreed to give it a go. We covenanted with Alice to work for us, and a Church Growth programme with a difference was born. *Liberal Evangelism!* We called it Mission 21. If it did nothing else, it cheered us up and helped us realise that there was something about us that was worth inviting others to join.

Mission statements were part of the rhetoric of the time, and the one I dreamt up for the Scottish Church seemed to sum us up, though it probably only summed up my own wishful thinking: 'We are the Church for people other Churches won't take in.' It sat well with another buzzword of the time. The Liberation Theologians of South America, soon to be on the receiving end of the Papal censor, had coined a phrase that spoke to me. They said the Gospel had a bias towards the poor. I agreed, but not just the economically poor. The ones who loved Jesus most were not just the economically poor, they were the ones who also understood their own moral and spiritual poverty; yet this man, this Son of Man, loved them and took them to himself just as they were. I couldn't see why this saving theme could not also apply to our poverty of belief. Was there a place around Jesus not only for the morally poor but also for the theologically poor, for those who were not able to afford the expensive packages on offer in the confident Churches? Was there a gap for a Church that accepted the theologically confused because it acknowledged its own theological confusion? Was there a gap for a Church that accepted the unacceptable because it knew itself to be unacceptable? As I thought about it, it did not seem to me to be an eccentric mission statement. It would have fitted the earliest days of the Jesus movement, when it consisted of the ritually and morally impure, the tax collectors and sinners, the ones excluded from the ranks of the righteous, the doubters and the uncertain. I belonged there myself. I was uncomfortable with high-octane believers and high-performance spiritual achievers. Of the priests in the province who caught the vision, a significant proportion were gay and were therefore already officially unacceptable. Like gay priests in most places, they were the ones working in the tough and struggling parishes, while the thriving evangelical parishes tended to be in prosperous neighbourhoods where holding the right kind of religion seemed to be another mark of success. My mission statement was a signal to those who felt themselves excluded by the more upmarket brands that our doors were open to them and we hoped they'd come and join us. Many of them did. But not everyone was happy with this theological downward mobility. There was the other Church, the Church of the elect, the Church of the redeemed, the ones who been fished from the sea of destruction. What kind of evangelist started swimming with the damned instead of hauling them into the boat? The warning signals were being hoisted again. And, consciously or unconsciously, I seemed to be going out of my way to provoke those who were running them up the pole.

Never good at guarding my tongue, I became more careless. Was I subconsciously sabotaging my own position, offering free ammunition to my enemies? I was becoming a riddle to myself and a scandal to others, some of them good friends. I was in a position of authority, but I had become anti-authoritarian. Ordained to defend the faith and uphold sound doctrine, I started trying to revise – if not actually subvert – key aspects of the Christian moral tradition. There was plenty of precedent for what I was doing, but it was not a popular role for a bishop. Reforms to Church and Society usually come from the edge, from those who are the victims of the cruel certainties of power, though they try to find allies at the heart of the institutions they are seeking to change. The victim's role on the margins is well understood, even by those in power; but what are we to make of people in power who start doubting their own position and subverting it in public?

The trouble was, I seemed to have a need to think out loud. A friend accused me of leaving no thought unpublished and wondered why I did it, when all it did was get me in trouble. I wasn't sure myself, but I went on issuing bulletins on how I was seeing things. I had started writing when I came to Edinburgh in 1968 and my early books were all slight and rather facile exercises in devotional theology, designed to help people struggling with issues of faith. You don't have to be Sigmund Freud to work it out. The most that can be said for those early books was that in knocking them off every other year, sometimes two a year, I was at least learning to write. When I became a bishop the tone changed and the books became less facile, probably because the struggle was becoming more existential. A turning-point was the book I published in 1988, a couple of years after becoming a bishop. The title was significant: *Crossfire: Faith and Doubt in an Age of Certainty.* The certainties I struggled with in the book were political as well as theological. This was the time of strong political convictions called up by Mrs Thatcher's premiership, but it was also a time of increasing theological conviction and conservatism. The tone of the book was troubled rather than subversive. It called for a change of tone in theological debate and for greater modesty in the claims we made. It asked disputants to recognise that no certainty was available to us as we wrestled with ultimate questions, though there were glimmers and whispers to encourage us. Nine years later in 1997, when we were well into the wars over sexuality that were dividing Christians even more violently than they were dividing secular opinion, I wrote a book that was intended to be frankly subversive and challenging. *Dancing on the Edge*,[97] which called for a re-evaluation of the Church's moral teaching on sex, particularly in its attitude to gay and lesbian people. I called for legalised same-sex partnerships in the State and saw no reason why the Church could not craft suitable liturgies for same-sex unions, different from but modelled on heterosexual marriage. The book earned me the soubriquet of the most hated clergyman in Britain. Fortunately, on catching sight of that headline I remembered Aneurin Bevan's nonchalant assertion that 'the smile of *The Express* was fatal'. If its smile could kill, maybe its scowl would turn out to be a blessing. Most people don't read the books of figures who find themselves in the glare of publicity, preferring the easy headline to the graft of following an argument, but I had only myself to blame for some of the other fixes I got myself into. I wrote books that gave people the opportunity to find out what I really thought, if they were interested, but I also had a fatal flair for off-the-cuff remarks that generated headlines. Two incidents went far to justify the Press's description of me as the current Barmy Bishop, a post in the national comedy that had become vacant on the retirement of David Jenkins from Durham.

During my brief sojourn in Oxford I had written a short book that set out to offer a positive exegesis of the seven deadly sins.[98] The idea behind the book was the background reports social workers prepare for magistrates before they pass sentence on offenders. Could we not explore the classic typology of sin with a view to understanding what prompted it and maybe get a better handle on how to deal with it? The New Testament encouraged this approach. One of the Greek verbs for *sin* was an archery term, *hamartano,* which meant 'missing the mark'. A sin was not an activity that was wrong in itself; it was misdirected effort, a good volition that went wrong or went too far. This exegesis was helpful in dealing with a sin like gluttony; it was also helpful in understanding *lust.* The book attracted little comment at the time, but I revisited the theme when I was Bishop of Edinburgh, and this time it caused an international brouhaha. I was invited by the Rector of Saint John's Princes Street to deliver a series of lectures on the Church and the Sexual Revolution. It was hard to resist a topic like that, one I'd been wrestling with most of my life. A week before the lectures, I was phoned by a stringer from the Press Association.

She'd seen a piece about the series in the Edinburgh *Evening News* and was intrigued. The journalist who'd done the piece she referred to was someone I admired, but his headline, as headlines usually do, had sensationalised what I had told him: BORN TO BE WILD, SAYS BISHOP. I'd been reading some of the new evolutionary psychology published in America at the time, especially Robert Wright's *The Moral Animal* and David Suzuki and Peter Knudtson on *Genethics*. Their theme was the tension between the reproductive imperative and our moral sense. Human contentment was found in ruling rather than being ruled by the sexual drive – not that it was ever going to be easy, as universal human experience could testify. The woman from the PA wanted to know more. I was about to leave for Lincoln where I was to give a lecture at the Theological College. I gave her a highly compressed version of what I'd told the *Evening News*, and rushed to Waverley for the train. The diocese had given me a mobile phone, but I rarely had it on and hardly ever used it. For emergencies only, was my policy. It went with me to Lincoln in the off position. As I was heading for bed in the college that night they brought me an urgent message to phone my press secretary, who'd been trying to contact me all day on my switched-off mobile. When I reached him he told me that a story had gone out on the wire reporting that I had said adultery was no longer a sin and the Church should remove it from the Ten Commandments. The world press had been on the phone all day and I'd better be prepared for the shit storm that was heading my way tomorrow.

On the train back my face stared out at me from the tabloids being read by my fellow passengers. I'd done it this time. LET US SIN, SAYS BARMY BISHOP. NINE COMMANDMENTS NOW! ADULTERY OFF THE LIST. And so on. When I got off the train at Waverley's platform 11 the Press was waiting for me, including television cameras and foreign journalists. There were about fifty of them, all shouting questions and shoving cameras in my face. My press secretary, wild-eyed as if he had not slept for weeks, hustled me into a cab. This won't go away unless you hold a press conference and explain yourself, he said, so we planned one for the next day. That evening Jeremy Paxman gave me an amused grilling on *Newsnight*, where I was up against one of the leaders of the Anglo-Catholic movement in England. I don't often wield Bible texts in argument, but I had a moment of quiet satisfaction as I watched him spluttering when I quoted the words of Jesus to those who wanted to stone the woman taken in adultery: 'He that is without sin among you, let him cast the first stone.' The press conference turned out to be a good-natured affair, and a more measured interpretation of my views appeared in the broadsheets. As well as the Press, I had to deal with letters from all over the globe, including one from a Turkish Muslim who advised me to convert to Islam because it took a more generous view of the imperious urges of male sexuality. I thanked him, but declined the invitation. When the time came for the lectures, the Press turned up in droves, as did demonstrators bearing placards denouncing me. I tried to make the lectures as boring as I could. But I was a marked man. There would be other occasions when, to borrow a metaphor from *The Godfather,* my office staff had to take to the mattresses to deal with a press blitz. Adrenaline got me through the uproar, but it left me feeling soiled and worried about my carelessness. And I knew it was tough on Jeannie, a reserved woman who did not enjoy seeing her husband make himself a laughing stock.

In 1983, when I was at the Advent in Boston and was still *persona grata* in Anglo-Catholic circles, I had been invited to lead a conference in Melbourne to help Australians celebrate the 150th anniversary of the Oxford Movement. Among the lectures I gave was one on the priesthood, based on a verse from the Letter to the Hebrews: 'We must pay the closer attention to what we have heard, lest we drift away from it.'[99] Using the image of a rowing boat that had slipped its mooring and glided silently into the mist, I warned them against drifting. Keep the rope tied tightly to the ring on the pier; secure the mooring, lest you drift gradually imperceptibly quietly away from the faith. Whether they acknowledge it or not, preachers are usually preaching to themselves. Was that what I had been doing then? I had been choked and tearful as I spoke. Was I even then anticipating my own drift away from disappointed friends watching from the shore? The image had now caught up with me and some of my friends began to worry that I was drifting towards real trouble.

If the sex fracas was created by journalistic mischief, the next one was all my own work, though it probably had roots in Random Street. I was on my way back from a meeting in London on 13 March 1996 when the BBC phoned to tell me about the massacre of children in Dunblane earlier that day. Would I extemporise a response to the tragedy on a television broadcast that evening from the cathedral? Words are useless at a time like that, yet we have to find them. Others found better words for the darkness that had engulfed us. I said what I could. What I said I cannot now remember. Jeannie, an accomplished versifier like her father, was moved to write a hymn for the memorial service on the Sunday after the killings. She found her own words.

Our children, innocent and dear,
Were strangers to a world of fear;
Each precious life had more to give,
In each, our hopes and dreams could live;
Enfold in love for evermore
All those we love, but see no more.

So brief, the joy since each was born,
So long the years in which to mourn;
Give us compassion to sustain
Each other in this time of pain;
Enfold in love for evermore
All those we love, but see no more.

Sung to 'Melita', her words gave grief a way of singing what it could not easily say. Neither of us could attend the service. We were booked for the Diocese of Bangor in Wales that weekend, where I was to speak at a conference organised by the Welsh movement for the ordination of women. Though the Churches in Scotland, England and Ireland had by then started ordaining women to the priesthood, Wales had not been able to gather the necessary majority among the clergy to get it through. The conference was meant to encourage campaigners for the struggle that still lay ahead. The other speaker was a young priest from England, the woman on whom the television series *The Vicar of Dibley* was supposed to have been modelled. In her talk she told of how the joy of the women who had been recently ordained in England had been officially confined. They had been told not to upset those who refused to accept what had happened and were behaving as if a profound tragedy had occurred. Rather than being able to celebrate a step forward in the liberation of women from yet another shackle, the newly ordained had to act as if they were at a funeral. The Church of England, in a characteristically generous but misguided attempt to appease the *refuseniks*, had given opponents of women's ordination separate little enclaves to live in, supervised by bishops whose hands had not been soiled by ordaining women. It was as if post-apartheid South Africa had provided racists with their own little *laagers* where they could continue the old segregations. Asked what I made of this dog-in-the-manger response, I replied – more in sorrow than in anger – 'Oh the miserable buggers, the mean-minded wee sods.' My words became a brief diary item in the local newspaper the following week. Soon they were everywhere, another example of my undisciplined tongue. If the previous debacle was caused by carelessness, this one was a clear example of criminal reck-lessness. What was I up to? I seemed to have cast caution to the winds. Was I trying to get myself cashiered?

This time it got serious. A formal complaint was submitted to the Scottish College of Bishops by a group of clergy in the province. The College was required by the Canons of the Church to consider and reach a judgement on the complaint. Normally the Primus would chair such a court, but since the Primus was the one in the dock, the bishop next in line of seniority presided. I did not attend. The bishops had no option but to find me guilty of using inappropriate language. 'Bugger' and 'wee sod' might have been terms of endearment in Random Street, but they were unbecoming in the mouth of a bishop. I must apologise or resign. My own legal adviser suggested resig-nation, but I was damned if I'd let them have such an easy scalp. I issued an apology for my language and moved on, but for how long?

Was my wee boat finally heading for the rocks? It certainly seemed to be gathering speed in the current of my own reck-lessness; and a number of friends on the shore shouted warn-ings about the white water ahead. It would be the Lambeth Conference of 1998 that would send me over the edge, and it was just round the next bend.

LEAVING ALEXANDRIA

In my fourteen years as a bishop I attended two Lambeth Conferences. I didn't particularly enjoy the first one in 1988, but I actively hated the second in 1998. Held every ten years, they are better defined in negatives than in positives. They are not legislative assemblies or parliaments of the Anglican Communion, although the desire to give them that kind of authority is beginning to creep in. They are more like family reunions than anything else, and to understand them you have to know something about the history of the Anglican Communion, excluding Scotland, a special case to which I'll return. Like the British Empire, the Communion grew by accident as clergy from England followed traders and colonists round the world and set up chaplaincies to minister to them. In the process they scattered their brand of religion around the globe much the way they spread the game of cricket. For a time these outposts considered themselves to be Church of England chaplaincies not independent ecclesiastical entities, but as the Empire evolved so did its religious counterpart. The closest secular parallel to the Anglican Communion is the British Commonwealth, the international club former colonies joined when they left the Empire. The result is a network of autonomous provinces held together more by affection and shared

311

history than by doctrinal or cultural conformity. In spite of that, the Anglican Communion has shown a tenacious desire to keep itself together, something easier said than done with such a loose structure of national provinces all at different stages of social and theological evolution. Over the years several formal 'instruments of unity' were evolved to keep this scattered family in touch with each other, and the first one to appear was the Lambeth Conference. In 1867 the Archbishop of Canterbury invited Anglican bishops to join him for a conference at Lambeth Palace in London to celebrate their friendship and discuss their common interests, and the ten-yearly gathering was born. As is the way with these things, the conference has accrued influence and authority to itself over the years, but it is not a legislative body. Its reports may guide the policies of individual provinces, but they have no power to command them.

The Conferences meet now at the University of Kent in Canterbury, not in London, though there is always a big London Day when the Church of England lays on a service in Saint Paul's Cathedral in the morning and a Garden Party at Buckingham Palace in the afternoon. The rest of the time the 700 bishops go from their student rooms in the Canterbury campus to worship services, keynote lectures and discussion groups in which they debate the issues of the day, especially if they threaten the balancing act of the Communion's integrity. The results of these debates are brought together in big set-piece plenary sessions where they are voted on. If they smell blood, the Press turn up to watch the spectacle. They came in their droves to Lambeth 1988 because the hot issue was the ordination of women and it was predicted it would tear the Communion apart. At that time there were few Anglican provinces where it had happened, but it was firmly on the agenda for discussion in many places, including the British Isles, and was already a done deal in North America. Opponents mustered their forces against the blasphemous advance of women, Conservative Evangelicals and Anglo-Catholics operating a pincer strategy in opposition. Before looking at how the issue was handled at Lambeth 1988, I want to reflect on why it was such a tough topic to deal with, because it provides us with a classic example of the difficulties religions face when they are confronted with moral challenges that come from outside their own sacred enclosures.

The problem for the Church in the twentieth century was that many of the pressures for human emancipation were coming from the secular rather than the religious sphere, and Christianity is always suspicious of moral imperatives it did not invent, seeing itself as the uniquely qualified conscience of humanity. It is hard for institutions that believe they are divinely inspired and guided to admit they are wrong about anything, especially in areas of moral evolution. This is why campaigners for reform within the Church have to go out of their way to prove that the new challenge is not only consistent with their old convictions but is actually mandated by them. The Church can never just do the right thing because it is the right thing to do; it has to find religious reasons for doing it. It can't just abandon its rigid code, like the Good Samaritan, and go to the aid of the needy person on the side of the road; it has to find theological reasons for doing so. Code always has to justify compassion. Nevertheless, to be fair to it, the Church usually does try to find ways of adapting its code to the needs of compassion, though its serpentine logic may baffle the under-standing of outsiders. I began to notice both the charm and the absurdity of this process when I was a member of the

Human Fertilisation and Embryology Authority, the body set up by the UK Parliament to license fertility clinics, invigilate upon their activities and keep an eye on new developments in the field.

The first successful 'test-tube baby' had been born in 1978. The process had involved removing an egg from the mother's ovaries and letting her partner's sperm fertilise it in a fluid medium outside her body. The embryo that resulted was transferred to the mother's uterus and established a successful pregnancy. This new reproductive technique was described as *in vitro* as opposed to *in vivo* fertilisation, because it involved cultivation of tissue in a glass container – *in vitro* – outside the body. The new reproductive technology presented many problems for religious groups, but I only want to look at one of the less profound issues it raised for the Catholic Church, because the way it got round the difficulty tells us a lot about religion.

One of the challenges IVF presented for Catholic moral theology was how to retrieve sperm ethically. There was physical discomfort involved in harvesting the egg from the woman, but there was no moral problem attached to the process: as far as religion was concerned, it was a surgical procedure with little moral resonance. However, the usual way of harvesting sperm was morally problematic because it involved masturbation, a sin according to Catholic moral theology. How was the Church to balance the good of helping a married couple have children against the evil of the masturbatory act without which it could not be achieved? The Catholic moral tradition often appears to be inflexible, but it does its best to accommodate change within its own parameters. That is what it did here. It suggested two solutions to the dilemma, two ways of capturing sperm without sinning. One was for the husband and wife to have sexual intercourse and for the semen to be retrieved from the woman afterwards by a process of aspiration. The other was the use of the canonical contraceptive, a pre-perforated, non-spermicidal condom worn by the husband during intercourse and placed immediately after withdrawal in a container and express-delivered to the clinic, where it was stored until the insemination procedure was carried out.[100] When I read about this attempt on the part of Catholic theologians to be helpful, I did not know whether to laugh or cry. I was moved by the fact that within its own worldview the Church was trying to be helpful. On the other hand, it seemed to be yet another example of the tendency, particularly strong in religious systems, to assert the primacy of abstract principle over urgent human need.

Farcical as this example of Catholic casuistry may appear to be, I quickly realised that we were doing something similar in the Anglican Church in our debate about the ordination of women. We could not bring ourselves to say that the Church's opposition to the emancipation of women was stupid as well as wrong and should be abandoned forthwith. We had to find *religious* reasons for doing the right thing. We could not say that our scriptures were wrong on this subject as on much else – which was hardly surprising, given their cultural lineage in late Stone Age society – so let us put them aside and agree that there is no justification for refusing women ordination and just get on with it. What we did was to twist ourselves in knots to find justifications within scripture for doing what scripture had previously been understood to forbid. And we found them, just as Catholic theologians found a sinless way to retrieve sperm. The exegetical equivalent of the pre-perforated, non-spermicidal condom was 'the canon within the canon' or the Bible within the Bible: in other words, bits of the Holy Book that were held to be more profound and important than other bits. A text latched onto from Paul, the main opponent where the liberation of women was concerned, seemed to do the trick:

> as many of ye as have been baptized into Christ have put on Christ. There is neither Jew nor Greek, there is neither bond nor free, *there is neither male nor female*: for ye are all one in Christ Jesus.[101]

This text referred to one of the Church's earliest struggles with another gang of importunate outsiders, in this case Gentiles seeking entrance to a community that had hitherto understood itself to be a sect within Judaism. The passage from Galatians became our canonical condom, but it did not persuade everyone in the Church. Conservative evangelicals refused to use it. Galatians had nothing to do with the status of women; it was about the baptism of Gentiles, something Paul was quite clear about. On the status of women, Paul was equally clear: Man is the boss.

> Wives submit yourselves unto your own husbands, as unto the Lord.
>
> For the husband is the head of the wife, even as Christ is the head of the church . . . Therefore as the church is subject unto Christ, so let the wives be to their own husbands in everything.[102]

For Anglo-Catholic opponents of women, who were on the other tine of the pincer, the Bible was not the problem. Anglo-Catholics didn't rate the Bible that highly. They claimed, correctly, that the Church was in existence hundreds of years before the New Testament, which was the Church's creation and over which it had interpretative authority. So Paul wasn't a problem. You could get round Paul. The Pope was the problem, and no one could get round the Pope except the Pope himself. It was not an inerrant text we had to contend with, they claimed, it was an inerrant institution.

> The Roman Pontiff, when he speaks *ex cathedra,* that is, when, exercising the office of pastor and teacher of all Christians, he defines . . . a doctrine concerning faith or morals to be held by the whole Church, through the divine assistance promised to him in St. Peter, is possessed of that infallibility with which the Divine Redeemer wished His church to be endowed . . . and therefore such definitions of the Roman Pontiff are irreformable of themselves, and not from the consent of the Church.[103]

That, as the insurance salesman said to Bill Murray in *Groundhog Day,* is a doozy. It might appear odd that a sect within a Church that came into existence to resist claims of Papal infallibility was now denying that same Church the right to order its own life without permission of that same infallibility. It *is* strange. Anglicanism has often been a coalition of the unwilling, but this took its incoherence to a new low. But there was enough in the backstory of the Catholic revival in Anglicanism to have alerted us. During the height of the ritualistic controversies in the nineteenth century, one journalist had noted that many Anglo-Catholics were 'endowed less with a great power of will than with an enormous power of won't.' As well as the romance of monasticism and the dedication of slum priests, in the DNA of

Anglo-Catholicism there was nostalgia for the strong leader who would navigate the flux of history and pilot the Church infallibly through its storms. This kind of nostalgia is not unique to religion. It is at the root of all totalitarian systems: religious, political, intellectual. And it is easy to find sympathy for the craving. It is the longing for permanence and stability in the chaos and tumult of history; the need for something that abides, something to cling to among the wreckage of time. Unfortunately, there are no magical deliverers who can deliver us from ourselves and our muddles. No infallible Bible. No infallible Church. No infallible anything. And there never has been. Nevertheless, I find it hard to deny others the consolation of believing they have found one that works for them. Anglicanism had never claimed that kind of infallibility for itself. It knew it was a muddle; a muddled Church for muddled people. And since there were lots of muddled people around, it had an honourable vocation. Fortunately, when the ordination of women was squabbled over at Lambeth in 1988, the Archbishop of Canterbury who presided over it was an intuitive Anglican who understood the theology of muddle and helped us muddle through.

Religions take a long time to negotiate change, and Robert Runcie bought the Anglican Communion enough time to come to terms with the ordination of women by wielding two theoretical devices: *reception* and *contextuality*. They were based on historical observation: it takes a while for new ideas and new social arrangements to be received by people; and cultures vary in their absorption of the new according to their social context. A change that was a no-brainer in Manhattan might be anathema in Mombasa. Let us therefore accept these differences in cultural time-zones and not expect Manhattan to set its clock by Mombasa, or vice versa. Meanwhile, let us appoint a commission to explore the difficulties the ordination of women will undoubtedly cause for the Communion as a whole and how we might best manage them. There was grumbling, but there was also relief when we followed this approach. No province was pressured either to stop or start ordaining women. The Press had predicted the break-up of the Communion and they alone were disappointed when it did not happen. Runcie, a keen cricketer, had glided the problem into the long grass. Over the next decade more and more Anglican provinces, including those in the British Isles, started ordaining women. Conservative Evangelicals learned to live with the change, but Anglo-Papalists never did. Most of them have now transferred to a secure unit within the Roman Catholic Church, where they know the Pope will protect them from the advances of women for the foreseeable future.

Runcie was a complex and attractive figure. Though temperamentally his opposite, I grew to love and admire him. He was an instinctive Anglican of the old English type that distrusted enthusiasm and ideology. A devout pragmatist, he believed that institutions were best kept together by adaptive changes subtle enough to prevent panic among the forces of reaction but serious enough to achieve real momentum. Though a brave man and a decorated soldier in World War II, in his retirement, visited by the regrets that come to all reflective men as they approach the end, he wondered if he should not have been bolder in his approach. His critics had often accused him of nailing his colours to the fence. In spite of my impatience for change, I thought his approach was wise. And it worked. The Anglican Communion did not hit the rocks over women. It was his successor who pulled off that navigational feat ten years later on the even more contentious issue of homosexuality.*

As with women's ordination, there was a wild variety of opinion on the subject. This time, however, the opposition's tone was uglier. And no canonical condom was available, no get-out-of-gaol text to help us fudge the debate. Paul had not told us in his Letter to the Galatians that in Christ there was neither gay nor straight. What references there were in the Bible to homosexuality were all hostile. Stick to the Bible and you were stuck with hatred of gays. Fundamentalists from the Bible Belt understood the logic: God hates fags. What I hadn't expected at Lambeth 1998 was to hear so many men in purple cassocks mouthing the same sentiments with the same ugly avidity.

I turned up not expecting the Communion to support gay rights, but I did expect a reprise of the Runcie strategy and I was firmly under the impression that the new Archbishop, George Carey, intended to steer us in that direction. There would, I assumed, be passionate debate, equally passionate disagreement, and ugly things would doubtless be said; a commission would then be appointed to consider the impact on the Communion of our disagreements – to report back before the Second Coming – and the problem would roll into the high grass for a generation. Meanwhile, provinces would deal with it in ways appropriate to their own context, as they had with women's ordination, and we would muddle through again. I turned up at the campus in Canterbury with little

---

* In the summer of my departure from the Episcopate, precipitated by the hostile reaction to my book *Godless Morality,* I got a hand-written letter from Robert Runcie, thanking me for the book and regretting not speaking out in its favour when it was under attack. For some reason the letter took a while to reach me. I received it on a warm July afternoon. I was moved when I read it. A few minutes later my secretary came in to tell me she'd just heard the news: Archbishop Runcie had died earlier that day.

enthusiasm, but with no idea that it would be as grim as it turned out to be. My own reception was not encouraging. As a patron of the Lesbian and Gay Christian Movement, I had invited the bishops to a reception in Canterbury to meet some gay Christians. I did not expect all 749 bishops to attend, but I thought we would get a representative sample. I was wrong. To be fair to him, George Carey was one of the few opponents of change to turn up. I was moved when a young man told him that it had taken more courage for him to come out to the gay community as a Christian than it had to come out as a gay man to his family and friends. The gay community's perception of Christianity was unsurprisingly negative, given the ugly things Christians said loudly about them. He hoped the conference would help to soften that perception.

In the event, the conference made it far worse, and the Archbishop of Canterbury, probably more out of naivety than collusion, allowed the African bishops to force an unconstitutional debate on a subject that had already been prudently dealt with by an official sub-group of the conference. He presided over the rout with smiling incomprehension as the damage was done. Bishop after bishop, mainly but not exclusively from Africa, got up to denounce the wickedness and animality of lovers of their own sex. There were some valiant African opponents of the coup, including the Archbishops of South and Central Africa, but it pursued its ugly course to the end. A resolution was passed by a large majority, denouncing homosexuality as a practice incompatible with scripture and refusing to legitimise the blessing of same-sex unions or the ordination of homosexuals. But it was the tone of the debate that did the real damage. One American bishop, a man with a big heart and a small body, told me that he had been physically menaced by the bishops around him whenever he had raised his hand to vote against their increasingly intemperate resolutions. Immediately after the rout, on a grassy knoll outside the conference hall, a Nigerian bishop attempted to cast out the demons of homosexuality from Richard Kirker, the Director of the Gay and Lesbian Christian Movement, who had bravely challenged him about what had happened. A demon *was* released that afternoon, but it did not come out of the brave young man being apostrophised by the African prelate. A South African woman present at the conference as a consultant, a university professor, told me that what we had just witnessed was not just about African attitudes to homosexuality; it was an imperious assertion of male control over sex. One aspect of this had always been the control of women by men, but the other had been the ancient prohibition of sodomy *because of the way it undermined the idea of male dominance in the sexual act*. Andrea Dworkin had addressed the problem years before.

> Can sodomy become a legal form of intercourse without irredeemably compromising male power over women, that power being premised on men being entirely distinct from women in use, in function, in posture and position, in role, in 'nature'? Or will the legalisation of sodomy mortally injure the class power of men by sanctioning a fuck in which men are treated like women; the boundaries of men's bodies no longer being, as a matter of social policy and divine right, inviolate?[104]

Behind Lambeth's contempt for gay men, there lay a deeper contempt for women themselves, because they too are incapable of the fuck in this primordial sense. Men fuck. Women get fucked. Q.E.D. That was the demon that was released that afternoon, and it will never go back whence it came. It began the unravelling of the Anglican Communion that has been gathering pace ever since, an unravelling that the saintly scholar who succeeded George Carey at Canterbury will never be able to halt.

A Nigerian bishop had been spreading the rumour at Lambeth that my support for gay liberation was because my daughters were lesbians. He made the mistake of repeating the lie to the rector of a church in Connecticut where he went to preach after the conference. The rector, who had been one of my curates in Boston, challenged him on the claim, but he insisted it was true. It would not have mattered to me and Jeannie if it had been true, but it wasn't. What it did was fortify my sense that there was a profound sickness at the heart of so-called Biblical morality, if it could lead to such hatred and cruelty. I wanted to get in my car and come home to Scotland. Michael Peers, the Archbishop of Canada, persuaded me to stick it out to the end. We helped put together a resolution apologising to the world's lesbian and gay Christians for what the Lambeth Conference had said about them. Out of the 749 bishops present, 182 signed it, including the Primates of Brazil, Canada, Central Africa, Ireland, New Zealand, Scotland, South Africa and Wales.

Finally the conference was over, with a sting in the tail, in the form of a meeting of the Primates who were asked to stay behind to review what had happened. I had a dust-up with George Carey during that fractious hour, but at last I was free to come north again. The only sweet memory I brought away with me was throwing my mitre into the Thames. I had announced my intention to do this two years before when I preached in Norway at a service to mark the signing of an agreement that brought together the Anglican, Baltic and Nordic Churches. In my sermon I had noticed that while the practice of the episcopate was increasingly personal and collegial, the theatre of the episcopate was still monarchical and hierarchical. We were too fond of the intricacies of address and title. We were too bound to the badges of office. And the more splendid our titles and the more gorgeous our robes, the more cautious we became. Saint Martin of Tours had said bishops came in two forms, shepherds and fishers: shepherds cherished the flock, but fishers pushed the boat out from the shore and launched out into the deep. The Anglican Episcopate had rarely pushed the boat out, but I hoped that this agreement would embolden us to be more daring and adventurous. I ended with a letter the Cistercian monk Thomas Merton had sent to the Polish poet Czesław Miłosz. Merton, a hero since my days in the Cottage at Kelham, had written about the need to undermine 'this comfortable and social Catholicism, this lining up of cassocks, this regimenting of birettas. I throw my biretta in the river.'[105] That had given me an idea. It was rumoured that during the 1998 Lambeth Conference the bishops were to be taken on a cruise on the Thames after the Buckingham Palace Garden Party. Wouldn't it be great if the bishops could be persuaded to bring their mitres with them and chuck them in the Thames as a collective gesture of commitment to a simpler episcopate?

My tongue had been in my cheek, but I had meant what I said. So I came to Lambeth prepared. I had an artist friend in Edinburgh make me four biodegradable mitres which I had with me on the boat that took us down the Thames after the Queen's Garden Party. I knew mitre-drowning was unlikely to become a mass movement like the feminists' bra-burning, because bishops liked their silly hats and even the women were wearing them now. But I had no difficulty getting a Scottish and an American bishop to join me in the gesture. That left one to go. I caught sight of the Archbishop of Canterbury downing a pint of bitter and I asked him if he'd like to join us. Smiling, he said he was game; so each of us stood at the stern of the boat and chucked a non-polluting mitre into the river. It was a joke for the others, but I meant it. I never wore the thing again. And there was a footnote to the tale. *The Times* had heard about the ploy, though not from me. One of their photographers followed us in a speedboat and snapped the Archbishop in the act. Next day I was told by a member of the Lambeth press team that *The Times* had phoned the Archbishop's press office to say they planned to put the picture on the front page, though they might be open to a deal: an exclusive interview with the eleven women bishops present at the Lambeth Conference. I did not check the accuracy of the story. However, no embarrassing photograph appeared in *The Times*; but an exclusive interview with the women bishops did.

Like downing a good dram, throwing my mitre in the Thames afforded only temporary relief. I was beginning to wonder how long it would be before I followed it. My problem was not so much with God as with increasing disbelief in religion's claim to possess precise information about his opinions, including his sexual and gender preferences. The ceaseless flow of history was a big problem for religion, especially in those versions that believed they had received a timeless revelation that answered every question and solved every problem. I was increasingly conscious of the circularity of the claim. How can we be sure these scriptures and their unchanging commandments are from God? *Because they themselves tell us so!* To believe them you had to believe them. Religion's old Catch-22. The problem with author-itative revelation was that, rather than stopping all the clocks of history, it only opened itself to constant challenges from the future. The strangers in the wings of Louis MacNeice's poem who were emerging onto the religious stage were women and homosexuals, neither of whom was prepared any longer to be defined by religion's Stone Age attitudes. Though I was completely on the side of the new challengers, in spite of myself I felt some sympathy towards those who argued against any accommodation with them. If you had been brought up to believe that sacred revelation had defined our identities for ever and that any alteration in understanding them would be blas-phemous, how can you be blamed for being loyal to your code even if your heart protests against its cruelty? Once you start pulling the threads out of religion's carefully crafted quilt of precedent and prejudice, the whole fabric might unravel.

That is what they accused me of doing when I published *Godless Morality* in 1999, the year after the Lambeth Conference. The urge to write the book had been provoked by the Lambeth debates on sexuality and the gulfs of incomprehension they revealed. Biblical moralists did not negotiate; they asserted their position – God's position – and denounced all others. It was God's role in moral debate that struck me as increasingly prob-lematic. Humanity had been inconclusively debating both the nature and possibility of God for centuries. God's history was under constant revision as humanity had constantly changed its mind about him. Had he once commanded child sacrifice? Yes, but that had been a mistake – our mistake. We'd misunderstood him. Had he once permitted slavery? Yes, but we got that wrong too – or maybe he changed his mind. What about the subordination of women to men, and stoning for sodomy? Is it possible we are getting him wrong on these things as well? Almost certainly, said some; definitely not, said others. Might it not be better, since God's opinions seem to be so constantly misunderstood or so varied, to leave him out of our moral disputes and debate them on good human grounds? Even without God, it was obvious that good people could disagree passionately about what was and was not the best way to live. And I was coming to believe that there was an inescapably tragic dimension to moral debate. Moral opinions were incurably plural, even within religious groups. I doubted if there would ever be a single version of the perfect life or perfect society. Life was manifold in the forms it took; it was gloriously and inescapably plural. That was why in practical daily life we made trade-offs between conflicting goods and evils; and there was no infallible system for measuring them. Isaiah Berlin had described this as the *Incommensurability* of values, and it was why he thought the struggle for humans to be wise and good was necessary but intractable. Things were tough enough without importing rival interpretations of God into our debates. That only made it more difficult to find ways forward. Wasn't it better to leave God out of the debate and find good human reasons for supporting the approach we advocated, without having recourse to divinely clinching arguments? In support of my case I quoted from the philosopher John Harris:

> For a moral judgement to be respectable it must have something to say about just why a supposed wrong action is wrongful. If it fails to meet this test it is a preference not a moral judgement at all.[106]

To meet Harris's test it was not enough to quote the authority of God, a move that had a tendency to extinguish rather than elucidate moral judgement. To say that God commanded or forbade a particular action gave you religious not moral information. It might illuminate your theological convictions; it would cast no *moral* light on the act itself. According to the Book of Joshua, the god of the Old Testament ordered the Israelites to massacre the original inhabitants of the land they grabbed in Palestine. Belief in a divine command like that might explain the motive for the activity, but it told us little or nothing about its moral status. There was nothing new in what I was arguing, though it may have been new coming from a bishop. As far back as Plato there had been arguments over whether a particular behaviour was right because the gods commanded it or whether the gods commanded it because it was right. I thought it significant at the time that my book was well received by philosophers and widely repudiated by bishops.

The most dramatic repudiation was a *fatwa* on the book delivered by the Archbishop of Canterbury in my presence in the good Scottish city of Dundee. Let me hasten to add that he did not call for an assassination squad to rid the world of my presence. The Salman Rushdie affair gave *fatwas* a bad name, which is why they are now erroneously associated with violence, whereas a *fatwa* is a religious ruling on a matter of Islamic law, such as whether a good Muslim is permitted to smoke tobacco or only marijuana. What the Archbishop did was deliver himself of an authoritative ruling on my book. It happened in Dundee because in September 1999 the Scottish Episcopal Church, of which I was then Primus, was playing host to a meeting of the Anglican Consultative Council, the only international assembly in world Anglicanism that contains lay people. *Godless Morality* had just been published, and it got things off to a bad start, placing the Archbishop of Canterbury between a rock and a hard place. Scotland was the hard place.

In many ways Scotland has always been the embarrassing wee drunk uncle at the Anglican dinner party. The Scottish Church is the exception to the rule of Anglican fusion I described earlier in this chapter. Unlike the other provinces in the Communion, the Scottish Church had never been an outpost of the Church of England. Scotland had had its own Reformation in 1560, but it took more than a century to decide between winners and losers. Because the Scottish bishops had supported the Stuart kings in the Revolution of 1688, and continued to support them in the Risings of 1715 and 1745, they were outlawed and penalised for their loyalty to the Jacobite cause. During this period of persecution an event occurred that can legitimately claim to be the real beginning of the alliance that came to be known as the Anglican Communion. When America declared its independence in 1773 it created a problem for its Anglican clergy. Who would now provide them with Episcopal oversight? To solve the problem, in March 1783 the clergy of Connecticut elected Samuel Seabury as their Bishop and sent him to England to be ordained. The Church of England refused to perform the task because as an American citizen he could not take the oath of allegiance to the King of England, who was also the Supreme Governor of the Church of England. So he turned to the Scottish Episcopal Church, which refused allegiance to the English king. On 14 November 1784 Seabury was ordained by three Scottish bishops as the first Bishop of the newly autonomous American Episcopal Church.

This means that the originating event in the creation of

LEAVING ALEXANDRIA

global Anglicanism happened in Scotland under the hands of Scotsmen who owed no allegiance to the Archbishop of Canterbury or the monarch of England who had appointed him. So I was not pleased when the English Archbishop upbraided me on my own turf like a colonial governor calling a junior officer to heel. But it was not just his assumption of authority over me that irritated; his attitude towards the search for truth annoyed me more. I do not mind being disagreed with. Had the Archbishop offered an analysis of my book, showing where he disagreed with it and why, I would have relished the opportunity to take the argument further and maybe even change my mind – God knows I've done that often enough. That is not what he did. He *pronounced* against it. He offered not argument, but a sort of quasi-papal judgement that my book was *erroneous*. And in doing so he angered the delegates to the Dundee ACC. Few of them had heard of the book, and most of them would have disagreed with it had they read it, but they considered it discourteous of the Archbishop to condemn his host in his own home. They asked that I be given the right of reply. I took the opportunity and pointed out that what bothered me was the implication in the Archbishop's address that he had the right to pronounce judgement on the doctrinal status of my book, rather than offering specific arguments against it. He *could* say authoritatively that seventeen plus thirteen equals thirty not thirty-three, but he could not apply arithmetical precision to complex matters of ethical evaluation. Let him argue, therefore, not fire anathemas.

To be fair to the Archbishop, he did have a point, though he chose to deliver it in an inappropriate way. He claimed that a morality without God could not be a fully formed *Christian* morality, which may be true, but is not what I was talking about

330

in my book. As I have already indicated, I was wondering whether the time had not come to leave religion outside our search for moral agreement – including agreement to disagree – since its presence inhibited rather than encouraged discussion. There were obviously many different moralities, including one that could be described as Christian – though Christians disagreed among themselves almost as much as they did with unbelievers – so would it not be better to leave religious justifications for conduct to one side and try to find good *moral* reasons for the approach we advocated?

If Scotland was the Archbishop of Canterbury's hard place, then his rock was Singapore. The city state that brooks no dissent from its citizens was the appropriate base for the Archbishop of South-East Asia, an icy authoritarian who resisted any modification in the Church's age-old persecution of homosexuals. In an encounter I had with him in the lavatory in Cumberland Lodge in Windsor Great Park, during a meeting of Anglican Primates, he had accused me of filling Hell with homosexuals because I was giving them permission to commit a sin that damned them to eternal punishment, since no Sodomite could enter the Kingdom of Heaven. I resisted the impulse to deck him and left him to go on pissing his wormwood and gall into the Queen's urinal. So I was not surprised when he too delivered a *fatwa* against *Godless Morality*. I doubted if he had read it, but its publication provided him with an opportune *casus belli*. Though supposed to represent the Province of South-East Asia at the Dundee ACC, he issued a press release to say that because the Scottish Primus had just published a heretical book he would not attend the assembly. And, in a nice guilt-by-association touch, he went on to declare Scotland to be a heretical province. This was tough on the Scottish Church

331

because, while it was more liberal and inclusive than most Anglican provinces outside North America, many of its members had become unsure of me as their Primus and would have swapped me for the man from Singapore any day.

In spite of these ructions, we got through the assembly in good heart, and I returned to Edinburgh to reflect on my situation. Was I so out of step with my colleagues at home and abroad that I should consider my position? Was this my midnight?

> At midnight, when suddenly you hear
> an invisible procession going by . . .
> don't mourn your luck that's failing now,
> work gone wrong, your plans
> all proving deceptive – don't mourn them uselessly:
> as one long prepared, and full of courage,
> say goodbye to her, to Alexandria who is leaving.[107]

I was in a reflective mood when Jeannie and I drove into the Borders one Sunday weeks later to visit one of my favourite churches. The rector had been one of my own appointments, and I was fond of him and his family. Through the generosity of my friend Nadir Dinshaw we had been able to help support his wife's sister through medical school and I had been at her wedding not that long before, so I felt secure in their affections even though I knew there were theological differences between us. On the almost infinitely nuanced continuum of Anglican theological positions, Paul would have been described as an open Evangelical, an intelligent conservative with a pinch of liberality in his make-up. I knew *Godless Morality* would not have been his cup of tea, but I did not anticipate any difficulties.

After all, there were lots of things we disagreed about, but they did not undermine the affection we felt for each other. Sure enough, when I arrived in the sacristy to get into my robes for the service he told me he'd been speaking to the *Scotsman* about my book. And I bet you denounced it as heresy, I joked. I was puzzled by his tense and nervous manner but thought no more about it, and we got on with the service.

The first warning bell rang during the giving of the Peace. I wandered over to the choir to shake hands in the usual way. Several of the singers turned away from me and refused my hand, including a local doctor I thought I knew well. Not everyone liked giving the Peace. It was too effusive for them, too casual. Maybe that was it. The bell rang louder during the administration of communion when a number of people, including the doctor, ostentatiously refused to take the sacrament from me. I knew something was really up when a number of people refused to shake my hand in the porch at the end of the service and gave me a dramatically wide berth. By this time Paul was really uptight. I asked what was up with the doctor who had shunned me. He disagrees with what you say about drugs in your book. Is that now an excommunicable offence, I wondered. We joined the congregation for a rather strained parish lunch till I alerted Jeannie to the need for a tactical withdrawal. We're not welcome; I think we should leave. We said our goodbyes and drove home through the soothing green countryside.

The day after the visit all became clear. After attending the Eucharist at the cathedral, I picked up my *Scotsman* from the local newsagent and found myself the headline. A posse of Evangelical clergy in the diocese – prominent among them the man with whom I had spent the previous day – had called for my resignation and declared the Diocese of Edinburgh vacant. One of the main plotters was at my table for dinner that same evening. He was on the Cathedral Chapter, my advisory council, and this was their annual dinner. He walked eagerly into our flat near the cathedral, a smile on his face. I did not allude to what he had done, but my friend Graham angrily challenged him. I felt no anger, only sadness and an increasing weariness.

It was not their fault. It was mine. I was a disappointment to them, a lost leader. Rather than sheltering them from the blast, I had broken open the windows and blown in the door. It was a cold night, and I had chased them out of doors. Who could blame them for their anger? I knew it was time for me to leave them. But I waited before acting. I would not be hounded out. I would go at a time of my own choosing. A number of clergy in the diocese rose to my defence against the plotters and told me to ignore them: there was still work to do. More encouragingly, I started getting affectionate letters from people outside the Church. I was beginning to suspect there was more forgiveness outside the Church than in. And I became grateful for what the American poet Wendell Berry called 'the magnanimity of the world'. One of his poems, given to me by a friend, came as an absolution I had not realised I needed till it was received.

> And we are lost in what we are. Our privilege
> is the unrelenting effort of renewal
> of sight and hope out of failure –
> out of impatience, anger, haste, despair,
> violence to strangers, unkindness to loved ones,
> disappointment at the failure of expectations

that were, at the outset, unreasonable –
out of greed, arrogance, and ruin. Our privilege
is our sorrow: to know by blindness, by falling short,
the magnanimity of the world.[108]

In the spring of 2000 I announced my resignation. At the end
of October I preached my last sermon as Bishop of Edinburgh
in Old Saint Paul's, and I used it to look back. I told them that
when I arrived as their Rector thirty-two years before I had just
emerged from a period of radical doubt and had fallen into a
very common trap. I reacted against my own uncertainty by
attacking doubt and uncertainty in others. A closet sceptic, I
condemned in others what I had been afraid to look at in
myself. My first book, written in the attic at Lauder House
thirty years ago, was an attack on the kind of theology I myself
now wrote and was condemned for. It was the deepest irony
of my life that I had ended up the kind of bishop in my sixties
I had despised when I was a priest in my thirties. Now I had
come back to where I started from and knew the place for the
first time. I could no longer talk about God.

I felt glutted with the verbal promiscuity of religion and the
absolute confidence with which it talked about what was beyond
our knowing. The irony was that in one of Paul's great poems,
God chose to empty himself of language and become a life. But
along comes Christianity and turns it back into words, trillions
of them, poured out incessantly in pulpit, book and on the
airwaves, reducing the mystery of what is beyond all utterance
to chatter. I told them I had come to mind religious over-confidence more than I minded its atheistic opposite, because atheists
did not claim to put ultimate reality into words. Speaking personally, and without wanting to universalise my own experience,

religious language had ceased to be able to convey the mystery of the possibility of God for me because it confidently claimed to make present that which I experienced as absence; though it was an absence that sometimes feels like a presence, the way the dead sometimes leave an impression on rooms they spent their lives in. I didn't want to go back to the days when I had to name that absence. Even then I had felt insecure whenever I was called upon to offer an account of it. The best I had been able to do was to persuade myself and others to choose to live as if the absence hid a presence that was unconditional love. That possible identification, I thought, was worth betting my shirt on. It was a relief now to name my belief as an emptiness that I was no longer prepared to fill with words. But though I had lost the words for it, sometimes that absence came without word to me in a showing that did not tell. It was the absence of God I wanted to wait upon and be faithful to.

I was well aware of the irony of using words to condemn words, and I was doubly aware that in my ministry I had poured out more words than most, in books as well as sermons. Since I was a boy I had loved words, but now I needed to purge myself of them. I was what in the trade they call a manuscript preacher. Over forty years of preaching I had carefully crafted hundreds of sermons onto paper. I still had most of them carefully filed away in folders. What did they mean now? What did they represent? An absence. On All Souls Day 2000 I gathered them together and put them in black bin bags for Edinburgh's newly privatised cleansing service to pick up on the sidewalk the following morning. I divvied out my library of theology among the younger clergy in the diocese: more words. It was time to leave Alexandria again.

Jim, my beloved chaplain, organised a big farewell party and asked everyone who came to write something for me, describing the difference I had made to them. I read what they had written the morning I ceased to be Bishop of Edinburgh. It hadn't all been clash and controversy. Things I never remembered saying had been remembered by those to whom I had said them and were now being said back to me. They knew how important poetry had been to me, so they wrote some for me now. This is from one who knew me well:

> The difference was
> Two priests in full fig
> Dancing down Jeffrey Street,
> So that the stained-glass window Jesus
> In all his youthfulness
> Danced across the hills of Judea.
>
> The difference was
> The catch in the voice
> Over Judas and his betrayal;
> And somewhere in the words,
> The charismatic laughter,
> The unauthorised version.
>
> The difference was
> Leaving safety
> Striding out across water,
> And somewhere in the deep
> Of doubt, of restless faith,
> A resting place of truth.[109]

Then I dried my eyes, and I headed for the hills.

EPILOGUE

EPILOGUE

SCALD LAW

The hills I headed for were the Pentlands, Stevenson's 'hills of home', the southern backdrop to Scotland's capital. Less dramatic than the Ben that dominated my boyhood in the Vale of Leven, they did not so much punch themselves out of the earth as flow in folds over it. It was their friendly indifference I required. I needed my feet to be moving over terrain they knew so well that I wouldn't have to think about where I was going. It was the going in my head I had to think about now. I had just walked away from the work of a lifetime. *Demas hath forsaken me, having loved this present world.* Yet I felt that I, too, had been forsaken. I had been bereaved. But of what? My reaction to the Lambeth and Dundee ructions did not trouble me. I wanted nothing more to do with the men in pink dresses and their vehement opinions. The very uniforms they wore repelled me. I took off my bishop's ring and shoved it in a box. It had never been a proper bishop's ring anyway. Old Saint Paul's had given me a real Episcopal ring on my election as bishop, but there was a problem with it. It was beautiful, a small, elegant knuckle-duster. At my first meeting of British bishops, self-conscious in my new jewellery, the Bishop of Bristol looked at it. 'You'll have problems with that,' he said. 'You'll be shaking a lot of hands and it'll be agony. You need one that won't crunch your fingers.' He was right, as enthusiastic hand-shakers soon demonstrated. Where could I replace it? Somebody suggested Carnaby Street. I took the advice and explored the options next time I was in London. The nearest thing I could find that was suitable was a Hell's Angel ring: silver, dark amethyst, fifty quid. I practised with it, shaking my own hand to the amusement of the bikers' jeweller who was selling it. It was comfortable. No crunched fingers. I bought it. I don't think it was an omen. But into the box it went. As did the pectoral cross Nadir Dinshaw had given me. I had never taken to the purple shirt and had been happy to go on wearing the old black numbers from my days as a priest, so there was no problem folding it away in the drawer. The mitre had already gone into the Thames. The badges were easy to let go. I didn't miss them.

But what else had gone? Was I in any recognisable sense still a Christian? Others had made up their minds about me on that score. What was my own mind telling me? It was in the hills above the Vale of Leven as a boy that I had made the decision to leave Alexandria. I had walked myself out of that life. Now I had walked away again. What had I lost? What had I kept? I knew the best way to walk my mind was for my feet to walk the hills again, with my new Border Terrier Daisy at my heels – and no one else. There were three trails I took, all at the northern end of the Pentlands; and I took them again and again. The most arduous was to walk in at Bavelaw, through Kitchen Moss with the sweet slope of Hare Hill to the north. Then up West Kip and East Kip to Scald Law, the highest hill in the Pentlands at just under 2,000 feet. There is always a wind up here. Edinburgh is over there to the north and behind me the hills fold away into the distance. Then it was down the steep descent of Kirk Road, through the winding Green Cleuch between Black Hill and Hare Hill, and back to the car at Red Moss. A gentler walk was through Cock Rig, up between Harbour Hill and Bells Hill, along the road past Glencorse reservoir, then a cut through the valley between Bells Hill and Black Hill to Threipmuir and down through the great beech-lined avenue to Red Moss again. Sometimes I'd carry on past Loganlee Reservoir to the Green Cleuch and back that way. Daisy ranged around for the first mile or two of the trail, and then she'd tuck herself behind my heels and follow faithfully. We rarely met anyone. I looked around a bit, but I was really unseeing, walking my mind, trying to find myself.

Was religion a lie? Not necessarily, but it was a mistake. Lies are just lies, but mistakes can be corrected and lessons can be learned from them. The mistake was to think religion was more than human. I was less sure whether God was also just a human invention, but I was quite sure religion was. It was a work of the human imagination, a work of art – an *opera* – and could be appreciated as such. The real issue was whether it should be given more authority over us than any other work of art, especially if it is the kind of authority that overrides our own better judgements. It was a massive issue for me, because it was from its claims to unique authority that its manifest cruelty arose – and it was its cruelty I could no longer stomach. It is one thing to be in a state of ignorance – to believe that women are inferior to men, that gays are an abomination – because that is the going opinion, the prevailing worldview; it is another thing to go on holding that opinion in the face of clear evidence to the contrary *because an institution, whether Bible or Church, claims not on any evidential base, but simply on its own authority that what is wrong is right because it says so.* Authority does not prove, it pronounces; rules rather than reasons; issues *fatwas*. It refuses to negotiate.

How old is the universe? Well, science painstakingly reckons it's about 14 billion years, give or take the odd billion. Not so, says religious authority: it is 6,000 years old. Where did you get that from? The Bible! What evidence? The Bible! I see: on what grounds do you trust the Bible? Because the Bible tells me so! I had long since grown tired of that kind of circularity. It left us with no way off the roundabout. The next one was trickier. What have you got against women, and why are jobs in the holiness business not open to them? The Bible tells us to keep women in a subordinate role. (And from over the walls of the Vatican Gardens comes another voice: and so does the Pope!) First it was the Bible; now it's the Pope. What arguments do they adduce, what evidence do they offer to support their point of view? Thebiblethepopethebiblethepopethebiblethepope. Don't you see that saying it over and over again adds nothing, except a sense of desperation on your part?

There's another thing: I don't mind you sticking to a 3,000-year-old myth of creation that says God made the universe in six days. It's eccentric, but I can live with it unless you try to impose your eccentricity on everyone else. But where women and gays are concerned it is not just an eccentric opinion, it is an active injustice, a sovereign cruelty. I have to withstand that. Your opinion has solid consequences for the lives of men and women, some of them terrifying. Your opinion gives hate crimes respectability. Another sad thing is that, because of asserting your authority rather than debating the issue, you open the whole religious enterprise to derision, even from those who might otherwise be disposed to look upon it with some sympathy.

344

Like other human enterprises, religion grew out of the human predicament. We are thinking animals. We may even be the only thinking creature in the unimaginable vastness of the universe, which means that in us the universe is thinking about itself, maybe for the first time! And we can't stop doing it. It comes with these big self-conscious brains of ours from which also come science and philosophy. And art! Art is what our imagination has conjured up to express the wonder and terror of life; the stories we have told ourselves, the dreams we have dreamt, the longings and fears we have woven together. And the great gallimaufry we call religion is one of art's greatest imaginings.

Religion is *human,* and like humanity it is both a glory and a scandal. It is full of pity and full of cruelty. Just like us. So is the Bible. If only we could stop using it as though it had any more authority than Shakespeare or Proust or Elgar or Gauguin or Tolstoy or Nietzsche! It belongs with them, with its yearnings and crucifying certainties. It was human, all-too human. Don't abandon it, any more than we ought to abandon the other great flawed cruel epics of the human imagination: but don't listen to its mad voices.

In my walks I discovered my real dilemma. I wanted to keep religion around, purged of cruelty, because it gave us a space to wonder and listen within. Purged of the explanations that don't explain, the science that does not prove, the morality that does not improve; purged, in fact, of its *prose,* religion's poetry could still touch us, make us weep, make us tender, and take us out of ourselves into the possibility of a courageous pity.

I needed somewhere to sit as well as somewhere to walk during my reveries, so my walks sometimes took me back to Old Saint Paul's. I went under the bridge, up the close, in the side door and through the curtain into the little chapel Aeneas Mackintosh had led me to when I was a sixteen-year-old boy at Kelham. I sat, remembering Aeneas not as a priest in the Diocese of Edinburgh, but as a footballer at Kelham, a forward, the ball glued to his right foot, sprinting towards the goal. He was gone now; with all the others I had led down the stairs and under the bridge to join the unnumbered dead. I gazed at the white light of the sanctuary lamp, my mind peopled with the dead. My mother had gone too young, in her sixties. I recalled the heat on the train as I travelled to the Vale to see her for the last time. I was amazed that the world did not notice. *Stop all the clocks!* My father made it into his eighties and died shortly after I became a bishop. Both were buried from Saint Mungo's, my mother inside, my father outside. Because he was always uncomfortable in church, we left him in the hearse outside on Main Street.

I remembered the last time I had seen Geoff Shaw. He got out of Cleland Street just ahead of the bulldozers and wrecking balls and went into politics, soon becoming Convenor of the vast and troubled Strathclyde Regional Council. I bumped into him one day under North Bridge. He'd been through for a meeting at Edinburgh City Chambers and was dashing to Waverley for the train. I was in black; he was wearing an old raincoat. We'd lost touch, but we greeted each other affection-ately. We talked about Scottish politics. He had recently been married. He was happy, but too busy, he said, stubbing out a cigarette. Then he was off for his train, down the stairs of the Market Street entrance. A few days later the paper told me he had died of a heart attack, aged fifty-one. Thousands came to his funeral.

The clocks stopped for Geoff. They did not stop for Lilias,

who died in her nineties, outliving the tower blocks that had evicted her from Gorbals. She died unremembered except by those who knew. Her memorial service at Saint Ninian's – where I was a curate when she asked for my help a lifetime ago – was filled with the grandchildren and great-grandchildren of her Gorbals family. Molly Harvey made gallons of Scotch broth for the party. I remembered Lilias's big soup pot in the kitchen at 10 Abbotsford Place. NOTHING COUNTS BUT LIFE-TIMES!

Then, as I continued to walk the hills, accompanied, or so it seemed, only by the dead, someone else was dying, a friend whose name I have written in this book. And I, a doubting priest, blessed and committed him to the care of the God I don't believe in. I did it, believing and not believing what I was saying, but doing it for his sake, who also believed and did not believe. It is the pain of our humanity to know that we are nothing that lasts, like the haar that blows along Jeffrey Street; yet to feel the pity of that because of the dreams we have dreamed, dreams that sometimes seem to be higher and better than the universe that so indifferently spawns them. That is the conundrum of our humanity, the place of living and losing we occupy. It is what led Canon Laurie up the stairs of Old Saint Paul's at midnight to mourn and remember, to doubt and to pity, knowing and not knowing, but calling out the names of his dead that they might not be forgotten for ever. And it is what takes me back to the hidden graveyard at Kelham to stand there and listen for the whisper.

It was Yehuda Amichai who taught me to listen for the whisper. Yehuda Amichai was the greatest Israeli poet of the twentieth century. He was a tolerant atheist in a city maddened by religion; a humanist in a nation driven to acts of terrible cruelty; but he was too compassionate an artist to be surprised by anything in the human condition. I sat with him in his house in Jerusalem months before his death, talking poetry and religion. I wrote a book that was an attempt to transpose the topography of the mountains of my mind onto paper. I took the title from one of his poems. I called it *Doubts and Loves,* because that is all I am left with after my long journey from Alexandria.

> From the place where we are right
> flowers will never grow
> in the Spring.
>
> The place where we are right
> is hard and trampled
> like a yard.
>
> But doubts and loves
> dig up the world
> like a mole, a plough.
> And a whisper will be heard in the place
> where the ruined
> house once stood.[110]

I am left in the ruined house listening for the whisper. 'This world is not conclusion,' said Emily Dickinson.[111] I know that too. I am tugged still by the possibility of the transcendent. But only whispers and tugs; nothing louder or more violent. Religion's insecurity makes it shout not whisper, strike with the fist in the face not tug gently with the fingers on the sleeve. Yet, beneath the shouting and the striking, the whisper can sometimes be heard. And from a great way off the tiny figure of Jesus can be seen on the seashore, kindling a fire.

I don't any longer *believe* in religion, but I want it around: weakened, bruised and bemused, less sure of itself and purged of everything except the miracle of pity. I know that the people who will keep it going will have to believe in it more than I do. Who could be persuaded by my whisper? Who could even hear it? Anyway, I no longer want to persuade anyone to believe anything – except that cruelty, especially theological cruelty, has to be opposed, if necessary to the death.

And a whisper will be heard. What else? What else have I discovered on these compulsive walks? Something about myself. Regrets, as well as knowledge of their futility. I have been a disappointment to many – and to myself – but I am beginning to realise I could never have been anything else. Old Updike always comforts me.

> Easy on the guilt trip.
> We didn't deal the deck down here, we just play the
>   cards.[112]

I was helped by an essay a friend sent me. A Norse scholar, she had been working on the metaphor of weaving in thinking about human destiny. She wrote, 'Referring to fate or destiny as something that is spun or woven is a well-known metaphorical image in both classical and Old Norse mythology.'[113] I had been taught that we build our character by our choices, and slowly create ourselves – and I had wanted to make myself a world-denying saint. There was never a hope of that. Norse mythology showed me again that the way we act does not so much make us as reveal us; our response to circumstance shows us not what we want to be but who we actually are. I was never constituted to be a saint. I had just fallen among saints by accident.

I don't want to exaggerate the impact of these different metaphors for the way life forms itself in us, but each of them can cast a shadow of regret over the past. The idea of the character that was slowly revealed by the choices we made can be distressing if we do not like the life that has been woven for us by fate. If we come at it from within the Christian tradition, the human story can also be heavy with regret, because it proved impossible to become what we set out to be. Looking back from either vantage point can bring sorrow, either because the character revealed to us through the choices we made, or the character that we ourselves slowly created by those same choices, may disappoint us. It is the idea that we were ever free to affect our own destiny that is the mistake here. I don't believe that some agency hands out destinies to us that we perform like actors on a stage, maybe free to interpret or embroider the role to some extent, but unable to alter its fundamental trajectory; but nor do I think we get a clean sheet on starting out that we sketch our lives onto. It is hard not to believe that much of our life is decided for us by the weight of antecedent facts over which we had no control. I left Alexandria but Alexandria never left me. Great fiction explores this truth better than anything else, though a good biography can achieve the same feat of revealing the inevitability of the way a life was woven. However, it is one thing to accept the inevitability of *another's* life and to see how, given its ingredients, it assumed the form it did; it is quite another to offer the same sympathy and acceptance to *oneself.* Nietzsche called the capacity for self-acceptance *amor fati* or love of fate.

My formula for greatness in a human being is *amor fati*: that one wants nothing to be other than it is, not in the future, not in the past, not in all eternity. Not merely to endure that which happens of necessity, still less to dissemble it – all idealism is untruthfulness in the face of necessity – but to *love* it[114]

I can't say I love what I made of myself or was revealed to be, but I have learned to accept it: losing Alexandria is something we all have to get used to.

I don't expect to meet my maker when I die, but if I do it won't surprise me if he comes smiling towards me over green fields. 'So that's what you made of the hand I dealt you? I know you were strongly tempted by determinism when you were down there, but it is not strictly correct to say the Dealer bears all the responsibility for the hand. You played it, after all, and some things you could have done differently. But there is no point in feeling shame about any of it now. Want to see what I thought I was doing when I dreamt the whole thing up?' As I say, I don't expect that to happen, but if it does I'll accept his invitation, because I am still curious about the mystery of it all.

What's left to say? Only this: when I die I hope my children will bring me back up here. I don't want a stone or a sign left anywhere to mark the fact that I had a life on earth before I went down the stairs to join the unnumbered dead. My name will be written in ink, and ink is the best symbol for a life. Brief. Defiant. Fading. But I hope that Ann and Sara and Mark will bring my ashes up here one October day. They can take turns carrying what's left of me in my old rucksack. Through Kitchen Moss up West Kip and East Kip to Scald Law. Because of the wind up here, they'll have to watch where they stand when they open the box to let me out to blow away into the heather. I know now that the three of them are what I was for. It has been a great purpose being one of the instruments of their becoming. I love them, and she who bore them.

Then they can make their way back down the Kirk Road to the Green Cleuch and the beech-lined road below Bavelaw and home.

And that'll be that. Well, almost certainly . . .

NOTES

PROLOGUE

1 Mark Girouard, *The Victorian Country House* (Yale University Press, New Haven and London, 1979), p.224.
2 Girouard, *The Victorian Country House*, p.235.
3 Girouard, *The Victorian Country House*, p.234.
4 Dame Felicitas Corrigan, *Helen Waddell* (Gollancz, 1986), p.357.
5 *Hymnal for Scotland* (Oxford University Press, London, 1966), Hymn 744.
6 Alistair Mason, *History of the Society of the Sacred Mission* (Canterbury Press, Norwich, 1993), p.13.
7 Mason, *History of the Society of the Sacred Mission*, p.16.
8 *Father Kelly and the Idea of Theology* (Society of the Sacred Mission, 1987), p.1.
9 Mason, *History of the Society of the Sacred Mission*, p 28.
10 *An Idea Whose Time Has Come?* (Society of the Sacred Mission in Australia, 2009), p.10.

CHAPTER 1

11 Lewis Grassic Gibbon, *A Scots Quair* (Hutchinson, London, 1946), p.130.
12 Vladimir Nabokov, *Lolita* (Penguin Books, London, 1995), p.170.
13 Edwin Muir, 'Transfiguration', in *Collected Poems: Edwin Muir* (Faber & Faber, London, 1963).

CHAPTER 2

14 *Hymnal for Scotland*, Hymn 20.
15 Dennis O'Driscoll, 'Missing God', in *Being Human* (Bloodaxe Books, 2004), p.97.

16 Helen Waddell, *The Desert Fathers* (Collins Fontana Library, London, 1962), p.172.
17 John Meade Falkner, 'After Trinity', in *The Oxford Book of Twentieth-Century English Verse*, edited by Philip Larkin, (Clarendon Press, Oxford, 1973), p.40.
18 V.S. Naipaul, in Patrick French, *The World is What it Is* (Picador, London, 2008), p.210.
19 2 Timothy, 4:10. (Demas was a companion of the Apostle Paul, who left him for the pleasures of the city of Thessalonica.)
20 Mason, *History of the Society of the Sacred Mission*, p.118.
21 C.P. Cavafy, 'The Great Yes', in *Collected Poems*, translated by Edmund Keeley and Philip Sherrard (Chatto & Windus, London, 1998), p.10.
22 Walter de la Mare, *The Collected Poems* (Faber & Faber, London, 1979), p.84.
23 T.S. Eliot, *Murder in the Cathedral* (Faber & Faber, London, 1936), p.85.

CHAPTER 3

24 Philip Larkin, 'Deceptions', in *Collected Poems* (Faber & Faber, London, 2003), p.67
25 Nabokov, *Lolita*, p.321.
26 Larkin, 'Annus Mirabilis', in *Collected Poems*, p.146.
27 Peter Brown, *The Body and Society* (Faber & Faber, London, 1990), p.424.
28 Steve Jones, *The Language of the Genes* (Flamingo, London, 1993), p.97.

CHAPTER 4

29 G.M. Hopkins, 'Spring and Fall', in *Poems* (Oxford University Press, 1948), p.94.
30 Paul's Letter to the Romans 6:12–13.
31 Paul's Letter to the Romans 7:19–21.
32 Hopkins, 'My Own Heart Let Me More Have Pity On', in *Poems*, p.110.
33 Hopkins, 'Heaven-Haven', in *Poems*, p.40.
34 Isaiah 6:8.

CHAPTER 5

35 Edwin Morgan, 'Glasgow Green', in *Collected Poems* (Carcanet, 1990), p.168.
36 Luke 6:21.
37 www.glasgowwestend.co.uk/out/outdoors/thegorbals.html

CHAPTER 6

38 Hopkins, 'My Own Heart Let Me More Have Pity On', in *Poems*, p.110.
39 Albert Schweitzer, *Out of my Life and Thought: An Autobiography* (Holt, New York, 1933), p.114.
40 *The Essential Tillich* (University of Chicago Press, 1987), pp.200–1.
41 Hugh MacDiarmid, 'The Two Parents', in *The Oxford Book of Twentieth-Century English Verse*, p.256.
42 James 1:17.

CHAPTER 7

43 R.S. Thomas, 'Introduction' to *Selected Poems of R.S. Thomas* (Faber & Faber, London, 1964).
44 Mason, *History of the Society of the Sacred Mission*, p.16.
45 Mark 2:27.
46 Friedrich Nietzsche, 'Human, All-too Human', in *The Portable Nietzsche* (Penguin, New York, 1976), section 224, p.54.

CHAPTER 8

47 Adam Phillips, *On Balance* (Hamish Hamilton, London, 2010), p.57.
48 W.H. Auden, 'Leap Before You Look', in *Collected Shorter Poems 1927–1957* (Faber & Faber, London, 1975), p.100.
49 Larkin, 'Days', in *Collected Poems*, p.98.
50 Nietzsche, *The Portable Nietzsche*, p.181.
51 Terry Eagleton, *On Evil* (Yale University Press, 2010), p.84.
52 R.S. Thomas, 'Kneeling', in *Collected Poems* (J.M. Dent, London, 1993), p.199.
53 The Epistle of James 1:13–17.
54 Hopkins, 'I Wake and Feel the Fell of Dark', in *Poems*, p.169.
55 Miguel de Unamuno, *The Tragic Sense of Life* (Dover Publications, New York, 1954), p.43.
56 The First Epistle to the Corinthians 14:8.

CHAPTER 9

57 Ian Frazier, *Great Plains* (Granta Books, London, 2006), p.41.
58 Jorge Luis Borges, *Los Conjurados*, translated by Nicomede Suarez Arauz in *24 Conversations with Borges* (Emecce Editores S.A., Buenos Aires, 1989).
59 Graham Greene, *The Power and the Glory* (Vintage, London, 2001).

60 Hopkins, 'My Own Heart Let Me More Have Pity On', in *Poems of Gerard Manley Hopkins* (Oxford University Press, 1952), p.110.

61 Adam Phillips, *On Balance* (Hamish Hamilton, London, 2010), p.47.

62 Robert Pogue Harrison, *The Dominion of the Dead* (University of Chicago Press, Chicago, 2003), p.137.

CHAPTER 10

63 Hopkins, 'I Wake and Feel the Fell of Dark', in *Poems*, p.109.

64 1 Corinthians 13:1.

65 Quoted in *Sojourners* magazine, September 2001.

66 D.H. Lawrence, 'The Song of a Man Who Has Come Through', in *The Oxford Book of Twentieth-Century English Verse*, p.187.

67 Matthew 11:3.

68 Matthew 11:6.

69 André Schwarz-Bart, *The Last of the Just* (Penguin Books, London, 1977), p.373.

70 Elie Wiesel, *Night*, translated by Marion Wiesel (Hill & Wang, 2006), p.65.

CHAPTER 11

71 James 1:8.

72 Kathleen Raine, 'If I Could Turn', in *On a Deserted Shore* (Dolmen Press, Dublin, 1973), Poem 95.

73 John Betjeman, 'Anglo-Catholic Congresses', in *Collected Poems* (John Murray, London, 2006), p.265.

74 Henry Scott Holland, *A Bundle of Memories* (Wells Gardner, Darton & Co., London, 1915), p.95.

75 Luke 5:39.

76 Louis MacNeice, 'Mutations' in *Collected Poems* (Faber & Faber, London, 1979), p.195.

77 Richard Holloway, *The Stranger in the Wings* (SPCK, London, 1994), p.147.

CHAPTER 12

78 *Hidden Gardens of Beacon Hill* (Beacon Hill Garden Club, 1987), p.3.

79 Betty Hughes Morris, *A History of the Church of the Advent* (Boston, 1995), p.135.

80 Morris, *A History of the Church of the Advent*, p.135.

81 I have taken several phrases here from Philip Larkin's famous poem 'Church Going', in his *Collected Poems*, p.58.

82 Hopkins, 'No Worse There Is None', in *Poems*, p.107.

83 Timothy O'Grady, *Divine Magnetic Lands* (Vintage, 2009), p.10.

84 John Cornwell, *Newman's Unquiet Grave* (Continuum, London, 2010), p.19.

85 Albert Camus, *The Plague* (Penguin, London, 1989), chapters 2, 3 and 4.

CHAPTER 13

86 Robert Browning, 'Bishop Blougram's Apology'.

87 Ludwig Wittgenstein, 'Journal, July 8 1916', in *Wittgenstein: The Notebooks 1914–16* (Blackwell, London).

88 Ludwig Wittgenstein, 'Tractatus, 6.52', in *The Tractatus Logico-Philosophicus* (Routledge & Kegan Paul).

89 A.S.J Tessimond, 'Heaven', in *The Collected Poems*, Hubert Nicholson, ed. (University of Reading Press, Reading, 1985).

90 John Betjeman, 'Anglo-Catholic Congresses', in *Collected Poems*, p.463.

91 John Meade Falkner, 'After Trinity', in *The Oxford Book of Twentieth Century English Verse*, p.41.

92 Richard Holloway, *How to Read the Bible* (Granta, London, 2006), p.90ff.

93 Virginia Woolf, *A Room of One's Own/Three Guineas* (Penguin Books, London, 1993), p.133ff.

CHAPTER 14

94 Jane Millard, 'Fragments of the Watch' (unpublished).

95 Albert Camus, *The Plague* (Penguin, London, 1960), p.297.

96 Matthew Arnold, 'Dover Beach', in *The New Oxford Book of English Verse*, chosen and edited by Helen Gardner (Clarenden Press, Oxford, 1972), p.703.

97 Richard Holloway, *Dancing on the Edge: Faith in a Post-Christian Society* (Fount, London, 1997).

98 Richard Holloway, *Seven to Flee, Seven to Follow* (Mowbrays, Oxford, 1986).

99 Hebrews 2:1 (in the Revised Standard Version).

CHAPTER 15

100 Anthony Hirsh, 'Post-coital Sperm Retrieval', in *Human Reproduction*, vol. 11, no. 2, p.245.

101 Galatians 3:27–8.

102 Ephesians 5:22–4.

103 John Cornwell, *Newman's Unquiet Grave* (Continuum, London, 2010), p.196.

104 Andrea Dworkin, *Intercourse* (Arrow Books, London, 1988), p.189.

105 Thomas Merton, *The Courage for Truth: Letters to Writers* (Farrer, Strauss & Giroux, New York, 1993), p.79.

106 John Harris, *Wonderwoman and Superman* (Oxford University Press, 1992), p.42.

107 Cavafy, 'The God Forsakes Antony', in *Collected Poems*, p.10.

108 Wendell Berry, *Sabbaths 1987–90* (Golgonooza Press, Ipswich, 1992), p.13.

109 Sheila Brock (unpublished).

EPILOGUE

110 *The Selected Poetry of Yehuda Amichai,* translated by Chana Bloch and Stephen Mitchell (University of California Press, 1996), p.34.

111 Emily Dickinson, *Collected Poems* (Courage Books/Running Press, Philadelphia, 1991), p.276.

112 John Updike, *The Witches of Eastwick* (Penguin Modern Classics, London, 2007), p.134.

113 Karen Bek-Pedersen, *Fate and Weaving – Justification of a Metaphor* (unpublished).

114 Friedrich Nietzsche, *Ecce Homo,* translated by R.J. Hollingdale (Penguin Classics, London, 1988), II.10, p.68.